SOCIAL CHANGE AND ECONOMIC DEVELOPMENT

SOCIAL CHANGE
AND
ECONOMIC DEVELOPMENT

Reprinted from the *International Social Science Bulletin*
Edited by Jean Meynaud

UNESCO

Published in 1963 by the United Nations
Educational, Scientific and Cultural Organization
Place de Fontenoy, Paris-7e
Printed by Sijthoff, Leiden

TABLE OF CONTENTS

---

1. The figures in brackets refer to the volume and number of the *International Social Science Bulletin* in which the article first appeared.

LIST OF CONTRIBUTORS

R.J. ..., University of Paris

C. ..., Oxford Inst... of Education

R.E. Backhouse, University of Reading

A. De..., University of Bristol

L. ..., Kaplan, ... University

H. Perry, London School of Economics and Political Science

M.H. Pesaran, Oxford University

O. Hirst, University of South Kent

P. Dasgupta, Swedish University, Konstanz, Uppsala

R.L. Harris, Chicago Law School

E. Hutchinson, American University, ...

R.N. Millar, Reserve Bank of ...

D.W. Pearson, University, Lancaster

M. Morishima, Centre National de la Recherche Scientifique, Paris

P. Mayo, Mehta University, India

J. Whitaker, University of Lausanne and Ecole Polytechnique Fédérale de Lausanne

S. Knox..., University of ...

S. Solomou, University of Glasgow

H.W. Simons, ... of the United Nations, New York

C.N. Vaish, University of Bombay

INTRODUCTION

J. Meynaud

Ever since its inception, the *International Social Science Journal* (originally *International Social Science Bulletin*) has devoted considerable space to the analysis of contacts between countries of differing civilizations, and, in particular, to the study of the consequences of technological progress in the underdeveloped States and territories. In view of the gravity and complexity of these problems, it has been thought advisable to bring together in one volume some of the most noteworthy of the contributions on this subject which appeared in issues now long out of print.

To those acquainted with the number, scope and variety of the papers which have dealt with these questions over the past few years, this decision may not appear, at first sight, to be one of absolute necessity. But there seem to be two decisive arguments in its favour. Unesco, as a world-wide organization, has often been able to enlist the help of scientists from countries overseas: the articles contributed by these specialists express original views and bear the stamp of authenticity which is sometimes lacking in the work of writers foreign to those countries. Furthermore, the Department of Social Sciences has always been more at pains than other research centres to take account of the views of anthropologists and draw upon the resources of their science. In such matters anthropologists obviously have a special message to convey.

Such being its origin, the volume I am privileged to introduce has a highly individual significance and value.

The backbone of this collection is formed by the group of reports drawn up for a round-table meeting on economic motivation and stimulation in underdeveloped countries. This meeting was organized in Paris, in March 1954, under the sponsorship of the International Social Science Council, by the International Research Office on Social Implications of Technological Change. The papers reprinted here are therefore comparatively old, but any reader of the general report by G. Balandier will perceive that the problems raised and the solutions proposed are by no means out of date.

In point of fact, the Office opened up paths and began a process of exploration which is still continuing, though all too slowly. It is not intended to question the importance generally attributed to the study of the group of social and economic factors which holds a dominant place in the destiny of the communities under consideration. But to ignore or underestimate the psychological variables is to neglect an essential aspect of the matter, and such neglect can easily result in omissions and tactical errors in the planning of practical activities.

The International Economic Association also organized, from 28 August to 2 September 1953, a symposium on problems of long-term economic development. Part of the time available was taken up with an analysis of the factors governing economic progress in the underdeveloped areas. In some respects, the similarity between the respective concerns of the economists and the anthropologists was striking, and it was therefore felt that it would be useful to include in this volume such of the reports of that meeting as dealt with underdevelopment.

The resultant collection, in itself impressive, has been augmented by various studies published in other numbers of the *Journal*. Several of these are monographs with a direct bearing upon the subjects discussed at the two meetings I mentioned above. Since their analyses of situations and the proposals they make have not lost their originality, it was thought that their authors should be given a fresh opportunity to stimulate research along the same lines.

Several of these articles deal with countries or territories which, at the time of the survey, had not yet attained political independence. Readers will make the necessary allowance for the decolonization which has since taken place, particularly in Africa. These studies have been reprinted without alteration, in order to leave them their value as documents describing phenomena typical of a particular period and its particular conditions. Attainment of independence naturally alters the factors of the problem, or at least some of them. Fresh prospects have been opened up, new motives are coming to the fore. But the transition from dependence to sovereignty, though of prime importance in some respects, does not get rid of economic difficulties, and from this standpoint much of the research undertaken in the colonial period retains its value today.

The interest of the studies included in this volume is such as to need no comment. I should like, however, to tell readers of this volume about the personal benefit I have derived from it. In my opinion, these papers make a definite contribution to the analysis of social change. They stress the resistance displayed by traditional communities when confronted with changes likely to disturb the behaviour they have learnt and the balance they have achieved. The volume also offers hints or suggestions regarding the circumstances in which measures to encourage these changes can be effective, and how far they can be carried. My purpose is simply to emphasize the value of the findings in these two spheres. By presenting matters in this light I am of course implicitly acknowledging that fuller knowledge helps to make action more effective.

I

One of the principal advantages of these investigations is that they show, by specific example, the scale and significance of the resistance aroused by attempts to introduce technical improvements in communities governed by principles which run counter to such improvements. These reservations or refusals have often been the subject of hasty analysis, not always devoid of racial prejudice. It is not really possible to give a lucid, impartial explanation of these phenomena unless we allow for certain factors which determine the behaviour and account for the reactions of the peoples confronted with the innovations concerned. Moreover, field studies have revealed the weakness and danger of generalizations based on pure theory; a particular variable may quite frequently produce different results in different environments. Here I should like to give a brief illustration of each of these points.

Such resistance exists, and is sometimes forcibly displayed. Rejection may be open and violent, or it may be widespread but latent. In many cases it merely takes the form of a lack of helpfulness or enthusiasm; the new practices are not rejected, but those concerned neglect or ignore the procedure required to make them effective.

This leads to charges of apathy in industrial work and to more general complaints about the attitude of the workers. Another matter that deserves attention is the exercise of responsibility at the employer level—for instance, the reaction to the fact that if capital equipment is to be kept in good condition, its value must be gradually written off and a reserve built up out of income. Neglect of such standards may be regarded as a form of resistance to the implications of an industrial civilization. Naturally this branch of economic management has attracted comparatively little attention, because few of the local population become managers of industrial firms, particularly in Africa; but the problem is now becoming a live issue, owing to the repercussions of the desire for independence and the eagerness for development.

It should be noted that traditional communities are not the only ones which erect barriers against technical progress; resistance to change is to be observed at all levels of technical advancement and in all environments. This tendency, and the innumerable laws and regulations to which it gives rise, are described in France by the term *protection du passé*. On a number of occasions, particularly during the decade from 1930 to 1940, voices were heard demanding that inventions should be put in cold storage, or at any rate prevented from expanding. The trade unions more than once took steps to prevent measures intended to lower prices by making economies in manpower (for instance, the mechanization of the entrances to the Paris underground railway system). The greatest obstacle to what is known as the policy of industrial decentralization has been the reluctance of workers to change their geographical or occupational position. In fact, one need only look around to find widespread evidence of attitudes which are commonly assumed to be confined to the population of the underdeveloped countries.

One more point. As several contributors to this volume explain, the refusal to adopt technical innovations was attributable in some cases to genuinely serious motives (unsuitability of the soil or particular climatic conditions, for which the foreign experts failed to make sufficient allowance). On other occasions these negative attitudes were engendered by the actual character of the instructions given to the local population by the colonial authorities; here we need merely mention the compulsory crop system which the Dutch attempted to establish in Java. In his study of the development of capitalism in Indonesia and Uganda, J. H. Bocke points out that the effect of this system was to make the Javanese farmer into a contractor in spite of himself; but a contractor of a special type, since he had to bear all the risks of the undertaking and provide all the labour.

By discouraging and demoralizing the workers, this system had a disastrous influence which endured even after it was abolished. On the other hand, the colonial authorities in Uganda succeeded, in the space of a few years and by different methods, in greatly increasing the production of cotton by the negro planters. One contemporary British observer remarked that these planters, once released from the shackles of established custom, increased their activities of their own accord, needing no official encouragement; they were spontaneously eager to earn more money in order to buy land, to clear it, or to take on extra workers.

These two examples show the value of a system of interpretation which makes it possible, in each individual case, to work back to the origin of the attitude or view observed. This, it seems, can be arrived at by combining the resources of psychological analysis and of the sociological survey.

SOCIAL AND PSYCHOLOGICAL FACTORS OF CHANGE

Here we must consider, on the one hand, the circumstances in which change is accepted—not always with satisfactory results—and, on the other hand, the factors making for resistance to the changes introduced. In other words, the system should enable us to understand why some attempts to make changes are successful, and why others fail. In both cases, change is the outcome of people's reactions to new types of activity. To realize the complexity of the problem, we need only read A. Doucy's study of the causes of instability among the local workers in the Congo, which was under Belgian rule at the time.

Explanations of the monistic type—particularly those based on alleged innate characteristics—are inadequate to explain a situation which remains confused and complicated in respect of all types of social activity (including the activities of the so-called primitive communities). In many cases, the sole purpose or result of such interpretations has been to provide a justification for measures which have been criticized (for example, the laziness of the native population is alleged as an excuse for the introduction of forced labour). That being so, what framework can be selected for an adequate list of the factors involved?

The concept of attitude—one of the key concepts of modern social psychology—may very well serve as a good starting point for such analyses. The social psychologist regards all behaviour, whether it takes the form of conduct (active behaviour) or of opinion (verbal behaviour), as a response to a situation. The attitude is the intermediate variable which explains the transition from the latter to the former. It is a propensity or readiness to act in one way rather than another. To put it more explicitly, the attitude of a person depends on his previous experience of the situation with which he has to deal.

Analysis of an attitude also extends, of course, to the conditions governing its change, or, if we prefer, to the search for stimuli by which such modifications can be brought about. We may distinguish three main categories of stimuli—those which derive from changes in the situation for which the subject is not directly responsible (development of education, urbanization, etc.); those which originate in the individual consciousness of the person concerned (changed outlook due, for instance, to foreign contacts, travel, etc.) and the third group—of growing importance—engendered by systematic efforts to influence other people. Unless there is some marked change in the situation or in the interpretation of it, these stimuli are clearly far from certain to produce the desired effect.

The difficulty here is to proceed from individual reactions to the general tendencies displayed in the particular community under consideration. The individual cannot be isolated from the world in which he lives except by a deliberate effort of abstraction. The study of cultural models helps us to situate the individual again in his social context. It is largely through the imitation of such models that attitudes become established and are handed on. Following this line, we are not far from the concept of the basic personality, which makes allowance both for the dynamism of the culture concerned and for the relationship between culture and individuality. Without entering into a controversy which is beyond the scope of this introduction, I may say that this interpretation is not incompatible with the recognition that the individual possesses a certain margin of autonomy, or in other words, an element of creative spontaneity. It means that attitudes are not invariably predetermined.

The method, of which I have just outlined the main principles, may be used to explore the different sectors of human relationships. It can be used, for instance, in analysing political behaviour, and it is equally applicable to the individual's attitude towards industrial work and technical improvements. The word 'attitude' belongs, generally speaking, to the vocabulary of social psychology, which accounts for the fact that it is not employed by the anthropologists who have contributed to this volume. The intermediate variable that they select for the analysis of change is that of psychological 'motivation', or alternatively, 'motive' (several writers use either word indiscriminately). But despite the variable terminology, there is a strong similarity of intellectual procedure.

As Herskovits points out, the adaptation of an individual to an economic environment results from the shaping of the component elements of his psychological motives by the traditional framework in which he lives. Regarded from this angle, the question of changes in the economic and technical structure represents no more than one particular aspect of the general theme of cultural readjustment. Despite differences of terminology, it is always the same problem that has to be stated and interpreted—that of the individual's responses (actions or opinions) through intermediate variables (attitudes or motivations), to the conditions of the environment (situation or framework) on which his existence is centred and to the variations produced therein.

The important thing is to grasp the impossibility of explaining the behaviour of individuals correctly without taking into consideration the whole set of factors or variables by which they may be prompted or influenced. But these factors and variables are normally the proper concern of several of the specialized social sciences, and frequently, indeed, of them all. Even if the survey is made by the workers in only one branch, it must necessarily be of an interdisciplinary nature. From this standpoint, and despite stubborn prejudices to the contrary, economic science and political science are on the same footing. It is impossible to account for the results of an election without considering a great number of social factors; nor are there many economists, nowadays, who would maintain that questions of investment should be decided merely on the strength of financial calculations. As for political economy, the point of juncture of the other two branches of study, the terms in which it is expressed are arrived at by criteria which are essentially mixed and heterogeneous.

It is from this standpoint that we must assess the effect on social attitudes of the accession to independence of the countries which were formerly colonies or political dependencies. The transfer of sovereignty means, in the first place, a changed situation which must naturally lead to the adoption by governments of a different set of criteria and a different order of priorities (see, as to this point, D. N. Majumdar's study on 'Tribal Rehabilitation in India'). This change should likewise lead to certain changes in the individual's interpretation of the situation, with a consequent restructuration of attitudes or motivations (this, admittedly, does not always have the effect of raising productivity). But the end of colonization does not in itself bring about any immediate and radical change in the various elements of the situation, least of all in the management of economic resources; this explains why old forms of behaviour are sometimes carried over into a new political framework.

This survival, where it occurs, is a generalized phenomenon. It may result from failure to perceive the changes that have taken place in the situation. In this respect we must not forget that the mechanism of perception is selective. It has frequently been observed that facts incompatible with the individual's attitude, or with his usual system of motivation, pass unnoticed, or are scarcely perceived; unfavourable facts are ignored, in all good faith, and attention is concentrated solely on the favourable ones. In other cases, the individual, after assessing the changes which have been made or are being demanded, comes to the conclusion that only appearances have changed, and that the old relationships survive intact (this is the state of mind of workers in nationalized enterprises in countries which, generally speaking, are still faithful to the capitalist system). The result is the survival of customary behaviour.

These remarks show that it would be undesirable to overlook the weight of objective factors, and, in particular, the state of the various forces within a society, when considering the factors that influence the disposition to take action. In other words, the adoption of a psycho-sociological system should not lead us to neglect or underestimate the influence of the social structure on human behaviour. Deviations do take place, usually under the influence of an ideological preference, but they are by no means a necessary consequence of the suggested method of analysis. In itself, the 'situation response' method of interpretation precludes any preconceived opinion; it is valuable only inasmuch as it leads to a detailed, and continuing, inventory of the factors involved.

This system has one drawback, which at first may appear very serious. While it enables us to list the different elements of a situation, and, as it were, justifies a wide investigation, it provides no special facilities for assessing the relative strength of the variables taken into consideration or, more simply, for arranging them in order of importance. But this is a difficulty or inadequacy by which very large areas of social analysis are still affected, and is not an innate characteristic of the particular system of analysis adopted. Thus the application of this system, as of any other, is influenced by subjective and theoretical judgements which detract from its scope, though without depriving it of all value.

UNIVERSALITY AND DIVERSITY OF VARIOUS SITUATIONS

One of the special features of present-day social analysis is its propensity to form large groups of concepts under which extensive sets of phenomena can be classified. It is true that no theories can be formulated without adopting some system for presenting them, and the elaboration of any doctrine entails some degree of simplification. But the result of these measures is to diminish the originality and variety of the situations considered. By stressing their common features, we are led to overlook the elements peculiar to each individual case: this adversely affects our understanding of the problems concerned, and lessens the practical value of the methods of action selected.

Expressions such as 'underdeveloped countries' or 'neutral States' are typical of this tendency. The communities usually included under these headings have certain properties or characteristics in common, and their resemblance becomes more marked if we contrast them with the so-called rich or affluent communities. But by juggling too persistently with general categories, we are led to forget that the various underdeveloped countries differ in many important respects—in their main problems, in their difficulties and also in their potentialities. Consequently, measures which may be desirable or acceptable for certain among them will not necessarily be so for others. Here again we find that inadequate theoretical analysis often has unfortunate repercussions in the sphere of action.

Anthropologists are usually preserved, by the area and nature of their investigations, from the propensity to oversimplification. Since they work in the field, they are naturally led to emphasize the traditional elements and the present-day behaviour which give a human community its individual stamp. The ambition of the social scientist is to classify scores, or even hundreds of individual situations in a few large categories, whereas the anthropologist is interested in certain selected communities, whose hard core of originality he seeks to express. By reminding us of man's individuality, anthropology gives a valuable hint to the other branches of social analysis. In particular, it puts us on our guard against the danger of premature generalization. In some territories, women exert a conservative influence, which slows down the acceptance of technical progress. Elsewhere, however, the women are found to be more dynamic than the men.

One factor of differentiation is strongly evidenced in countries which have recently acceded to independence. This is the weight of the colonial heritage. It is reflected in the retention of a number of economic structures (industrial firms) or intellectual institutions (schools), which enable the former colonizing country to maintain a privileged relationship with the new States which have arisen on the ruins of its empire. This factor is particularly influential in cases where the behaviour of the local people itself is affected by what they learnt under colonial rule. The use of the language of the former colonizing power is the most obvious instance of such a situation, and its implications are perhaps apt to be underestimated. Then there are phenomena such as the African trade union movement, which cannot be satisfactorily accounted for if we overlook the part played in this respect by the colonial governments and the central authorities in Europe. The maintenance of special relations after the transfer of sovereignty (particularly economic assistance and cultural exchanges) has the effect of consolidating these tendencies.

I think I have said enough to show that the papers in this volume form an interesting contribution to the explanation of social phenomena. I shall now turn to their value for the establishment of programmes of economic and social development.

II

The second great merit of these studies is that they compel us to make a close examination of the measures adopted with a view to bridging the technical and economic gulf which is at present widening between the different countries. In the face of inadequacies and setbacks, it is easy to become critical. But we cannot fairly expect scientists to reveal talents and a grasp of the situation which the government authorities do not possess, and, above all, we should not jump to the conclusion that errors are necessarily due to the failure of the latter to consult the former. History is not so simple as that, and responsibilities are more evenly divided.

Cases of resistance to technological progress should obviously not be treated as established and unchanging phenomena, but as obstacles which can always be by-passed, reduced, and ultimately eliminated. Admittedly, the transformation may be accompanied by chaos and suffering; we too readily forget the price paid in the nineteenth century for the industrialization of what are now the economically advanced countries. But it is desirable for the changes to be effected under a long-term social policy. It is clear that scientific analysis, if it does not wander off into mere abstract theorizing, can help the workers in the field in two different ways—by defining the importance and scale of the resistance (for experts are not in agreement as to its intensity), and by considering what inducements can be offered to encourage productive effort. These intellectual measures are in any case the necessary preliminary to any attempt to direct traditional motivations along new lines if they are to be planned and followed without arousing the hostility of the workers.

Such responsibilities are a delicate matter. They cannot be discharged without reference to some criterion by which efforts can be guided and co-ordinated. In the long run, moreover, external help can be no more than a supplement or auxiliary. The main effort must inevitably rest with the countries concerned—which brings us back to the problem of the means by which a desire for change can be awakened, organized, and guided along the chosen lines.

CONTRIBUTION OF THE EXPERTS

It is evident that, until very recently, economic and political experts concentrated mainly on the economically developed parts of the world. It was in the light of the needs and problems of these regions that theories were established and machinery set in motion. When the time came to deal with a different environment, a dearth of means of study and action was revealed in most cases. Since the governments could not slow down their intervention to the pace at which academic knowledge was increasing, they were compelled to take impromptu action and in several cases the final result was unfortunate. For instance, development and equipment plans were drawn up more or less regardless of the attitudes and motivations of those whose activities they were intended to direct.

It is true that the universities joined in the movement. In the course of a few years, a large amount of teaching and research work was carried out in connexion with problems which had hitherto been ignored, or with vast areas of the world which had been completely forgotten by all but a handful of men. The former colonial governments and, later, the national authorities of the young States, which were grappling with countless difficulties, very naturally enlisted these expert services which in many cases had only recently become available. Economists were invited to draw up programmes for long-term expansion, political scientists were asked to draft constitutions or electoral laws, and sociologists were urged to turn their attention to the varied problems raised by industrialization and urbanization. In all fields, from the choice of seeds to the organization of education, experts were at a premium.

It would be unfair to say that the confidence thus shown in technicians was invariably misplaced. But it would be a distortion of the truth to claim that the results secured were always commensurate with the sacrifices accepted, let alone with the hopes raised. One of the most obvious causes of the setbacks thus encountered was the inability to devise novel solutions, suited to the special features of the situation. In all too many cases, the suggestion proffered amounted to no more than the transfer—sometimes with minor amendments— of institutions or practices which had proved satisfactory elsewhere, or, at any rate, were in regular use in other places.

Those who consider that this procedure is dictated by ideological preferences are forgetting one factor of prime importance—the force of routine, which very few specialists escape, and the general weakness of the creative imagination.

Combined with the desire to protect certain interests, this tendency has created regrettable and sometimes absurd situations. For instance, during the years between 1950 and 1955 the people of French Tropical Africa, where industrial life was still at the most rudimentary stage, were equipped with a trade union system which was a faithful replica of the metropolitan pattern, down to the smallest detail.

If experts are to render more effective service, they undoubtedly need more experience in the field. But the improvement of social analysis would also have its effect. In this respect, the papers in this volume bear witness to one point of prime importance—the danger of the present splitting up of the social sciences into isolated fields of study. The progress of our research will depend, to a great extent, upon the scale and quality of the efforts made to remedy this defect. The question is, in my opinion, sufficiently important to warrant a few comments.

The division of social analysis into a number of branches of study is too well known to call for comment. It is as evident in education as in research. Yet despite all the appeals and declarations made in favour of interdisciplinary contacts, relations between the separate branches of study remain rare and superficial. The relationship between two departments, or two Chairs, is marked by indifference and even, at times, by suspicion or hostility. In the alleged interest of efficiency (this is always the excuse for specialization), each individual sticks to his own field and tends to ignore the results achieved by his neighbour.

Many charges have been laid against this voluntary isolation. The value of such separatism is all the more doubtful since the present division is purely empirical in character and varies at different times and in different places. By clinging to it, the universities are causing themselves to lag regrettably behind current developments. Though it may have been understandable at a time when social life was at the mercy of spontaneous mechanisms and influences (but has this ever been the case?), this sub-division loses all logical justification when so many authorities— public, professional and private—are striving to direct the course of events. In several respects, our universities continue to reflect a liberal view of institutions whose champions, once they are in power, discard it themselves.

Most of the contributors to this volume avoid that inconsistency. At the beginning of his general report, G. Balandier emphasizes the decisive importance of psychological and cultural factors in economic development. He unhesitatingly declares that underdevelopment is not primarily a matter for the economist. The same view is expressed by Melville J. Herskovits, who follows K. Polanyi in asserting that man's economic life is an inseparable part of his social life. S. Herbert Frankel, in his turn, clarifies the point at issue by suggesting that technological and political factors should not be regarded as fortuitous causes, independent of one another, but as interdependent phenomena. And the perception of these connexions, on which the value and significance of our analyses depend, is contingent upon the restoration of some degree of unity to social reflection.

Over-specialization narrows the scope of scientific analysis; it disperses the factors which must be assembled before the actions of the agents can be explained. But the consequences of this situation are of more than theoretical interest. In cases where correction or reform are required, it leads specialists to propose or agree to the transfer of institutions to an environment ill-fitted to receive them. Those who are in control end by forgetting that no system for organizing or regulating one branch or aspect of human relations has any value in itself; the essential question is whether it will function properly and produce the desired results.

It is true that the parts and the whole are constantly interacting and that a change made at one point may have general repercussions and help to alter the context in the desired way. However, it equally often happens that the effect of the innovations thus introduced is cancelled out or completely distorted by variables whose existence, or at least strength, had not been revealed by an analysis which was incomplete. The monographs presented in this volume give many examples of such distortion. To their evidence, we may add a fact now universally recognized: when universal suffrage is introduced in a community where certain feudal features (large landed estates) are still well established, it does not—at the first stage, in any case—curtail existing privileges, and may even serve to consolidate them.

It is hardly necessary to point out that the drawbacks of over-specialization have been denounced for a long time past. Auguste Comte, for instance, sharply criticized the artificial isolation of political economy, which he regarded as indicating a survival of the metaphysical spirit. In terms which could not be bettered today, Comte protested against an explanation which attempted to ignore all the manifold tendencies present in human nature except the principle of self-interest. On the other hand, Marxism, whether we accept or reject it, has one immense advantage over all the doctrines which preceded or have followed it, in that it offers a unified picture of human activity. There is no point in continuing the list of these reminders: by showing us how strongly even the scientific mind is influenced by social conditions, the sociological approach to knowledge affords decisive proof of the epistemological weakness of the sub-divison of social analysis.

The only arguments which can be advanced in favour of the present situation are empirical not to say opportunist. The anthropologist may find himself in a position to undertake a complete study of the so-called primitive communities and in analysing these he is following his original, or at least his initial vocation. Many people consider that this is not possible with large communities, which are so complex that a division of the work between several specialists may be desirable and is at all events inevitable. I am inclined to concur with this view, on condition that the present situation is regarded as merely a stage, though perhaps a fairly long one, on the road to the reunification of social science studies. This position, which refuses to commit the future, makes it necessary to follow carefully all attempts to find a way of escape from the present over-specialization (for instance, the *behavioural* sciences).

Pending the completion of this stage, it rests with each branch of social science to arrive, by its own efforts or in collaboration with other disciplines, at a complete explanation of the problems for which it has the academic responsibility—as a result, I repeat, of a mere convention. Economic under-development cannot be correctly interpreted merely by reference to the strictly economic structures and mechanisms of the advanced communities. For we are here confronted by basically different communities, and the divergence of levels and of methods of exploiting resources constitutes one of the factors of cleavage.

Economists are aware of this problem, and try to get round it by enumerating the typical features of underdeveloped communities. But this mere enumeration, apart from the fact that it varies with different writers, and never includes any weighting factor, is purely superficial and sheds no light on the question. In reality, these factors are as much the cause as the result of underdevelopment. Until this mutual dependence—which testifies to the social character of the phenomenon—is properly emphasized, the suggestions made are bound to be incomplete and in some respects misleading. This is particularly true of the attempt to establish general criteria for a policy.

We are so convinced of the virtue of our own methods and rules of life that we cannot conceive the future of other nations except as an effort to abolish, or at least to reduce, the technological gap between them and ourselves. We have, of course, read books in which the consequences of technological fever are deplored or condemned; but we do not really believe them, and we continue to delight in mechanical improvements. Technical efficiency thus becomes the touchstone of economic progress and even, in the long run, of progress as such.

This view, while apparently justified by our attainment of a wealth of material satisfactions, reveals a particularly narrow form of egocentrism. The short article by C. Gini on the different concepts of economic progress has been included in this volume, because its author had the courage to compare the distinctive attitudes of Oriental and Occidental theorists, and to declare that the West is doomed to disappointment in striving to convert the Orientals—not a small *élite*, but the mass of the people—to its ideas. But it is undoubtedly D. P. Mukerji's study of the views of Mahatma Gandhi which will give Western readers the greatest shock of surprise and, to put it frankly, of discomfort.

The birth and advance of our civilization is sometimes explained in terms of the myth of Prometheus—that is, as a constant effort on the part of mankind to unveil the secrets of nature and put them at the service of the human race. This refusal of the intelligence to submit to obscure, blind forces, is thought to lie at the root of the lust for conquest and adventure which seems so universally typical of man at the present day. It is considered responsible for the determination—sometimes latent, but often openly expressed—not to accept things as they are, but, if necessary, to change the universe in order to make it more agreeable for human beings—effort being concentrated chiefly on the physical aspects of our environment, but on social structures as well when they get in the way of the attempt to correct and adapt. And the machine is the most glorious symbol of the mastery thus acquired, the instrument through which, it seems, the world can gradually be rid of its ancient scourges. If the Promethean symbol has any meaning, mechanical civilization is certainly its most perfect expression.

Yet here we have a man—and one who successfully defied the forces of an immense empire—rejecting, with imperturbable tranquillity, the myth on which our daily efforts are founded. The machine is thrown down from the pedestal on which we usually place it. According to Gandhi, the indiscriminate introduction of modern technology into India could have only one effect—the disruption of the structure of human relations. By substituting the idea of output for that of skill, it would put an end to the love of work and the satisfaction of work well done. In short, the widespread use of machines for profit-making purposes would destroy the scale of values peculiar to India and the principles of that country's social organization. D. P. Mukerji shows his whole-hearted agreement with these views by presenting the absenteeism of Indian workers, their inattentive, casual attitude and their unpunctuality, as sound, normal reactions.

Many readers may be tempted to shrug their shoulders at these observations, which are far from universally accepted by the Indian *élite* (as will be seen, in particular, from the study by C. N. Vakil and P. R. Brahmanand). They may regard it simply as an example of the same wish to glorify the past which led Péguy, at the height of the Promethean period, to praise the work of the man who mends chairs. They should, however, wait to make up their minds until they have read K. Motwani's study of the influence of modern industrial technology on the social structure of South Asia. This is a merciless indictment, and I should not like to be given the task of refuting it. The author describes the big cities, those vast mausoleums of coal, smoke, iron and steel, filth and destitution, where coolies live herded into huge barracks. Then there are the indirect consequences to be reckoned with, including the breaking up of the village communities, as described by B. K. Madan in his article—the decay that has resulted from the pressure of a market economy and given rise to the scourge of usury. Considered in the light of these disastrous consequences, Mahatma Gandhi's views on machines and technological progress no longer appear untimely forebodings.

Moreover, Gandhi's attitude does not amount to a downright rejection of our mechanized civilization. All that D. P. Mukerji asks is that mechanization shall be preceded by a survey enabling it to be carried out in a manner consonant with the needs and aspirations of the people—which means, in his opinion, that the State must own the machines and direct their use. This is a recognition that economic activity, at every stage of technical development, has no value except as a contribution to a social aim. And it would not appear that the Promethean spirit has always made full allowance for this demand, which is both deep and elemental, meaningful and commonplace.

It is particularly difficult for those who live in an advanced capitalist civilization and enjoy the immense material advantages of the system, to give advice to nations which have not reached the same level of productivity. The introduction of technical progress into a freely developing economy leads to appalling, unspeakable wretchedness; yet after a certain point is reached—the point where consumption can expand without impeding the accumulation of capital—it has an undeniable corrective effect. Though they do not enjoy that 'affluence' which has been adopted as a propaganda slogan, the present-day industrialized communities are nevertheless able to eliminate or reduce a great deal of poverty.

To advise others against the use of machines, on the ground that it would imperil the purity of their ancient institutions and the stability of their traditional balance, would be intolerably pharisaical. Few attitudes are so contemptible as that of well-fed, comfortable people, holding forth about the blessedness of poverty. Yet we know that the conquest of material advantages is invariably offset by spiritual retrogression or repercussions, and that from this point of view technical improvements are by no means always synonymous with moral advancement. The representatives of the young States often express their resolve to modernize their countries without lessening the originality of their own particular traditions and modes of behaviour. This search for an individual path towards industrialization—a road which shall avoid all the disturbance and suffering that marked our own development—springs from a most optimistic view of man's capacities. If such a plan should succeed, it would be a red-letter day for the human race. But it would be disingenuous to conceal, or even to underestimate, the immense difficulty of such an undertaking.

Access to political independence is the very factor which can—or should—enable the necessary decisions to be made with open eyes. The first decision relates to the degree of mechanization or industrialization to be aimed at; and here it may be supposed that the competitive spirit and the instinct of imitation will lead the responsible authorities to aim at the highest level compatible with the resources of the country and the amount of external aid available. While admitting that this is a subjective view, based on one particular attitude towards human progress, I think that such a stand deserves approval.

It then remains—and this is the second decision—to adopt a system and institutions by which the entire nation can reap the benefit of its efforts, without unnecessary sacrifice or wastage. Twentieth-century experience, by destroying doctrinaire prejudices, has shown that in this respect there is a considerable margin of choice. But in any event, the underdeveloped countries are bound to meet with obstacles which cannot be surmounted without a hard struggle. Hence the need for governmental machinery which can encourage, co-ordinate and sustain their efforts.

IMPORTANCE OF THE POLITICAL SECTOR

Here we find in action the theory that economic development is affected by all the other factors of social life. The development of resources undoubtedly facilitates the formation of a stable, honest government; it is difficult, for instance, to fight against corruption when the Treasury cannot guarantee the regular payment of civil service salaries. But if there is no effective administrative machinery, economic achievements will be unsatisfactory and incomplete. This interdependence, which is in danger of developing into a vicious circle, is a clue to the difficulties now confronting the underdeveloped countries.

For several reasons, the value and effectiveness of the political sector constitute an important factor of economic progress. This is true of all countries, but it applies with particular force to backward regions where there is a temporary shortage of educated leadership. In many cases, these countries are unacquainted with the distinctions we are accustomed to draw among the ruling classes, and which facilitate the fair division of tasks and responsibilities. For instance, in many African countries there are practically no employers drawn from among the local people. Moreover, the trade union movement in that continent is limited in scale, and frequently in a position of subjection to the State. It thus inevitably rests with the latter to provide the chief, if not the only impetus to economic development. These considerations, which may seem obvious but are often overlooked, should help us to realize the absurdity of transplanting to Africa the discussions about 'isms' (capitalism, socialism, etc.) which are customary among ourselves.

Very few social scientists nowadays imagine that the expansion of the backward countries will take place according to the precepts of liberal economy (which the developed countries themselves gave up long ago, and, indeed, never applied in full). If the backward States wish to expedite their development, the only possible method would seem to be a central, or centralized organization of economic life, sufficiently strict to ensure that essential priorities will be observed, and sufficiently flexible to avoid discouraging the executive units or invalidating their efforts. We have learnt, often to our cost, that successful planning is extremely difficult. The paradoxical fact is that planning is needed most urgently in those very countries which are least prepared to undertake it (poverty of demographic and economic statistics, weakness or in many cases complete absence of geological surveys). In fact, the initial problem is that of doing high-precision work with clumsy tools.

The centralized organization of the life of the community not only requires the presence of skilled, unselfish and courageous statesmen, but also calls for a bureaucracy equipped to put the instructions received into daily practice. The application of administrative methods worthy of the name is prerequisite for effecting the desired improvement, and it goes without saying that results cannot be achieved merely by transplanting the methods in favour in the highly-developed countries. This transposition has already led to so many failures that it would be superfluous to criticize it here. The study by B. F. Hoselitz contains some

interesting observations on the recruitment of personnel to undertake such responsibilities.

The main thing is to devise solutions in keeping with the needs and possibilities
of the countries concerned. If they can shake off the usual prejudices, forget the
ideological controversies in which the highly-developed countries are so apt to
indulge, and reject the pressure of material interests (even should they be common
to an entire nation), the experts could make a valuable contribution to an effort
at reorganization which, if it is to be effective, will require preliminary or simultaneous changes in attitudes and motivation systems. But the decisive impulse can
only come from within, and that is how the basic lines of the new trends must be
laid down.

What I have said is enough to demonstrate the interest of this volume. Even so, I
have touched on only a few of the questions discussed or referred to in it. I am not
sure, however, whether I have made clear the greatest merit of these studies, which
is that they help us to understand a world different from the one to which we are
accustomed. Contact with that world engenders a feeling of unfamiliarity which
we must accept, for it is the prerequisite for a fair and accurate interpretation.
But things which demand from us an exceptional effort make up the natural and,
so to speak, daily intellectual fare of the anthropologist. It is in that respect that
this book, which is greatly indebted to anthropology, can be exceptionally helpful
by showing us the outside world as it really is.

Lausanne, December 1961.

ECONOMIC MOTIVATIONS
AND INCENTIVES

COMPARATIVE STUDY OF ECONOMIC MOTIVATIONS AND INCENTIVES IN A TRADITIONAL AND IN A MODERN ENVIRONMENT

General report on the round table organized by the International Research Office on the Social Implications of Technological Change (Paris, March 1954)

G. BALANDIER

When they decided on this topic, the organizers of the round table were attempting to deal with two very different types of difficulties. They were taking up, in the hope of clarifying it, a concept which, though it has come into widespread use, is nevertheless still very far from precise—the concept of motivation. And, secondly, they were embarking on the study of a whole group of problems—arising out of economic development and, in particular, out of the process of industrialization—which are at present shared by great areas of the world where there are enormous demands for equipment and modernization. There were therefore likely to be many difficulties, both on the theoretical and the practical side; but at the same time, those very difficulties were indicative of the scope and potential usefulness of research along these lines. The object of the meeting organized by the Research Office was to assist in this work by listing the main questions involved, making a critical assessment of the notions most commonly encountered, and formulating a few suggestions to serve as a guide in further investigations.

The economic development schemes are now in progress in the so-called 'underdeveloped' countries, and the technical assistance programmes carried out in certain territories have shown the decisive part played by psychological and cultural factors when financial and technical problems have been newly solved, at least for the time being. This has led certain observers to take the view that underdevelopment, as such, is only partly a matter for economists—and possibly, as one of them puts it, 'only in a very small degree'. Similarly, comparative studies undertaken, for instance, on the specific revenues of certain countries have shown what serious errors in assessment may result from concentrating attention on numerical data alone. It is absolutely necessary that cultural features, affecting the production, distribution and consumption of wealth, should be taken into account. It is therefore not surprising that several writers, when considering the concept of revenue to which we have just referred, make allowance not only for the 'accounting aspects' but also for 'psychological' (and cultural) aspects, which they are sometimes inclined to regard as playing a very special part. Forms of behaviour which have been developed in a traditional civilization still operate long after technical and economic changes—whether as regards attitudes to modern labour and the products of that labour or the ability (or inability) to accumulate capital and to embark on business undertakings—have overthrown the old social order. The sudden introduction of industrial civilization which, in one form or another, is the necessary condition for material progress, not only gives rise to a problem of technical adjustment: it calls for a new balance in motivations and thus necessitates a very real 'conversion' in the individual. This constant intervention of the cultural factor explains why, in his paper, Professor M. J. Herskovits considered the problem of fitting the individual into a new 'economic environment' in the light of two 'key concepts': the concept of motivation and the concept of the cultural pattern. Neither of these two factors operates alone and they can only be considered in close association.

From another point of view, it is important to make it clear that the idea of motivation, as elaborated by the psychologists, relates to the physiological conditions peculiar to the human system as well as to the nature of the experience already acquired. If it relates to fundamental (or primary) human needs, it requires much more reference to the framework of experience, whether natural or cultural. It therefore makes an interdisciplinary approach essential and it was for this purpose that the Research Office took the very useful step of arranging for co-operation between different specialists (anthropologists, sociologists, psychologists, economists and geographers) with a view to limiting the use of the concept to the economic field. Thus at the outset, a problem of adjustment among different branches of study had to be faced, and this experience has taught us much that may be extremely useful in the future.

The comparison between the nature and interrelations of the economic motivations operating in a traditional environment, on the one hand, and in a 'modern' environment, on the other, leads to the discussion of the incompatibilities and changes encountered in various types of situation. In particular, it shows, as Professor D. Kresch has already noted with reference to psychological theory, to what an extent motivations in general consist of closely interrelated factors, and that they can not vary in any particular without affecting the whole. This explains the 'chain reaction' which comes about, for instance, when a peasant previously living on a subsistence basis in an agricultural society moves over to the paid employment sector. Moreover, such a comparison is of practical use so far as it gives us material for answering the basic question: What types of economic situations induce workers to engage in the modern forms of economic activity? There can be no question of confining attention to cultural and psychological considerations, such as resistance to changes which seriously disturb social relationships, an inadequate degree of adaptability, comparative inertia in the matter of innovation, etc. At this point in the investigation, the idea of the general situation (with due regard for the direct or indirect compulsion suffered, the opportunities for access to the riches of modern economy, the opportunities for organization open to workers and producers, etc.) and that of differential variation (according to ethnic and social categories, age-group and sex, etc.) should guide research. The discussions that took place at the meetings of the round table made this abundantly clear.

It is thus impossible to carry out a too narrowly-defined investigation bearing mainly on attitudes towards the modern techniques and economic machinery being introduced into the so-called underdeveloped countries. Such a study is really useful only if it is based upon comparative data and if advantage is taken of the special methods peculiar to the various branches of study involved. The discussion meetings organized by the Research Office were designed to bring out this fact and, at the same time, to enable a first assessment to be made of the knowledge already at our disposal. The organization of the discussions was inspired, as the chairman, Professor R. Firth, had asked, by the desire to furnish guidance for the conduct of further investigations and to carry out a dynamic study combining the theoretical and the practical approaches.

It was clear, from the first, that problems of terminology and the interpretation of concepts were bound to play a very important part. The reason for this, as we have just suggested, is to be found in the present needs of research and the necessity for listing the existing material and making a critical assessment of it.

GENERAL INTRODUCTION TO THE SUBJECT OF INVESTIGATION

There are objections to the term 'underdeveloped country', in so far as it appears to imply that progress consists in technical and economic advance alone, and to reflect a somewhat ethnocentric outlook on the part of the economically powerful peoples. Professor D. P. Mukerji criticized this term, which has been adopted by the various international organizations, and suggested that a more 'dynamic' term should be used in its stead, taking into account all the socio-cultural and economic aspects of life which characterize the 'development' of a society.

Professor C. Lévi-Strauss warned against the dangers of a unilateral outlook, pointing out, in particular, that the so-called underdeveloped societies cannot be simply receivers but also have something to give. Where we find that there are no economic incentives, or very few, we may assume that there is often a different balance of incentives. We must beware, moreover, of regarding our own system as the only good one; it has not come into being without serious disturbances and at a high cost to certain social groups. Societies which are at present engaged in the processes of economic development and industrialization may, with the help of their own specific cultural wealth, build up their own systems of motivations and incentives; and before these are criticized by reference to the criteria peculiar to the industrial societies of the West, they must be subjected to minute examination. They also offer us a rewarding field of study.

Many psychologists, by centring their research on the industrial environment, have, as Professor Herskovits remarked, been working inside Western societies; what matters now is to observe carefully the variations that arise from the diversity of cultural contexts. Indeed any study of behaviour entails reference to these, and most psychologists would like to see research conducted along the lines of comparative studies and the investigation of series of variations. Dr. O Klineberg pointed out how far psychologists have moved from an explanation linking economic motivations with biological requirements only. He drew attention to the tendency to investigate how the latter 'operate' in particular societies, cultural systems and historical contexts; at the same time, he affirmed the urgent need for defining the most favourable conditions for an interdisciplinary approach. Dr. A. Ombredane, in the light of his investigations in the Belgian Congo, emphasized the need for comparing the criteria appropriate to work done in a 'white' (modern) environment with those appropriate to work done in a traditional environment. He urged that incompatibilities and discordances should then be noted: the latter were particularly to be found in connexion with the nature of the work (which in the 'white' environment is split up into a number of separate operations whereas, in the traditional environment, it was 'complete'), and the destination of the product of labour (in the 'modern' system, the worker is a stranger to the consumer of the product). All the preliminary observations show that economic motivations cannot be considered in isolation and indeed emphasize the need to regard them as forming part of 'configurations' or 'systems' of motivations.

According to Professor G. Balandier, when we speak of economic motivations, we know that we have to do with incentives born of necessity, social and cultural stimuli, and direct or indirect compulsion, but it is not easy to isolate these various factors and to classify them in order of importance. The first point to remember is still that the problem of economic motivations cannot legitimately be simplified by relating it to a theory of needs. The second major point is that a problem of this kind cannot be considered apart from the situations in which the motivations operate.

This concept of the situation relates to the conditions of the natural environment, technological standards, and the socio-economic and cultural systems. When we speak of traditional and non-traditional environments, we have in mind a broad distinction between two very different types of situation; for purposes of scientific observation there should clearly be much greater precision in the definition of types, by reference to the three factors mentioned above. Mr. J. Malaurie emphasized the geographer's point of view and laid most stress on the first of these factors. He pointed out how necessary it is to remember that all civilizations are linked up with the phenomenon of 'adjustment to a place', and urged that the study of economic motivations and incentives should not be divorced from a survey of resources, which enables a whole group of boundaries to be defined. Eskimo and Tuareg societies, on which this writer has concentrated, are cases in which these natural boundaries are particularly striking. A first hierarchy of motivations can thus be made by reference to the conditions of the environment.

While the geographer deplores that proper attention is not always paid to environmental conditions, the psychologist complains that in certain investigations (conducted by anthropologists and sociologists) there has been no interdisciplinary co-operation, in which his own special techniques could have been useful. Dr. O. Klineberg mentioned that useful experiments could be carried out on the problem under consideration and, in particular, drew attention to the need for a differential examination. Although motivations appear as 'configurations', it is nonetheless true that some of them predominate—and that the predominance varies according to the social group concerned and the particular situation with which we are dealing. To the idea of the hierarchy of motivations must therefore be added the concept of the relativity of the hierarchies.

The very fact that this comparative study of conditions in a traditional environment and conditions in an industrialized environment had been suggested raised the problem of adaptation to the latter type of environment. Taking up this question of the reorientation of motivations, Professor B. Hoselitz emphasized the importance of research relating to 'marginal' individuals and groups. The individuals who are classified as marginal may either react in a rigid manner that betrays a failure to adjust, or, on the contrary, they may show a plasticity that reveals them as active promoters of innovation. This latter attitude may offer the best opportunity of investigating the conditions most conducive to a genuine change in motivations. Owing to its vagueness, however, the concept of the 'margin' gave rise to a considerable number of objections, particularly from Professor Herskovits. The term is ambiguous because its use in both economics and anthropology creates confusion and because the social groups to which the expression may be applied are not precisely defined. Professor R. Firth, while laying emphasis on the idea of marginal groups, endorsed Dr. Mukerji's proposal that research should be organized on the basis of the 'intermediary groups' which come into being as industrialization proceeds.

Some of the objections just mentioned brought out the fact that, in investigations undertaken on the basis of the marginal concept, greater attention has been devoted to the negative aspects ('disadjustment', failure of motivations to respond to the needs of economic progress, etc.) than to the positive aspects. Professor Herskovits emphasized the latter and, in particular, mentioned the case of the Chagga (Tanganyika) who have adapted themselves to coffee-growing, organized agricultural co-operatives and set up a bean-drying business. This adjustment has been achieved without degrading the people's religious concepts or code of values and without disorganizing the traditional society. Illustrating his remarks with other examples drawn from Africa, Professor P. Gourou also directed attention to the phenomena revealing a trend towards adaptation. He said that a better knowledge of African institutions, and a conviction that 'social' considerations should take precedence over 'technical and economic' considerations, might have been very helpful in securing success in a greater number of cases and in facilitating modernization. He recommended that a study be made of occupational groups (such as railway workers or the staff of shipping companies in Equatorial Africa) which, for reasons that are not yet clear, constitute a framework within which the calling in question is effectively pursued.

All these observations are linked with a more general problem, namely: in what way are behaviour patterns conditioned by a new situation? What types of situation are most conducive to a change in the trend of behaviour? What are the ends (traditional and new) for which the economic motivations serve as means. The investigation of these motivations cannot be separated from that of the values they 'serve' and of the resulting forms of behaviour. The phenomena of adjustment and disadjustment cannot be clearly grasped except at the level of the connexions between these three factors, and many economists who are specially interested in the problems of the underdeveloped countries have drawn attention to the fact that these problems are only 'partially economic'. The main conclusion drawn from the first day's discussions was therefore that an interdisciplinary organization of research was necessary. There can be no doubt that many projects undertaken in the field of economic studies are still based on the concept of the 'economic man'. They have more or less overt psychological implications which call for meticulous examination and which may prove completely false when applied to very different cultural contexts, as in the case of the so-called underdeveloped countries. Dr. O. Klineberg, for instance, emphasized the need for a psychological approach, which has so far produced only a very few noteworthy studies.

THE IMPLICATIONS OF MODERN ECONOMY

The introduction of a modern economy into traditional societies gives rise to a dualism which was very clearly brought out by Professor J. H. Boeke in his comparison of the two economic systems. This dualism can also be seen in the pairs of concepts suggested by various members of the round table as a means of clarifying the terms 'traditional environment' and 'modern environment'; there is no need to mention them all, but the following are examples: non-industrialized society and industrialized society, pre-capitalistic society and capitalistic society, closed society and open society, etc. It is difficult to pick out any one of these pairs of concepts as being fully satisfactory. Two lists of more or less parallel features might, however, be drawn up as follows:

Non-industrialized environment	Environment in which industrialization has begun and is proceeding
Predominance of a subsistence economy	Very much reduced importance of a subsistence economy
Maintenance of a relatively 'autocratic' control by the members having authority over the basic groups	Trend towards the development of individual control of income and of the consumption of wealth
Importance of exchange and of 'give and take' etc.	Importance of competition, etc.

These are the opening terms in the parallel lists suggested by Professor G. Balandier, which may lead to a definition of the types of situation and which, in any case, show how profoundly this dualism affects the whole socio-cultural complex.

Professor J. H. Boeke, after reminding his listeners that there is no possibility of a choice between a subsistence economy and a market economy, sought to define the general conditions of an economy which might lead to a more satisfactory analysis of the problem. The fundamental change is obviously the increasing circulation of money. The first problem to be considered is that of people's reactions towards money and the possibilities of accumulating capital. Some members of the round table pointed out how closely consumption is bound up with cultural characteristics as a whole. Forms of remuneration may have a negligible incentive value not only because of the low level of remuneration but also because they are not adjusted to the characteristic forms of behaviour. Dr. A. Ombredane, for instance, referring to his research in the Congo, mentioned that, in that region remuneration implies an idea of prestige which is more important than that of gain and is related to immediate consumption, being a factor in a 'very special type' of organization of consumption. Moreover, irrespective of the local opportunities for saving and accumulating capital, one of the major problems is how to train producers as entrepreneurs 'in the European sense'. Certain forms of behaviour with regard to capital (predominance of expenditure on consumer goods, circulation of money for the purposes of usury alone, hoarding, etc.), and certain ideas of what is or is not an economic proposition, may create conditions militating against economic progress. In this connexion, it is important to take into account the time factor, which has a very profound influence on socio-economic phenomena: in the underdeveloped countries, short-term results and short-term efficacy are preferred to medium- and long-term undertakings. This attitude is to be accounted for, in many cases, by the influence of cultural systems (those which we call 'traditional') that set very little store by activities whose results are deferred for any length of time. Mr. H. M. Phillips' question: 'Are we working for next year or for the next generation?' reflects the dilemma with which we are faced.

The study of reactions to modern economy again brings to the fore a second problem to which we have already referred, namely: What are the prevailing attitudes towards work? What benefits is it expected to produce? Dr. O. Klineberg said that this question was of great interest and suggested that the hierarchy of motives—money, security, prestige, interest in the work, attachment to the social contacts formed through work—should be studied in relation to cultural contexts, situations and social groups. Such a study should reveal a set of variations which could be analysed in detail and thus provide useful guidance for further work. It was clear to all the members of the round table, however, that far too little material has so far been assembled in this sphere; it is therefore essential that attention should be drawn to the gaps in the information available, and Professor Ombredane made a practical suggestion when he asked that sociologists, anthropologists and psychologists should be given an opportunity of co-operating in drawing up a questionnaire to provide a framework for future investigations.

After the discussion of these preliminary problems, Professor D. P. Mukerji asked that the studies should be conducted dynamically, and that all the various types of reactions to new techniques and new forms of economic organization—hostility, indifference or preference operating in favour of a particular change—should be considered. Remarks made by Professor B. Hoselitz opened up new prospects here, suggesting that resistance to change is not as active as it is generally said to be. Contesting certain anthropological views, which attach special importance to systems of values, he stated that what matters is not so much to 'change' fundamental values as to 'change' economic and social institutions so as to make them more receptive to innovations. He mentioned the emergence of new needs—the major stimuli of economic activity and invention—and pointed out how little resistance these needs encounter when they are reflected in terms of entirely new goods and services, unless religion or unreasonableness puts obstacles in the way. On the other hand, he pointed out that, when the need for commodities which improve living conditions, or the need for more efficient techniques, does not prevent resistance to certain changes, there can be no doubt that the reasons accounting for the resistance are perfectly rational. In this connexion, mention may be made of the introduction of the plough into Equatorial Africa, or of the clearing of stones from cultivated fields which was recommended by agricultural experts in Turkey. There were very good reasons for the rejection of these changes by the local peasants, since the proposed improvements involved serious dangers owing to the friability of the soil and the climatic conditions.

Mr. B. F. Hoselitz indirectly suggested a useful comparison which, so far as the problems of adaptation to modern economy are concerned, shows the contrast between a trend marked by a reasoned optimism and a trend marked by extreme caution. Mr. J. Malaurie, referring to the very special example of the Eskimos of Thule, stated that, in no case of this sort, can there be 'any reason for restricting modernization'. Anthropo-geographers and economists tend to subscribe to the first of these trends, whereas certain anthropologists, being doubtful of the adaptability of typical modes of behaviour and giving first place to cultural aspects, may invest the second of these trends with a fundamentally pessimistic character. Mr. J. P. Lebeuf raised some major objections, dwelling on the preponderant part played by religious factors, on cases of the 'wrong use' of manufactured commodities and cases of the hoarding of money. Professor Ombredane suggested the need for caution in making judgements, pointing out that it sometimes takes more than a generation to secure the acceptance and efficient use of a new tool or an alien technique. He laid particular stress on the conservative influence of the native woman, which, in many cases, puts a check on innovations. This observation, which calls for a series of special investigations, deserves consideration by research workers. There can be little doubt, however, so far as these controversial points are concerned, that a comparative approach of the kind to which attention has already been drawn several times is for the time being the best attitude for research workers to adopt. Incidentally, the interest of certain members of the round table (as revealed, in particular, by the remarks of Professor Mukerji) in 'intermediary' phenomena, was characteristic of their desire to concentrate on 'average' cases and so avoid being led to extremes in either direction.

Professor R. Firth rounded off the consideration of this group of problems by stating and clarifying the subjects on which further investigations are necessary. He suggested, in particular, that a study should be made of the foreseen and unforeseen effects of the introduction of foreign tools; of the problem of reactions towards mechanization; of the assessment of the social costs of innovations; of the formation and use of capital and the social implications of these processes. This last point, to which various observers drew attention (Mr. H. M. Phillips, Governor H. Deschamps) and on which Professor Firth was anxious that comparative studies should be organized, is a most important factor in any study of the phenomenon of the expansion of monetary and market economies.

THE RURAL ENVIRONMENT 'IN TRANSITION'

It is in connexion with the introduction of so-called 'cash' or 'commercial' crops that the extent to which peasant reactions are modernist can best be grasped. As several contributors noted, the increased cultivation of these crops intended for the foreign market gives the land a new value, creates a new relationship between man and the soil, and, in certain regions, gives rise to particularly serious questions of land reform. There is no doubt that the form and rate of these changes vary from territory to territory. Professor Hoselitz reminded his listeners of this by drawing a distinction between two fundamentally different types of development: the gradual introduction of cash crops, or the sudden complete transformation of the old subsistence economy, associated with the rise of urban centres (e.g., in China). Professor Hoselitz also laid stress on another feature of these changes, which is of particular interest for the study of economic motivations: the introduction of commercial crops makes the small producers more dependent on the big farming concerns and subjects them still further to the whole economic system associated with these concerns. In a process of this kind, the problem of the organization of the small producers— for instance, in co-operative societies—becomes of primary importance.

The moment we started comparing notes, it became clear that situations differ greatly. Professor Doucy quoted the example of the Belgian Congo, where the new crops were introduced by European settlers or by the government, which was endeavouring to create a 'peasant class'. The difficulties, in this case, were due not only to the instability of the village settlements and to low productivity, but also to the fact that the measures taken failed to make due allowance for the special conditions of the physical and social environment. The development of a peasant class resembling (in theory) the peasant class in the Western countries may produce disappointing results, especially when it is associated, in a colonial territory, with measures initiated entirely by the government. Governor Deschamps made a point of warning us against the signal failures in which attempts to establish a 'pre-fabricated peasant class' may end. He pointed out that the most constructive experiments have been those resulting from spontaneous movements.

Instancing the development of cacao plantations in the Fang country, the Gaboon and the South Cameroons, Professor Balandier showed that the major problems were only partly technical, having been caused mainly by the nature of the traditional economy itself (transition from a system based on conquest, followed by the slave trade, to an agricultural economy) and of the traditional society. The introduction of the new form of cultivation was hampered in the first place by the customary division of labour, by the mobility of the communities, which have only the slightest bonds with the soil, and by a social organization marked by equalitarian trends militating against the emergence of a land-owning middle class and the development of a wage-earning class within the clan or tribe. In such cases, collective systems create the atmosphere most conducive to the modernization of agriculture. To achieve the best conditions, moreover, not only must there be technical training proper, but also the villages must be trained as sellers (need-ing to defend themselves against powerful buyers) and consumers. Similarly, Mr. J. Malaurie pointed out the importance of internal social factors, quoting the case of certain Saharan peoples with a highly organized society, where the peasants hold no land of their own at all but farm on the *métayage*, or sharecrop-ping, system; the social and environmental conditions combine to restrict farming. Mr. Malaurie summed this up in the phrase: 'The peasant is compelled to regulate his work by his own under-nourishment.'

The problems involved in the 'modern' organization of the peasants (especially on co-operative lines) occupied the attention of several of those taking part in the round table, who reported on the results of experiments in Peru (Professor Matos Mar), Indonesia (Professor Boeke), North Africa (Professor Leduc) and the Pacific region (Professor Firth). Professor Boeke drew up a particularly useful system of references by recalling the weak points of the rural co-operatives organized in Europe—a tendency towards expansion and centralization, which reduces the sense of practical co-operation at the local level, inability of the peasant members to manage and supervise the organization, tendency for these institutions to turn into 'companies', which restricts the opportunities for new members to join, etc.— and urged that these lessons should not be forgotten in present efforts to foster co-operative systems in the underdeveloped countries. After making these general observations, which are applicable to any form of co-operative organization, Professor Boeke drew a distinction between two forms of co-operation which are peculiar to these countries: one being of the 'European' or 'Western' type, organ-ized on 'capitalist' lines and essentially intended for economic purposes, and the other 'local', limited in extent and, in fact, representing a real reorganization of village life. In this connexion, he drew attention to various examples to be seen in Asia and asked that help should be given to 'these co-operative societies which have no funds and no specific aims but are seeking to instigate joint action in the interests of a better and a fuller life'. In so doing, he made us aware of a type of situation which is likely to lead to a new balance of economic motivations and the other motivations associated with them.

Professor Firth pointed out that a useful starting point for future investiga-tions would be a comparative study of social structures and organizations which may (as in New Zealand) or may not (as in Malaya) provide a basis for the develop-ment of the co-operative system. This question of the relations between traditional organizations and 'modern' organizations was in the forefront of the minds of all those present. Dr. Klineberg drew attention to the consensus of opinion on this point and accordingly proposed that research should be undertaken on the following questions: In what circumstances is it possible to introduce new methods of cultivation and new forms of organization by building on the existing socio-cultural foundations? On what conditions is it possible to break with tradition and to introduce an entirely alien type of organization? To what extent is such a break the price that has to be paid for progress?

Professor Firth spoke on much the same lines, suggesting that an assessment should be made of the degree of 'success' achieved in modern experiments neces-sitating a complete break with the past, that the conditions conducive to a desire for 'change' should be determined, and that the nature of the changes desired should be clarified. Referring to examples drawn from Africa, Professor G. Balan-dier emphasized that, at least at the outset, the solutions adopted must be specifi-cally adapted to the differing situations. In some cases, powerful chiefs may be able to lead the movement for modernization; in some, the process of adaptation may start from characteristic features of the tribal system (e.g., certain communities in the South Cameroons); while, in others, typically capitalistic reactions and changes may actively develop. From another point of view, Mr. G. Balandier drew attention to two other problems: adaptation means that any innovation must have a clear significance for the villagers and that, in a country which has been colonized, it must not be part of a system which is almost exclusively controlled by the colonists.

Professor Herskovits pointed out that all these questions raise a general problem which is of great importance in relation to theories of culture. He reminded his listeners that institutions and types of behaviour which are in line with the customary background have a better chance of being adopted. This led him on to a question of the utmost importance in cultural anthropology: How, and to what extent, is it possible for societies which are very different from one another to co-operate? From this point of view, certain parts of Latin America seem to offer an interesting field of study owing to the importance of the 'mestizo culture' there. The investigations, mentioned by Mr. J. Matos Mar, on which the University of San Marcos, Lima, is at present engaged may produce some invaluable information on this point.

The reorientation of motivations related to a rural environment in the course of modernization is a question too wide to be covered by a few research 'subjects'. This became quite clear in the two meetings devoted to this question, though various studies that might be undertaken were also suggested at the same time. New data might be collected, bearing in mind the 'technically optimum size', the possibility of combining the extension of cash crops with that of food crops (B. F. Hoselitz), the relations between the development of industrial crops and changes in systems of land tenure (D. P. Mukerji), the reactions of villagers towards cash incomes and, in particular, the part played by hoarding and the immobilization of currency in 'dowries', and the emergence in a rural environment of an 'intermediate' or 'middle' class (R. Firth). It should be added that a study of the migratory movements commonly referred to as the drift from the land, which are of considerable importance both in Asia and in Africa, ought to be undertaken in relation to the topic we have been considering above. What are the practical motivations that induce people to seek an urban environment in which to live and work?

ADAPTATION TO THE BUSINESS UNDERTAKING AND TO THE
INDUSTRIAL ENVIRONMENT

The industrial undertaking and its offshoots, in the form of workers' camps or services established by the firm, make up a social complex to which the newly-arrived villager cannot adapt himself without some difficulty. Professor G. Friedmann explained that this introduction to the industrial environment causes a 'shock' by forcing the individual to become a member of new communities that have a far-reaching influence on behaviour. He makes a distinction, in this respect, between the so-called formal groups, represented by the various 'shops' or 'departments', work-gangs, organizations necessitated by the hierarchy within the undertaking, etc., and the so-called informal groups which come into being outside the environment of working life and are based on ethnic affinities, the fact that individuals come from the same place, religious affiliation, etc. So far as the native worker is concerned, the significance and the influence of these two kinds of groups differ. The first, which spring from production requirements and technical considerations, are beyond his control; the second take account of his needs, offer comparatively wide scope for initiative on his part, and keep alive in the industrial environment some of the cultural features characteristic of the traditional environment. As will be realized, these latter groups provide a good field for anthropological research. They help to bring about the 'transition' and act as a kind of buffer.

To help in the discussion of general problems, Professor Hoselitz instanced two 'cases' studied by the Research Centre in Economic Development and Cultural Change. In a Mexican village (Paracho), with about 2,000 inhabitants, two or three villagers managed to set themselves up as industrial entrepreneurs. The problems which then arose were not so much technical—i.e., connected with the introduction of machinery—as social, resulting from the emergence of a wage-earning class, the development of employer-workman relations, and a status of dependence which had hitherto been unknown. The second survey dealt with a village in Guatemala (Kantal), where there is a modern business, founded about sixty years ago, employing 1,200 Indians from the plateaux. In some cases, two or three generations of the same family are employed. At the same time, the part of the village which has no connexion with the business goes on living as it has done in the past; the cultural system has been strong enough to 'hold' the villagers in spite of the importance of the factory and the time its influence has been operative. These two cases show how necessary it is to broaden our terms of comparison and to extend the series of variations on fundamental problems. Why do certain societies seek new forms of organization while others, in the same circumstances, do not? What are the personal characteristics which, in one case, lead to conservatism (often purely formal and of no practical significance) and, in another, to a readiness to accept innovations? These questions open up the whole problem of a differential study of reactions to change.

Referring to the results of recent surveys conducted in India, Professor Mukerji also noted that the development of a wage-earning class (e.g., in mining concerns) did not necessarily, of itself, bring about a rapid change in types of behaviour. He mentioned that such a change seems to be linked up with two groups of factors: the proximity of urban centres and the closeness of contacts with those centres; and the influence wielded by Christian missions, which may weaken and reduce the sway of the traditional religion. The weakening of the caste system and its conversion into a class system is accentuated by the operation of such factors which, as it were, accelerate the effects directly due to technological and economic changes.

This consideration of the degree of aptitude for change leads on to the problem of the part played by women as an impediment to the adaptation of the native worker. Professor Doucy, referring to observations carried out in the Belgian Congo, dwelt on the conservative influence of women—the 'clan pressure' is exercised through them—and their responsibility for the degree of instability shown by African workers. Mr. Lebeuf agreed with these observations and quoted other examples drawn from Central Africa. Professor Friedmann cited facts which he had had occasion to note when carrying out an inquiry, in North Africa; he found that the native worker is in a transitional state, 'hesitating' between the traditional environment from which he comes and the modern environment found in and around the business undertaking. Such workers are therefore extremely 'sensitive' to any influences operating in either direction. The influence of the women in the family group is still very considerable and Mr. G. Friedmann did not think that the progress of industrialization would become easier until a change had been brought about in the women's attitude.

Professor Herskovits reverted to the cross-cultural approach, characteristic of all anthropological study. He pointed out that, in certain societies, women display genuine dynamism and assert their personality more than men. Professor Klineberg took the same view, adopting the idea of differential receptivity, and uttering a warning against the temptation to generalize with widely differing situations. He observed that women may be more receptive with regard to certain socio-cultural changes and less so with regard to others, and that similar differences were to be found between varying age-groups or occupational categories. In this problem of receptivity, we thus had variables requiring systematic investigation.

Following up these general remarks, Professor Hoselitz suggested that problems of basic importance should be approached indirectly, from the standpoint of commitment to the industrial way of life, this concept being one that could give relative unity to the research in question. In order to observe the 'mechanisms' characteristic of this commitment, and the ensuing reactions, it would be well to take into account important variations depending on whether the commitment was total or partial. The latter made for instability, maintained the influence of the traditional environment (particularly in the case of women), and gave rise to faulty adjustment within old family units that had been preserved with all their ramifications.

Professor Firth was also concerned with these concepts and advocated defining them more precisely, by reason of their very complexity. The expression 'commitment' could be considered from the psychological angle—the individual's desire, for various reasons, to take part in the industrial sector—and from the socio-economic angle; the evolution of industrialization forcing individuals, sometimes against their will, to follow the new way of life. As for the expression 'industrial way of life', Professor Firth made it clear that a distinction should be drawn between at least four types of situation: work in an industrial environment, which raises the problem of adaptation to machinery and to industrial discipline; production intended for the 'industrial market', though with no commitment to the industrial way of life; consumption of manufactured goods, again with no commitment to the industrial way of life; impact of industry as a dominant economic factor, although certain social groups may escape its direct influence.

No single term could cover all these various possibilities. This was conceded by Professor Hoselitz, who however made it clear that the expression frequently employed referred to the first of these possibilities; it implied the technical relationship between man and the machine and the accomplishment of one portion of a task, and also pointed to a definite state of dependency on the level of social relationships.

Professor Herskovits drew a further distinction by asking that cases where industrial activity had been imposed should be clearly distinguished from cases where this was an entirely spontaneous development, a definite desire for progress. However, the dividing line was never quite so sharp, and criteria for evaluation seemed difficult to define; this distinction appeared to be drawn indirectly, on the basis of the degree of adjustment to the demands of the industrial environment, and the strength of the reaction against that environment. Professor Mukerji directed his criticism along these lines, suggesting a severe scrutiny of terminology and a precise definition of the meaning of the ever-growing list of technical expressions employed.

The problem of adaptation to the specific conditions of any industrial concern immediately raises the question of accustoming employees to rhythms of work and also the question of the discipline these rhythms require. Prof. Friedmann stressed these different aspects and showed how they might help to define the scope of research. The development of the industrialization process in a traditional environment or in contact with such an environment implies the introduction of new rhythms of life; it brings to light a transitional phenomenon calling for psychological and physiological examination. Certain features of labour in underdeveloped countries—turnover, absenteeism, occasional low production, etc.—are partly explained by lack of adjustment to the new work rhythms.

Similarly, the enterprise concerned should be organized in such a way as to facilitate transition, prepare men to accept work of a different rhythm from that to which they are accustomed, and to establish teams of individuals all working at the same rate, etc. Hence the importance of studying industrial psycho-sociology from the very start of the industrialization movement. These studies should be specially concerned with the very controversial question of output in an underdeveloped country. Professor G. Leduc stated this problem when he remarked that a rise in the standard of living depended on a rapid improvement of output. But to what extent were the shortcomings in question to be regarded as the result of physiological conditions, poor adaptation and lack of education, or of certain forms of social relationships?

Mr. A. Braunthal suggested an answer to this question by recommending that the relationship between low salaries and low production should be examined, as well as the reactions (spontaneous or organized) against productivity drives which engender fear of industrial unemployment—as is already happening in certain regions of South-East Asia. He also emphasized that the existence of a colour bar within and outside the enterprise concerned, and even in certain trade unions, could greatly affect the strength and the form of economic motivations.

Moreover, these motivations are undoubtedly linked with the opportunities enjoyed by native workers to organize themselves in occupational groups. This fact was emphasized by Mr. Braunthal, who drew attention to the importance of trade unionism during the 'modernization' of traditional societies and to the special characteristics of trade unionism in underdeveloped countries. In such countries the movement, like most of the changes affecting society and culture as a whole, bore the characteristic features of a transitional phenomenon. In this connexion, Professor G. Balandier drew attention to the difficulties encountered by the first trade union organizations introduced into the French Congo after 1946. These difficulties arose from the following: distrust of a method of organization completely alien to the country and associated, to some extent, with the whole European system of control; a concept of efficiency calling for short-term results; and growth of a large number of small trade unions each with its separate interests. Moreover, where native workers are concerned, internal causes as well as outside influences often militate against the development of effective trade unionism.

Study of these problems of adaptation to the industrial environment should not, however, cause us to exaggerate the difficulties noted or to consider progress impossible: it should not lead to any kind of conservatism which, moreover, would run counter to the present desire for progress on the part of most traditional societies. The orientation of comparative research towards the best adjusted occupational groups, as advocated by Professor Gourou, would help to provide the necessary corrective to any such tendency.

RESULTS AND SUGGESTIONS

Professor Firth, in his capacity as chairman of the round table, gave a general summary of the discussions and exchanges of views; he stressed the fact that agreement had been reached on many points and that despite the diversity of experience, progress was being made with studies conducted by much the same methods. He then considered the results obtained in relation to the aims set by the members of the round table.

Definition of the research topic

In the first place, he commented on the outstanding interest of the material used which, gathered as it was from most of the representative regions, was very varied; and observed that it was thus possible to define more clearly the problem of economic motivations. One implication of the subject under consideration was the possibility of a new balance of motivations, and of a reorientation to meet the needs of economic development. It further raised the question of the time factor, in that the results of short-term observation were liable to be very different from those of long-term observation. The absence of historians and the lack of data made it impossible to give adequate consideration to that aspect of the problem, but its true importance was realized and awaited the attention of future research workers.

Although the concept of economic motivation was not analysed from the strictly theoretical standpoint, it nevertheless formed the background of all discussions and was approached in connexion with the broader phenomena and situations considered. Moreover, it was discussed from the particular angle of each branch of study represented. A co-ordinated approach of this kind, by collating very different systems of reference, brought out the need for comprehensive study and served as a warning against the shortcomings of any one-sided investigation. Several of the members repeatedly emphasized that motivations cannot be discerned separately, but only as part of a whole set of factors whose aspect varies according to circumstances. This illustrated the necessity for interdisciplinary investigations.

Inventory of completed and current research projects

Professor Firth dwelt on the importance of the examples discussed during working meetings and their value for purposes of comparison. To meet the wishes of all members, a short bibliography is to be drawn up to serve as a guide to the material used.

Orientation of further research

The meeting felt the need for additional research outside the actual topic of discussion, in order to obtain a clearer general view of the problems under consideration. A list of research projects was drawn up by Professor Firth (chairman) and Professor Balandier (rapporteur). It covered three types of problem: study of motivations and their characteristics; study of processes; and study of groups (vocational and co-operative, etc.). It should lead to a consideration of the problems arising from industrial development and the modernization of economy, and should be the first step in the gradual elaboration of a general theory of social change.

Professor Lévi-Strauss observed that the need for increasingly precise and specialized research methods had been consistently stressed. He defined the task ahead as 'clarification of our modes of thought' and offered suggestions for a theoretical approach to the problems discussed during the working meetings.

38

To begin with, he pointed out that research was all too often organized as if the problem of socio-economic change 'were suddenly appearing on the historical scene'. However, the so-called underdeveloped societies had had technical and economic contacts with each other long before the expansion of Western civilization. Why were they so deeply affected by the changes now taking place? To answer this question, there must be taken into consideration: (a) the change of scale factor involved in 'modernization' processes within traditional societies. This problem was now under consideration by the International Social Science Council, which had just organized an inquiry into the 'effects of change of scale on the characteristics of social groups'; (b) the factor of the differential divergence between societies that have been brought into contact with one another; there were 'natural partners' with which creative symbiosis is possible, while in other cases there might be incompatibilities giving rise to pathological situations.

On the other hand, Professor Lévi-Strauss cautioned against the tendency to think that immediate, sudden contacts could be made, without any previous preparation. He emphasized that industrialized societies exert a remote influence before forcing their way into any traditional society, and may thus have a destructive effect jeopardizing any possibilites of latter adaption. Apart from the oft-quoted case of conflicting incentives, consideration must be given to cases in which this negative influence affects old types of incentives before the 'introduction' of new types; a vacuum is then created, which makes any subsequent readjustment more difficult.

In conclusion, Mr. Lévi-Strauss asked that 'the relative influence of the various elements in any one society on another society with which it establishes contact' should be borne in mind. All changes were not possible to the same degree, however receptive a society might be. Study of 'natural partners', selected in accordance with the techniques peculiar to the groups thus brought into contact, might enable a revealing investigation to be carried out along the lines of the differential research frequently referred to during the discussion. Lastly, Mr. Lévi-Strauss suggested recommending a study in which problems would be considered within the framework of a series of societies 'in contact' but presenting increasing differential divergencies.

During each of the working meetings, special attention was given to theoretical considerations, which were also linked with the suggestions for research made by all members of the round table. Collaboration between specialists in the various branches of social science, approaching the same question from the angle of their respective techniques, raises a difficult problem of adjustment.

The terminology and specific capacity for elaborating concepts, peculiar to each discipline, no less than its equally individual study methods, did not lend themselves to immediate co-operation. This question was raised by Dr. Ombredane who inquired how the social sciences could continue practical co-operation on a common research theme? Professor Doucy nevertheless stressed the illustrative value of the first results obtained and said that the round table had given him the idea of organizing a seminar at the Solvay Institute of Sociology in Brussels.

It was not only through this problem of adjustment that attention was directed to questions of methodology. The cases referred to by all members of the round table showed the quality and quantity of the results achieved by a wide variety of investigations covering most parts of the world. But at the same time it revealed the lag between the present state of scientifically assembled documentary material and the present possibilities for the elaboration of theories. An effort to achieve critical assessment and harmonization is necessary not only for the purpose of interdisciplinary collaboration, but also within each discipline. This may be expected to bring about real progress in research. Our concern for efficiency, however, should not cause us to overlook the fact that where the application of the sciences is concerned, it never pays to go too fast.

MOTIVATION AND CULTURE-PATTERN
IN TECHNOLOGICAL CHANGE

M. J. Herskovits

The adaptation of an individual to an economic milieu reduces itself to the components of his psychological drives as these are shaped by the traditional setting in which he lives. When a total society is under consideration, this becomes a problem in the study of the psychology of culture, or psycho-ethnography. Our key concepts, in terms of this approach, are motivation and cultural pattern. Situations involving changes in the economic and technological structure are but phases of the broader problem of cultural re-adaptation, to be analysed by the investigation of any questions lying in the field of acculturation.

The relevance of our basic concepts has become apparent to students of industrial psychology, even though they have worked exclusively in Euro-American society. Stagner, for example, in discussing the causes of industrial disturbances, puts the case in this way: 'The problem of industrial conflict is the problem of what people want and the methods by which they try to get it.'[1] Or, again: 'The problem of industrial conflict is the problem of democratic self-assertion versus self-assertion without democratic controls.' Though the approach here is culture-bound, his phrasing can readily be translated into psycho-ethnographic tems. The fact that people 'want' things, in the first statement, the element of 'self-assertion', in the second, lie on the psychological level of motivation.' What they want', 'the methods by which they try to get it', and the mechanism of 'democratic control', represent the cultural directives given these drives. That the problem of motivation, in such cases, 'must be analysed in terms of specific human beings', and that 'it cannot be analysed effectively in terms of industry and labour as collective groups', reduces the question to the least common denominator of the individual, whose reactions, as we shall see, may not be neglected if we are to strike to the fundamentals of any problem where the dynamics of culture are involved.

The position of Polanyi, who holds that 'the outstanding discovery of recent historical and anthropological research is that man's economy, as a rule, is submerged in his social relationships', indicates how students concerned with general principles of economics are setting their findings in a broader matrix. Polanyi's statement, because of its relevance for the present discussion, may be quoted further: 'He does not act so as to safeguard his individual interest in the possession of material goods, he acts so as to safeguard his social standing, his social claims, his social

1. Ross Stagner, 'Psychological Aspects of Industrial Conflict', reprinted in: *Readings in Industrial and Business Psychology*, bv H. W. Karn and B. von Haller Gilmer, pp. 1-11 (from *Personnel Psychology*, Vol. III, 1950, pp. 1-15).

assets. He values material goods only in so far as they serve this end. Neither the process of production nor that of distribution is linked to specific economic interests attached to the possession of goods, but every single step in that process is geared to a number of social interests which eventually ensure that the required step be taken. These interests will be very different in a small hunting or fishing community from those in a vast despotic society, but in either place the economic system will be run on non-economic motives.'[1]

Moore has investigated economic motivation and incentive on a cross-cultural basis,[2] marking 'a comparative analysis of the social preconditions to industrial development, particularly with respect to the motivation of workers'. His investigation, he finds, 'does not lead to a conclusion that would deny central relevance to the established values and institutional structures of divergent social systems. On the contrary, it has documented their relevance in considerable detail'. On the other hand: 'Despite all that may be said about incompatibilities between non-industrial societies and the industrial way of life, the modern industrial system has a rather overwhelming record of penetration into and even conversion of these societies.' The economic evaluation of rewards in 'newly developing areas', in all cases, must take into account that 'wages are always to be viewed relatively to (a) alternative means of support; (b) alternative systems of social valuations; and (c) alternative or correlative rewards within the industrial system itself'.

The present paper will develop a theoretical structure for the study of economic motivation and incentive under conditions of technological change that was suggested in earlier discussion of a number of aspects of the subject as it pertains to sub-Saharan Africa.[3] In this previous analysis, the relation of certain 'consistent characteristics' of the 'indigenous productive systems of the continent' to the question of the adaptation of societies to new tasks was examined. These had to do first with the rhythm of work; then with the manner in which the available supply of labour can be mobilized so that a newly industrialized economy can function; and finally with the 'motivations for labour, the factor of incentives', which more particularly concern us here.

The psycho-ethnographic approach of this earlier study is exemplified in the following statement where the point is made that developmental projects in Africa 'must build on ways that make sense to the people involved in them if incentives to active participation are to result in the effective attainment of stated ends'. The basic problem was further stated in terms of the need 'to consider how what is brought to a people is integrated into their ways of living, as against the manner in which their established patterns of behaviour are adapted to the requirements of a new economic and technological system. Here we are confronted with the question of the meaning of a way of life for those who live in accordance with it. This, in turn, can be understood only in the light of the findings of that phase of psycho-ethnography that has to do with the mechanisms of learning and conditioning which shape the characteristic motor habits, reaction patterns and accepted modes of thinking of a people'.

In developing our thesis, we will first consider the nature of culture and cultural conditioning, and then proceed to an analysis of the motivational phenomena as they operate in the context of their cultural setting. On the basis of this theoretical

1. Karl Polany, *The Great Transformation*, New York, 1944, p. 40.
2. Wilbert E. Moore, *Industrialization and Labor, Social Aspects of Economic Development*, Ithaca and New York, 1951, pp. 5, 174, 310-11.
3. M. J. Herskovits, 'The Problems of Adapting Societies to New Tasks', in: B. F. Hoselitz (ed.), *The Progress of Underdeveloped Areas* (Proceedings of the 27th Institute of the Norman Wait Harris Memorial Foundation, University of Chicago), pp. 89-112.

structure, some suggestions for research, with particular reference to the African area field, can then be essayed.

The importance of the concept of culture is reflected in the fact that, as Kroeber and Kluckhohn[1] point out, 'in explanatory importance and in generality of application it is comparable to such categories as gravity in physics, disease in medicine, evolution in biology'. Many attempts have been made to define it, these authors citing more than one hundred and fifty definitions, a figure that is doubled if the statements as to its nature and functioning, which can be regarded as extended definitions, are included. There is general agreement, however, that culture is the learned, man-made part of the environment, derived from the unique ability of human beings to employ language and to use tools. Language is at the base of the cumulative character that differentiates human learning and cultural behaviour from the responses of the infra-human forms that are circumscribed by inherent behaviour norms; the use of tools has enabled man to range more widely and to exploit the resources of his habitat more effectively than any other creature.

The totality of human culture, however, has as many manifestations as there are peoples; indeed, when we take individual variation into account, as there are human beings. Each of these group manifestations has its own characteristic modes of behaviour, which is what we mean when we speak of a culture. We are concerned with these latter modes when, as at present, we consider the effects of contact between groups having differing ways of life. In this sense, an understanding of the culture of a group entails comprehension of its material equipment and social institutions, together with those underlying sanctions, expressed in systems of values, that guide the conduct of its members. When we treat of culture as a whole, we stress the unities in the behaviour of human beings; in studying a single culture, we discover the things that differentiate the behaviour of a given group from that of others. On a more sophisticated level, the study of the unities in culture has given rise to the concept of the universal aspects of institutionalized behaviour, while the study of the differences between cultures has enabled us to plot the range of variation in the differing ways human groups achieve similar ends.

There is general agreement as to what these common ends are—the exploitation of the resources provided by the habitat, and the distribution and consumption of what is produced; the regularization of social life to provide for the care of the young, see to it that they are properly trained, and assure equable relations between the members of the group and its protection from hostile forces that may threaten it; some modes of adjustment to the universe, however this may be conceived; means of providing aesthetic satisfactions; a language; a system of values which renders the cultural forms meaningful and welds them into a functioning whole. What is not agreed upon is the reason for these universal aspects of culture, a point of no minor importance for a cross-cultural theory of economic motivation.

It will be apparent that these aspects sort themselves out into two classes, those that represent efforts to comply with the demands set by the biological nature of man, and those that have a derived, psychological character. The problem under consideration here, in terms of the psycho-ethnographic approach, has facets that fall into both categories. No cultural forms more clearly fulfil biological needs than those which constitute the economic and technological phases of culture. To what extent the effectiveness of a particular form in fulfilling such needs determines its acceptability to a given people, is, however, by no means clear

1. A. L. Kroeber and Clyde Kluckhohn, 'Culture, a Critical Review of Concepts and Definitions', *Papers of the Peabody Museum of American Archaeology and Ethnology*, Harvard University, Vol. XLVII, No 1, 1952, p. 3.

when viewed objectively. This is to be seen in the cases where, in situations of cultural change, a people have proved reluctant to accept a technological device, or an economic mechanism, or a more favourable diet, that will provide them a richer store of goods, or more adequate subsistence than their established ways could ever yield.

It is apparent that while we must recognize the role culture plays in satisfying needs, we must not disregard the fact that it is the sanctions of a culture that stabilize the particular manifestation of the way in which a given need is satisfied. Because of this, we must look to the force these sanctions exert if we are to understand the devotion of a people to its pre-established modes of solving a given problem. On what other ground, for example, can we explain why so many agricultural peoples in the world have rejected the plough?

Since man is one of the social animals, it follows that culture is a social phenomenon. Phrased somewhat differently, this means that there is no such thing as a culture which is restricted to a single individual. As has been indicated, individual behaviour varies, but it varies within the limits set by the institutions and sanctions of the society to which individuals belong. Problems lying in the field of culture must therefore be studied in terms of their social setting, which at once brings to the fore the much discussed point of the relationship between the concepts of society and culture.

Reduced to their fundamental components, the positions that lay stress on either concept would seem essentially to involve differing emphases, each having its own historical derivation. That is, students whose principal point of orientation is the concept of society may be thought of as following the path set by such scholars as Spencer and Durkheim; those who organize their investigations in terms of culture as holding to an approach expressed in the work of Klemm and Tylor. Depending on the problem under study and the methods employed in studying it, however, either concept would seem to be fruitful, and both, in actuality, do enter to a greater extent than is ordinarily realized into studies having either orientation.

One can hold, that is, to the position that cultural behaviour can best be understood if studied in its social framework; or emphasis can rest on the total body of traditions, the social institutions of a people in this case representing a special aspect of their entire body of custom, their culture. However, it is as unrealistic to attempt to understand social organization without setting it in the cultural totality of which it forms a part as it is to study any aspect of a culture in disregard of the structure of social institutions in which it functions. From this point of view, if a society is defined as any interacting aggregate of individual organisms, then in the case of an interacting aggregate of human individuals, the totality of their accepted modes of behaviour is their culture.

The very fact that culture is defined as learned behaviour makes an understanding of cultural learning essential. This process, called enculturation, may be thought of as cultural conditioning, so pervasive that for the most part it takes on a quality of painless psychological absorption of the forms of behaviour prevailing in the group into which the infant is born. Enculturation begins at birth, and continues throughout life. By the time early childhood has been reached, much of the individual's behaviour has been taken entirely out of the area of conscious response, and has become automatic. As the individual grows older, the area of automatic reaction to cultural stimuli widens, so that the normal adult literally can be said to function much more of the time on this level than on that of consciously determined responses to the situations he meets in everyday life. At first glance, such a

44

statement may seem overdrawn, but only a slight consideration of the facts is necessary to dispel the illusion that conscious thought predominates in guiding behaviour.

Thus, for example, it is rare that reactions to any aspect of linguistic structure rise above the level of consciousness, any more than does the phonemic system employed in pronouncing the words of one's language. The same is true of the meaning of these words. This frees the individual to give conscious thought to what he is going to say, and makes it unnecessary for him to pay attention to the mechanisms of speech he must use in saying it. This statement also applies to music, to systems of etiquette, to moral codes, to canons of value, to aesthetic responses. These, it should be noted, are cultural elements in which conscious thought enters least. When it is realized that the same principle holds, to some degree, whenever an individual reacts to any culturally derived stimulus that does not involve the element of choice between alternatives, it becomes clear to what extent the human being lives on the plane of automatic behaviour, and thus how effectively he is enculturated.

Cultural responses, moreover, tend to represent reactions to total situations than to stimuli arising from fragmented elements of experience. This is a way of phrasing the fact that every mode of life is patterned and not haphazard; that the individual units of custom, the cultural traits, so-called, that can be discerned in a culture by the student of it, are in actuality interwoven into a series of interrelated groupings called cultural patterns. This patterning of culture, the outer expression of its regularity in organization and functioning, is the means by which a particular culture develops those special configurations that permit us to differentiate it from other cultures. In psychological terms, cultural patterns are to be regarded as consensuses of the individual behaviour patterns of the members of a given group, that distinguish their characteristic reactions from those of the members of other groups. On the level of the objective analysis of culture, cultural patterns are to be thought of as providing the institutional framework for behaviour, as when we speak of the pattern of marriage of a people, or their patterns of production or distribution, or their patterns of religious worship.

Besides conditioning the individual to the modes of behaviour of his group, the enculturative experience creates for him a 'behaviour world' to guide his perceptions no less than his overt acts. Time and space and distance, colour and rhythm, are thus culturally defined for him; the continuum of nature is structured in terms of the conventions set up by his culture.[1] The spectrum is arbitrarily divided into colours which vary in their interpretation from society to society, but which, within a given society, have a common meaning for all. The gamut of the musical scale offers another telling example of how the infinite physical progression of wave-lengths is similarly divided into socially acceptable intervals, or the division of time is guided by linguistic devices employed to mark off one socially conceived unit from another. The endless merging of natural phenomena comes to be subsumed under categories that make the world comprehensible to the individual, and permit the character of reality to be transmitted from one generation to the next, so that the particular type of reality to which the individual is enculturated becomes self-evident to him.

This, however, does not tell the tale of the results of enculturation. In addition to freeing man to think by permitting a large proportion of his responses to be automatic, and by shaping perception so that the world in which he lives is provided

---

1. A. I. Hallowell, 'Cultural Factors in the Structuralization of Perception', in: J. H. Rohrer and M. Sherif (eds.), *Social Psychology at the Crossroad*, New York, 1951, pp. 164-95.

with dimensions with which he can cope, enculturation also gives to human experience an emotional 'loading' that aids in achieving individual adjustment and cultural stability. This element of affect comes into play whenever cultural change is in process, whether through internal or external innovation, especially where a reorientation in the system of values of a people is involved. The operation of these emotional responses can be witnessed in any situation where some sanction of thought or behaviour is challenged. To analyse them, however, is far more difficult, since the phenomenon strikes some of the most involved problems in the study of human psychology. It represents a type of reaction to culturally determined guides to conduct which, institutionalized as social taboos, and internalized as unconscious feelings of guilt and compulsion, constitute a powerful mechanism to hold the acts of men and women within culturally sanctioned bounds.

This provides the basis, moreover, for the phenomenon of ethnocentrism, the quality in human psychology that not only causes the individual to be attached to the cultural modalities of his own society, but to accord them a higher value than he concedes to the ways of other peoples. The attitudes engendered by ethnocentrism assume practical importance in a number of dimensions. As a prime psychological process making for ego-involvement, it permits an extension of the ego structure which yields major satisfactions to the individual who identifies himself with the achievements of his people. And, since in his thinking, the modes of behaviour and the values to which he has been enculturated are not only the best, but the only proper ways in which the ends of living can be fulfilled, ethnocentrism thus becomes a powerful force making for individual adjustment and the emergence of a rounded personality. Where cross-cultural comparison is welded to a structure of power, however, ethnocentrism rationalizes a justification for the imposition of a way of life on those whose cultural patterns are oriented in a different fashion. And where this occurs, or where peaceful penetration convinces a people that their antecedent customs are of an inferior order, it is an equally powerful instrument in causing individual maladjustment and social disorganization.

The place of this emotional content of the enculturative experience in a theoretical formulation of the problems of economic incentive under conditions of change is underscored by the relation of these emotional drives to the phenomenon of motivation. This relationship is so close, indeed, that some psychologists find it difficult to disentangle the two. At this point, therefore, we may well turn to the next term in our equation, and examine the place of the factor of motivation in its cultural context as this bears on our problem.

It may be well, in discussing motivation, to clarify our approach, as was done with the concept of culture. There, it will be recalled, the multiplicity of phrasings that mark attempts to define the phenomenon was indicated; and this attack might have been pursued further to include some exposition of the differing explanations of the source and nature of culture—whether it is biologically or geographically determined, whether it has an independent existence or is a derived reality that lodges in the minds of observers rather than in the phenomenon itself.

Controversies of this order mark the approach of scientists in any field to their data, and turn on questions of the highest importance as means by which fundamental research is oriented. For those outside the field, however, the relevance of these differing positions is of a lesser order. Thus, in studying problems of the psychology of culture, it is more important for us to analyse the cultural component in terms which represent agreement as to the nature and function of culture than it is to enter into the peripheral areas where concept and method are under refinement. Conversely, in studying the same interdisciplinary problems from the psychological point of view, those principles that represent the core of agreement among psychologists must not be subordinated to any particular position that has been taken regarding them. We have seen that the learning process is fundamental in culture; but in studying the cross-cultural manifestations of education, for example, the varieties of learning theory come to hold a place of secondary importance. On the other hand, in an investigation of this type, the general principle that social behaviour is essentially learned, while the genetic, instinctual component is minimal, a question where controversy has been resolved into agreed principle, is of primary significance.

Whatever the approach to the problem of motivation, it is agreed that one of its important functions is to aid the organism continuously to reach the adjustment required by the total situation in which it finds itself. In terms of gestalt psychology this represents at any given moment a striving for the achievement of equilibrium in the total field situation. There are many theories about its nature and development, one of which, that stresses the factor of need, being strikingly similar to the hypothesis we have encountered in discussing theories of the nature of culture—one which, it may be said, is subject to quite similar reservations. For our purpose, we recognize that to the extent motivational drives arise out of the psycho-physical make-up of man, they are universal, and can be thus held as constants in analysing the variables represented by their socially and culturally derived manifestations. The physiological universals, that is, enter only in terms of the manner and degree to which the experience of the individual, as expressed in the cultural and physical setting, shapes his choices between alternatives, providing him with the values which direct his approaches to given situations and guide his reactions to them.

Whatever the approach to the problem of motivation, it is agreed that one of its important functions is to aid the organism in reaching adjustment of the kind which may be thought of as the psychological equivalent of the physiological state termed homeostasis. In terms of gestalt psychology, this represents the achievement of equilibrium in the total field situation. It is obvious that the needs of the organism figure prominently in determining these reactions, as where the individual is motivated to look for food, or to find shelter from extreme heat or cold, or to seek sexual gratification. Yet, in the final analysis, there is relatively little of human behaviour, in the precise terms in which this behaviour is manifested, that can be immediately attributed to this source. Even in such elementary responses as those to food or thirst or sex, the intervening term of social convention always enters.

It is cultural conditioning that determines at what time of the day a person feels hungry and what types of food he will seek to satisfy his hunger drive, or the techniques he will employ in drinking, or the ideals of beauty that will stimulate him sexually.

In terms of the bio-psychic requirements of the organism, cultural imperatives represent derived needs; but the responses to them are none the less powerful because they are derived and not primary. One of the outstanding characteristics of the human infant is the generalized character of his patterns of behaviour. His motor habits are unco-ordinated, his emotional structure generalized and his motivational system immediately related to drives for the satisfaction of his physiological requirements. Since the infant is entirely dependent on adults to satisfy these requirements, his development in one very significant aspect consists of a series of responses to those with whom he is in contact. We thus come to that aspect of the process of enculturation called socialization, especially as this occurs in infancy and early childhood. As we have seen, socialization provides the mechanisms whereby the infant is integrated into his group, experiencing increasing degrees of control over his modes of behaviour and thought which are taken over first from the members of his immediate family and then, as he grows older, from a widening circle of associates.

As the patterns of motor behaviour and emotional responses become more sharply structured in the growing individual, so does the motivational system. Freud and his followers have demonstrated how large a role the motivational forces that determine the behaviour of the individual play in shaping his personality structure. From a developmental point of view, their findings have demonstrated how early in his existence the resulting pattern of responses manifest in later life are laid down. As one psychologist has phrased it: 'While personal histories differ in details, most of them suggest that a predominant motive is established in childhood, largely through the influence of social contacts. As the individual gets older, one activity after another may be taken up while others, which no longer contribute to the satisfaction of the predominant motive, or which contribute less than the new activity, are dropped.'[1]

The emphasis here is on the individual, but if we approach the question from a cross-cultural point of view, we find, in overt behaviour as in these underlying psychological drives, that individual variation is limited by a culturally defined framework. Though the problem of the degree to which these fundamental aspects of the human personality structure are culturally influenced has been studied only for a relatively short time, our growing knowledge of how the individual responds to the cultural situation into which he is born has forced acceptance of the principle that culture is a major factor in shaping responses on all levels.

For our purpose, the key in the formulation that has been cited is that the predominant motives which rule the lives of individuals are established 'largely through the influence of social contacts'. Into cross-cultural terms, this brings into play the factor of consensus. For since methods of infant care and child training will, within the limits of individual and regional variation, follow reasonably consistent patterns in achieving the enculturation of the individual, it follows that each member of a given society will have been exposed to similar experiences in the early years of his existence, when so much of his personality structure is under formation. The implications of this fact take us over the entire range of problems that are contained in the simple statement of everyday observation that peoples differ from one another. These problems, however, despite their importance, have scarcely been more than adumbrated, and because of their complexity face the student with methodological difficulties that are far from resolved and which, therefore, need not enter into this discussion.

What is important is that the common elements in the enculturative experience of the members of a given group set up particular drives that characterize the responses of those who make up its adult components, as against equally characteristic responses of the members of other groups. It is out of this fact that derived needs, however expressed in a society, come to carry the same conviction to its members as those which are patently determined by biological requirement. This explains in large measure why the ends sought by men and women of a particular society are patterned, since from a cross-cultural point of view these are no more than socially sanctioned responses to prevalent motivational drives.

---

1. Norman L. Munn, *Psychology, The Fundamentals of Human Adjustment*, 2nd ed., New York, 1951, p. 291.

The configuration of common motives and goals that dominate the behaviour of the members of a group thus become the equivalent of what, in the analysis of culture, has been termed cultural focus, the sum of the institutionalized forms of a culture which, in commanding the interests of a people, represents those of its components which most highly motivate the people and in which the goals toward which their activities are directed bring the richest rewards, as culturally defined.

An approach to the problem of motivation that has significant implications for the cross-cultural analysis of problems, such as those with which we are concerned here, is found in the concept of the 'dynamic system' advanced by Krech[1] to account for the continuity of characteristic responses found in the individual. He holds, first, that the 'so-called motivational and cognitive attributes will be involved in every one of our experiences and behaviour', and that 'the so-called motivational attributes of any experience will be intimately related to all other attributes and will change as they change'. Continuing, he states: 'If we wish to speak of a "hunger motive" for example, we must simultaneously speak of the so-called perceptual, cognitive, memorial and other attributes of the experience. My "hunger" is not the same as yours, because my dynamic systems re food and eating are not the same as yours. And neither you nor I can have any "pure" sex motive—they are both sullied by cognitive factors.' Therefore, since 'dynamic systems are relative enduring structures', it follows that the given system of an individual functions in any situation in which he finds himself, so that 'behaviour' will show both variability and consistency in its motivational and emotional and intellectual aspects.

It is apparent that, if we accept this postulate that knowing and wanting form a single psychological unit, and agree that, in cultural terms, both knowledge and wants are established for the individual through his enculturative experience, we have here a principle of some importance for cross-cultural study. This is especially the case where we are concerned with economic factors in cultural change, since here both means and ends must be taken into account where either the technological system, or the system of production, distribution and exchange, or both, are involved. At this point, we return to the concept of cultural focus, which, as we have seen, is the manifestation on the social level of those elements in the total experience of the individual members of a group which hold most interest for them. From this point of view, the fact that focal concerns of Euro-American society lie in the economic and technological aspects of its cultures, something that is true for only a relatively small number of the societies which it has come to dominate, at once brings us a sharper formulation of the psycho-ethnographic problem we are considering here. The utility of this approach is underscored, moreover, by the fact that we are enculturated to total situations, and do not learn our culture piecemeal. Here, on the cultural level, is the equivalent of the psychological unity which Krech formulates in his concept of the dynamic system of response of the individual. Taken together, we have a theoretical frame of reference with which to attack a problem whose fundamental importance in achieving the unities of a world economic order has brought questions of this kind to the forefront of scientific concern.

One of the major aspects of our problem has been phrased by Moore;[2] 'What kinds of circumstances will induce workers to leave traditional modes of production and modern economic activity, and what additional circumstances are necessary to

1. David Krech, 'Cognition and Motivation in Psychological Theory', in: Wayne Dennis et al., Current Trends in Psychological Theory, Pittsburgh, 1951, pp. 131-2.
2. Wilbert E. Moore, Industrialization and Labor, Social Aspects of Economic Development, Ithaca and New York, 1951, p. 297.

secure skills and services essential to the industrial mode of production with its attendant specialization?' Let us extend this formulation by phrasing some of the ancillary questions that the study of economic change, in its broadest ramifications, involves.

A comprehensive approach must include a consideration of how economic expressions of value are re-ordered into terms of money where money did not previously exist; or to currency where the tokens used in effecting exchange were not pecuniary ones. It should take into account how people are introduced to the concept of saving as related to the allocation of income, so as to provide capital funds for industrial development, with future rather than immediate return the end in view. New attitudes towards the acquisition of unfamiliar goods of all kinds must be probed, and how patterns of the validation of social position by the consumption of valuable goods in excess of daily needs are changed. The attitudes toward the degree of specialization under industrial development, that so materially alters the satisfactions a worker derives from participation in an industrial order based on the handicraft system, must also be analysed.

One caution, arising out of the record of past research, should be drawn. This concerns the tendency, undoubtedly a reflection of the unconsciously enculturated ethnocentrisms of the student, to overweight the power of the industrial tradition to impose itself on technological and economic orientations of peoples who live under less complex systems. Where the approach is primarily from the economic or technological point of view, this is understandable in view of the differences in complexity and achievement between the systems of non-industrial peoples and that of Euro-America. This difference is demonstrably so great that, without an appreciation of the power of established tradition to define ends, it appears self-evident that the 'weaker' mode of organization must give way before more efficient methods of production, with the greater material rewards and higher standards of living that those bring. What is often not taken into account is the fact that we are here confronted with a question of ultimate values, where material gain may be discounted, despite the very considerable 'pull' of positive incentives that Moore has documented in his research.

Certainly it is much simpler to study the acceptance of change than the rejection of new ways. One of the most difficult problems faced by students of any aspect of cultural change is the methodological one of how to bring the pre-established elements in the scene into proper proportion in analysing the resultant situation. The lesson may be in the way of being learned in the hard school of experience. We need not go to the various large-scale 'schemes' to see this. We need only take the case of the American Point Four agricultural expert in Liberia who, intent on increasing the production of food, encouraged the cultivation of individual plots in place of co-operatively worked village land. The repercussions, in terms of the strife engendered between the women of a village, were as vigorous as they were unexpected. We hear much of the disorganization which industrial development produces, and especially how those who have received European education tend to lose their cultural anchorage and drift at a loss, dissatisfied with the old because they have rejected it, with the new because they cannot attain it. Yet the number of 'educated' Africans is not small who would agree with the sentiment expressed by such a person concerning one product of the pre-existing technological system, its wood-carving: 'If we don't take steps to save these things, we will have nothing. We'll be like people who don't have anything they can call their own culture'.

This does not mean that undue stress should be laid on the force of these pre-existing patterns, for this would be as unrealistic as is the prevalent tendency to neglect them. Thus, in the regions where a positive appreciation of established custom is found, one also is confronted with the phenomena of urbanization, people leaving their villages to live in towns and accepting the new discipline of employment in industry or trade, or going to mine compounds where the reorientations in customary behaviour are even more extensive. New prestige patterns develop under these situations that must be studied; otherwise, for example, why in the mines of Katanga would the young men prefer training as mechanics and artisans rather than as masons and carpenters? Or, for example, how do we explain the reorientation in motivating factors that causes a miner on the Rand to leave the security of the mine compound for the competitive labour market of secondary industry? Beyond this, what motivations in this segment of the South African economy lie behind the turnover in labour of those who have apparently accepted this method of earning a living, a turnover that is one of the highest in the world?

The variety of responses to the developing industrial scene, coupled with the differences in the pre-existing cultures and the range of different economic policies and practical measures to implement them to which they are exposed, is what makes of Africa such an excellent laboratory for the study of our problem. In studying it, the factors which are operative in most of the continent give the controls essential for the comparative analysis of attitudes that accompany the changing economic, no less than the changing social and political scene. Or, again, granting acceptance of certain aspects of the new, what is the role of the non-economic habitudes in pre-existing custom, particularly those that concern the supernatural; what forms do they take in situations dominated by the scientific approach that marks industrialization; how do they influence the attitudes of Africans who come to participate in the industrial scene? What precisely is the effect of the colour-bar in industry, as manifest in unequal wage scales, segregation in jobs, differing approaches to unionization, differentials in housing? What is the relation of these to the 'culture-bar' that arises out of the differences in opportunity to reach those standards of living and education set for persons deemed fully prepared to participate in the direction of affairs? Must we not also recognize the need to study the prevalent attitudes and motivations of the Europeans in the scene, something that has been quite overlooked in the emphasis laid on the need to concentrate on the position and reactions of the native people?

It is illuminating to read the exposition of the total problem, as exemplified in the approach to the practical issue of housing Africans in the city of Elizabethville, that has been given by Grévisse.[1] Here full recognition is accorded the importance of taking pre-established attitude and social behaviour, on the part of Europeans and Africans alike, fully into consideration in attempting to manipulate prevalent points of view, as when he says: 'Modifier ces habitudes serait difficile, sinon impossible, et réellement dangereux.' On the positive side, however, Grévisse recognizes the need for Africans who are in process of becoming urbanized, through being newly brought into the industrial situation, to have adequate motivation that will make of them not only socially but psychologically fully functioning members of the evolving social whole: 'Sertis dans un cadre de vie à tout le moins conforme à leur degré de développement et à leurs saines aspirations, assurés de la paix des esprits et des cœurs, soixante-quinze mille habitants pourront évoluer dans l'ordre, se stabiliser, se détribaliser et jeter les bases d'une structure sociale qui, sans plus être tribale, n'en conservera pas moins un caractère original, reflet de

---

1. F. Grévisse, 'Le Centre Extra-Coutumier d'Elizabethville', *Bulletin Trimestriel du Centre d'Étude des Problèmes Sociaux Indigènes* (CEPSI), No. 15, 1951, pp. 18, 439.

l'âme bantoue et des constantes physiques et historiques du milieu africain.' That is, the objective for the African is: '. . . étoffer une solide classe moyenne ancrée par la propriété et stimulée toujours davantage par des capacités professionnelles sans cesse accrues . . .'.

Let us briefly review the theoretical scheme that has been presented in these pages. The principal concepts with which we have dealt are motivation and cultural pattern. Motivation, even on the biological level, we have seen to be structured by the cultural setting in which behaviour occurs. Enculturation, the process of cultural conditioning, provides the mechanism of learning which permits the individual to act in accordance with the accepted modes of his society, with the promptness and decisiveness that so largely comes from the automatic character of his responses. These patterned reactions thus both satisfy the requirements of his primary biological needs and secondary drives, and make possible his physical well-being and psychological adjustment.

Every culture, however, is made up of aggregates of patterns. These consist of cultural elements which, to the members of a society, appear as integrated units. Behaviour thus takes on its configurational quality, and as objectively discernible, represents overt responses to the internalization of culturally patterned experiences. From this, it becomes apparent that the study of any segment of a culture to the exclusion of other elements, or of the psychological base, makes for a distorted view, whether on the level of cultural stimulus or socially patterned response. Hence analysing economic or technological factors alone is not sufficient to develop scientific formulations that strike deeply enough into the causal relationships involved, or point toward workable solutions of the problems of changing conditions.

When we take an inventory of our resources in the way of available data, we find that our knowledge of the cultures of the non-Euro-American world is well advanced, but that comparable psychological materials do not exist. The methodological problem for attacking the questions arising out of contacts of peoples having differing habits of work and systems of value thus becomes one of welding to our ethnographic knowledge the results of interdisciplinary investigations, which will reveal the psychological patternings that underlie the behaviour, individual and institutionalized, that has been observed and reported. To those studies in personality type that have dominated much of the cross-cultural approach to the psychology of culture must, however, be added intensive research into the nature and functioning of the differentials in perception and motivation which define the world for a people, inform their behaviour, and shape their aspirations. Through the intensive use of all the resources of the psycho-ethnographic approach, then, we may anticipate not only that we will move towards a more basic knowledge of human behaviour, but that we will control and interpret more effectively the data that are essential to provide adequate scientific guidance for drawing and implementing sound policy in solving the problems of individual and social adjustment.

SOME CONCEPTUAL ASPECTS OF
TECHNICAL CHANGE

S. H. FRANKEL

When I was privileged to receive an invitation to contribute this article I hesitated for some time before accepting it. I wanted to try to define more clearly in my own mind the problem involved, and the contribution which an economist might make to a discussion of it at the present time.

I came to the conclusion that perhaps the most useful approach would be to examine some of the conceptual ideas which, consciously or unconsciously, provide the framework of controversy in this field of study. In doing so, I shall not confine myself to any particular stage of economic development, or any particular region, except for purposes of illustration.

As a starting point it may be useful to draw attention to certain semantic peculiarities which, I think, are in themselves indicative both of the present climate of opinion, and of some confusions which seem worthy of further examination.

The first of these semantic, or definitional, peculiarities is the fact that we so readily tend to speak of 'the social consequences of technical change', and not of 'technical change as a social consequence'. This is very significant. It shows that we have formed the habit of regarding technical change in mechanistic terms—as an independent force, which, by impinging on society, sets in motion certain desirable, or undesirable, reactions. These reactions, since they are regarded as the inevitable consequence of the external force, are then presumed to require study in the same fatalistic spirit in which one might try to cope with the destruction left in the wake of a battle or of an earthquake.

A parallel can be drawn between the use of the term 'the Industrial Revolution', with its undertones of cataclysmic suddenness and consequences, and the frequent implication that technical change necessarily takes a similar form, and shatters all around it. But, as an eminent contemporary economic historian[1] has reminded us: '. . . the changes . . . spoken of as the Industrial Revolution . . . were not merely "industrial" but also social and intellectual . . . . The word "revolution" implies a suddenness of change that is not in fact characteristic of economic processes'. He remarks that 'the phrase Industrial Revolution has . . . become so firmly embedded in common speech that it would be pedantic to offer a substitute'. Let us hope that the term technical change is not yet as inseparable from its present and narrow mechanistic connotation.

The Oxford Dictionary defines technique as the 'manner of artistic execution

---

1. Professor T. S. Ashton, *Industrial Revolution 1760-1830*, Oxford University Press, 1948.

or performance' and the word technical as 'belonging or relating to an art or arts'. None of these (or other available) definitions indicates the presence of any exogenous forces affecting the work of individuals concerned with changing techniques. On the contrary, they refer to the ways in which certain activities are conducted. But as Professor Oakeshott has emphasized in his Inaugural Lecture on Political Education to 'understand an activity *is to know it as a concrete whole; it is to recognize the activity as having the source of its movement within itself.* (Italics not in the original.) An understanding which leaves the activity in debt to something outside itself is, for that reason, an inadequate understanding. And if political activity is impossible without a certain kind of knowledge and a certain sort of education, then this knowledge and education are not mere appendages to the activity but are part of the activity itself and must be incorporated in our understanding of it'.[1]

In the same way, I submit, it is important to recognize that an activity (or performance) which, for convenience, we describe as technical, does not consist as it were of two parts, namely of (a) knowing how to do a thing, and (b) of doing it. It consists essentially of one process as a whole, i.e., that of conducting of the activity itself. This can be illustrated by the arrestingly simple example which Professor Oakeshott has used in support of his thesis that 'political activity comes first and a political ideology follows after'. He takes the example of cookery: 'It might be supposed that an ignorant man, some edible materials, and a cookery book compose together the necessities of a self-moved activity called cooking. But nothing is further from the truth. The cookery book is not an independently generated beginning from which cooking can spring; it is nothing more than an abstract of somebody's knowledge of how to cook: it is the stepchild, not the parent of the activity. The book, in its turn, may help to set a man on to dressing a dinner, but if it were his sole guide he could never, in fact, begin: the book speaks only to those who know already the kind of thing to expect from it and consequently how to interpret it.

'Now, just as a cookery book presupposes somebody who knows how to cook, and its use presupposes somebody who already knows how to use it, and just as a scientific hypothesis springs from a knowledge of how to conduct a scientific investigation, and separated from that knowledge is powerless to set empiricism to work, so a political ideology must be understood, not as an independently premeditated beginning for political activity, but as knowledge (in an abstracted and generalized form) of a traditional manner of attending to the arrangements of a society. The catechism which sets out the purposes to be pursued merely abridges a concrete manner of behaviour in which those purposes are already hidden.'

Similarly, if we are to speak meaningfully of the effects of technical change we must, I suggest, be very careful to avoid falling into the common, and facile, error of thinking that changes in knowing how to do a certain thing can be separated from changes in the actual doing of it. This is the type of error which is frequently introduced when we speak of making available to a backward society the 'know-how' of a new technical process. In doing this we are not making available two processes, namely, a mental process of abstract technical knowledge on the one hand, and of the actual performance on the other. We are speaking only of the one process—the performance itself. The idea that technical change is somehow an exogenous force altering the established day-to-day activities of society springs, I suggest, from this erroneous way of speaking and thinking. It consists in the fallacious belief that a society's activities proceed in two separate compart-

1. *Political Education*, An Inaugural Lecture by Professor Michael Oakeshott. Bowes & Bowes, Cambridge, 1951.

ments: the first containing the process of abstract willing or knowing, the other containing the application of such willing or knowing. It is on the basis of a similarly erroneous conception of the nature of economic activity that we so readily conclude that technical change is a kind of abstract force which has certain social consequences, and fail to see that what we describe as the consequences of this imaginary force is simply part and parcel of the activity itself. When, for example, there is a change from farming to coal-mining, this will involve the development of new aptitudes and new habits of work over a wide range of new economic and social activities. The change will not be completed until it has resulted in a community all of whose activities (and not only those directly related to the production of coal) have been rearranged of have grown into a new pattern of life and work. If now we regard the introduction of coal-mining as a purely mechanical process, which will have certain social consequences, we fail to see that what we regard as the result or consequence is but the continuous, and necessarily uneven, process of change itself. Thus, if the workers in the coal-mine are inadequately housed, or suffer deficiencies in the standard of nutrition, education, or recreation now necessary in their new environment, these are not the consequence of the process of change to coal-mining, but rather of a failure to complete it. Even the direct activity of extracting coal cannot be brought to optimum efficiency unless all the other economic and social activities, to which that task must be related and with which it must be integrated, have been developed. Indeed coal-mining cannot even begin until some change in the previous aptitudes, habits, and patterns of social organization have taken place.

Let us examine for the sake of illustration a highly simplified example of what, presumably, would nowadays be regarded merely as a technical change. Let us assume that it is desired to increase the productivity of a subsistence cattle-owning African community which has never engaged in the production of butter or cheese either for sale or for its own consumption. It is hoped not only to get this community to consume these products itself, but also to market some of them so as to enable the society to increase its income by selling the surplus dairy produce, and buying other goods with the money so obtained.

At first sight the problem might appear to be merely one of introducing new methods of production, and the instruments, tools or machines appropriate thereto. But what is really involved is a vast change in social beliefs and practices—if, that is, it be assumed that the society in question is to remain intact as a society— an assumption which, as we shall see, raises questions of quite another kind. Here let us, for the moment, consider only what far-reaching social changes will have to be made to enable technical change—which we nowadays so readily tend to abstract as the prime mover—to be introduced at all. The utilization of cattle as a source of income in a monetary and accounting sense presupposes a basic alteration in the economic structure of the society. It presupposes not only the introduction of money, but a complete re-casting of the traditional values of the community. Thus it presupposes a change in the system of land ownership and use; in the laws and conventions governing access to it, and in the traditional beliefs as to how, and by whom, it is to be cultivated—whether by men or by women, by individuals working for themselves or for others. Moreover it presupposes an aptitude, ability, and willingness to tolerate, recognize, and provide for the emergence and training of groups in the community which are not attached to the land at all. This, in turn, presupposes the growth of new aptitudes and patterns of behaviour which will regulate their social and mutual relations not in accordance with the customs suited to shifting subsistence cultivation, roaming cattle herds, and the thrill of the chase, but to those of a settled agricultural and urban population. There is presupposed, therefore, the parallel emergence of a group of persons concerned not only with dairy production itself but with the transport, distribution, marketing and finance of all that the new producers have to buy and all they have to sell. These, however, necessitate a political structure—local, provincial, national and trans-national—suited to the establishment of these complementary economic, scientific and financial activities; they presuppose therefore the willingness, aptitude, and ability of the community to permit, and indeed to promote, the growth of all the legal, political and administrative institutions necessary to harmonize the rights and duties of the persons engaged in this new complex interdependent economy.

The purpose of this long list of social adjustments is to show that whatever it be that we may care to designate as technical change, it is but one aspect of mutually determined, and determining, processes of growth on many fronts of the social structure as a whole. It is idle to endeavour to ascertain which change is the innovation or cause, and which is the effect. For when we designate one change as cause, and another as effect, we are but examining the process of change itself from different points of observation.

The attempt to establish particular absolute causes of change is misleading, for it misconceives the very nature of the process of change or growth itself.

Let me revert again to that commonplace view of technical change which regards it as resulting from the application of new knowledge—of technical 'know-how'. Such a view presupposes a kind of mental certainty as to the change which is required in order to bring about a particular consequence in the near or distant future. Basic to this way of thinking is the implicit assumption that the 'know-how' exists, as it were, as a stock of techniques—like a stock of raw materials—which can be drawn upon at will and applied to any situation in order to produce the desired, and therefore foreseeable, end. It is because we tend to think in such abstract terms that we are led to imagine that somehow economic development, or the lack of it, can be explained in terms of the presence or absence of adequate quantities of factors of production; as when it is suggested that all that is required to assist the development of backward societies is to give or lend them part of that accumulated technical knowledge and capital—just as one might give an injection to a patient to cure him.

This way of speaking is based on a profound misconception: technical knowledge, the machine and other capital goods never exist in the abstract but always only in the relatively fleeting form suited to the momentary situation, and to that complex of unique problems to which they have been adapted. They have no power independent of the performance of which they are capable. They are the expression of man's response to the changing problems set by the environment and by his fellow men. When the problems which constitute man's framework of reference change they become useless. That is why they cannot be readily transferred from one situation to another. For meeting any new situation, new thoughts, new aptitudes, new action will be required. But knowledge has to grow; capital has to be created afresh on the basis of continuous experiment; and new hopes and beliefs have to evolve to urge men and women forward—for in the last resort they alone are the carriers alike of past experience, and of new endeavour. It is because all these new activities are not independent of the existing institutions into which they have to be fitted, and which have in turn to be adjusted to them, that the process of change is so complex and—if it is to proceed harmoniously—necessarily so slow.

It is the attempt to simplify that process—to avoid the gradualness of change in order to pluck the quick fruits of endeavour in one direction, at the expense of inactivity in others—which accounts for social maladjustments. In a society in which all changes were to take place at rates so well adjusted to each other as not to disturb the basic harmony and integration of its constituent parts, there would be no social consequences of change but only harmonious change itself. When, however, rates of change are very discontinuous it may well happen that one sector of the society cannot be meaningfully integrated into the social life of the community at all—so that, as far as that sector is concerned, society as a whole no longer exists.

The most extreme case of failure to achieve a balanced rate of change is that of slavery. It illustrates in its most terrible form the deliberate disintegration of established patterns of social and human values in order to pursue an immediate objective. Slavery not only detaches men and women by force from an established pattern of social relationships but, by using them as chattels for the ends of others, denies them both the opportunity to reconstruct a new society for themselves, and the right to become an integrated meaningful part of the society of their masters. In a society based on slavery the uneasy and unstable rule of force takes the place of that social harmony necessary for the full development of each part of the disrupted whole.

Slavery is an extreme case of the establishment of new structural patterns which by their very nature prevent further economic and social growth. But there have been, and continue to be, many less extreme yet parallel situations.

The large movements of indentured labour during the nineteenth century—like the migration of some recruited labour in Africa today—illustrate the consequences of attempts to use labour in pursuance of an immediate objective without considering the need to integrate the individuals concerned into a new meaningful social pattern.

In South Africa, for example, the need to obtain Indian labour for the Natal sugar industry arose because it was not possible to detach Africans for the purpose from their own indigenous society. The structure of the sugar industry was thus established on the basis of supplies of unskilled labour, and the Indians were forced to remain separated from both the European, and the African, social structures. This not only inhibited the evolution of a meaningful society for Indians in South Africa but also froze the economic pattern of the sugar industry itself. The whole economic evolution of Natal was retarded by the failure to establish the Indian immigrant as creative part of South African society.

I suggest that when we view the problems of change in the light of these considerations we shall accustom ourselves to focus our studies, to a greater extent than heretofore, on the historical evolution of the structural patterns of developing societies. By so doing we shall, I believe, be able to place the emphasis in studies of change where it belongs, namely on the need to discover to what extent rates of change in different parts of the society are moving towards, or diverging from, that minimum degree of social and psychological harmony necessary for its maintenance of evolution.

In using these terms I am aware of the fact that I am begging many questions. However, what I have in mind is something far simpler than the necessarily vague terminology I have used may at first sight indicate.

To illustrate this let me again refer to the lessons of the Industrial Revolution and quote again from Professor Ashton's valuable judgement: 'Experience has taught us', he writes, 'that an industrial society needs a framework of public services if it is to operate without social discomfort. . . . With the best will in the world, the transition from farms and cottages to factories and cities could never have been smooth. If the legislative machine had turned out statutes with the same speed as the mules turned out yarn there would still have been social disorder. For much of the overcrowding and squalor was the result of the fact that progress in science was then, as today, more rapid than in administration. 'The remote influence of arrangements has been somewhat neglected', wrote Dr. Kay in 1832, adding to this meiosis that the neglect arose 'not from the want of humanity, but from the pressure of occupation and the deficiency of time'. Not until the whole apparatus of government had been drastically reformed and a body of qualified public servants had been called into being could life in urban areas be other than squalid. If the Industrial Revolution was not able to bring its rewards in full measure to the ordinary man and woman it is to the effects of administrative, and not of economic processes, that the failure must be ascribed.'

What, I suggest, is most required now, in relation to the thought and practice of our predecessors, is a new awareness, not only of the need to adapt administrative and social arrangements to the pressure of economic and political events, but also of the fact that the political and economic pressures themselves so largely depend on those arrangements. Thus we should envisage neither the pressure of technical, nor those of political happenings as accidental, in the sense that they are independent causes of our problems. Instead we should accustom ourselves to see them as mutually interdependent processes. For that reason we must discipline ourselves to examine them everywhere in sufficient detail to lay bare their mutual relations. By so [doing we may perhaps hope to quicken that sense of social inventiveness and responsibility which makes change not a burden but an adventure in the art of government and mutual adaptation in free societies. For the sting of change lies not in change itself but in change which is devoid of social meaning.

Let me conclude with a final example. All over Africa, and, indeed, in many parts of the underdeveloped world, erstwhile members of simple rural economies find themselves drawn into urban centres of industry. For many of these men and women these centres are only the places in which they work; their social self remains located with their families, which are still eking out a precarious livelihood in rural conditions as yet unadapted to modern forms of production or the basic needs of health, education and the like. Even when these families come to the towns they find themselves psychologically and socially ill-equipped to establish satisfactory patterns of living there. Yet we know little so far about the administrative arrangements which must be evolved to cope with the changing activities of these wanderers in the twilight of newly emerging social structures. Very few detailed studies of their thinking and their needs exist; fewer still of their psychological reactions, and least of all of the ways and means of emancipating them to grapple with their problems by that most basic form of all political education—the conscious sharing in the governance of affairs by trial and error.

We know little of the processes involved in the vast change of aptitudes which these developments require, of the time they take, and the obstacles they encounter. There is need of carefully documented comparative studies of them in different regions. Moreover, only experience and a knowledge which exhibits clearly the full burden of change can prevent needlessly hasty development in this or that direction. All too often a socially uneconomic development is embarked upon because those who initiate it are unaware of its cost, or not responsible for its unavoidable accompanying economic and social changes. But change which is not in harmony with the social resources and needs of a community may well prove to be not a blessing but a curse.

It is here that the economist can be of help in examining the relative individual and social costs and benefits of alternative choices, and in disentangling the real from the apparent expected effects of the fiscal and economic burdens involved.

LONG-TERM
ECONOMIC DEVELOPMENT

MAHATMA GANDHI'S VIEWS ON
MACHINES AND TECHNOLOGY

D. P. MUKERJI

This paper comes out of the conviction that any study of the social changes brought about by technology should be based primarily on an understanding of the conditions of both the society which introduces technology and the society to which it is introduced. If these conditions are crystallized in two systems of values, one which has accepted, and the other which has not accepted 'technical progress' as desirable or technological advance as 'a self-evident good' (R. K. Merton, *Social Theory and Social Structure*, Chap. xiii, p. 317); and further, if the strains of technological advance, which any scheme of technological assistance brings in its wake, must be reduced or eliminated so as to render the assistance genuinely effective, then one of the chief concerns of the sociologist as well as of the technical administrator is the discovery of the terms of the normative system of both countries concerned. This does not preclude the various types of specific researches on the social effects of technological change; on the contrary, the normative study may be fortified by their scientific conclusions. What is stressed here is the methodological issue. For example, with regard to the impact of machines or technology (associated with Western Europe) on Asian countries (believed to belong to a pre-technical stage) the underlying assumption that technological advance is a 'self-evident good' should be brought to the surface so as to clear the way for the comparative normative approach. It is heartening to know that eminent Western sociologists have recognized the importance of this approach.

But it is disheartening that no formulation of the Eastern value-system has been made by an Eastern sociologist. One reason for this may be that Eastern people are still too deeply involved in their system and, therefore, the technological impact on their basic values is as yet superficial. Another reason may be that those who could formulate and compare the value-systems are the very people who believe in technical advance as a 'self-evident good' and, therefore, do not worry about the problem beyond the stage of annoyance with temporary maladjustments which, in their view, a welfare state, or a similar agency or agencies, would benevolently remove sooner or later. Certain economic interests in India, in particular, also seem to be far too committed to technological advance to be anxious to study the conflict of value-systems involved in the resultant strain. Though one hears about cottage industries and their place in Indian life and notices earnest administrative encouragements, the importance attached to them seems to be mainly on the score of their being able to provide 'some' employment to those who are being thrown out of 'employment' by technological advance. Gandhi, however, was deeply and primarily concerned with the value-systems. There were others too, but they are less known. Gandhi put his views very sharply indeed. One may not like his manner of posing the problem, one may consider it as partial, one may dismiss it, if one chooses, as many 'educated' men and industrialists of India have chosen. But his statements remain a challenge to the entire problem of technological change and schemes of technical assistance. They should be taken seriously because many new disturbing features of Indian life cannot be explained or removed otherwise. From them one might also infer that the term 'underdeveloped economy', which is the excuse of technical assistance, was inappropriate in so far as it confused the co-existence of two different value-systems by placing them on the assembly-line of historical development in which economic growth, being the supreme value, was subservient to and dependent only upon technological advance. Perhaps, Gandhi was unfair to the European civilization; it may also be that he did not subscribe to the unilinear concept of history. But it is certain that he had other values and his understanding of India, at least, was unerring. We Indians love to think that Gandhi's views correctly represent the unformulated values of the vast majority of the Indian population towards social changes. They, as he would say, would welcome change on their own human terms.

Let us know exactly what he said in regard to machines and when. (He never used the word 'technology', but it is clear that he meant it.) Much misunderstanding of his position prevails everywhere. But he did not want to be misunderstood; in fact, the very clarity of his style leaves no room for misunderstanding. The first unequivocal statement of his position occurs in *Hind Swaraj* or *Indian Home Rule*, written originally in Gujerati, on the return voyage from London to South Africa in 1908 'in answer to the Indian school of violence and its prototype in South Africa'. It was first published in the columns of *Indian Opinion of South Africa*, in the form of the editor's answers to readers' queries. In this period Gandhi was finding himself through many a personal and a few social experiments. Violence had become the desperate creed of Indian nationalists. He was analysing this creed all the time, digging its base, so to say, and reaching towards an alternative moral creed. *Hind Swaraj* was the first formulation and bears all the marks of religious conversion. The subsequent history of the book is interesting, but not quite relevant here. But it is on record that in January 1921 Gandhi would 'withdraw nothing except one word of it, and that in deference to a lady friend'. As Mahadev Desai wrote in his preface to the 1938 edition: 'Even in 1938 he would alter nothing in the book, except perhaps the language in some parts.' We will see, however, that certain alterations were made, but they were more in the nature of elaboration in terms of reality, e.g., the relative unpreparedness of Indian people for the practice of 'a higher simplicity and renunciation', which he knew to be India's values, than as deviations from a fundamental position.

His writings show (letter to a friend quoted in *Mahatma*, Vol. 1, pp. 129-30) that his opposition to England or to the Western or even the European civilization was not merely on the limited ground of political and economic subjection, but on the much wider issue of the conflict between the values of different civilizations. *Hind Swaraj* discusses this issue with eloquence and poses the conflict between Indian values and Western values in pure white and pure black. Many historians and sociologists would be more cautious about India's ancestry, about her deliberate wisdom in rejecting machinery, city life and the evils thereof. They would question the latent virtuous assumptions about India's past and her society. They would attribute them mostly to lack of opportunities and the incurable human habit of making a virtue of necessity. Nor would they fail to detect a high order of spiritual values in the Western, European, or modern civilization and a low order of social values prevailing in the East, in India old and new. But here at last was the Indian positing of a felt contrast in the fierce clarity of exaggeration. The exaggeration was similar to that of a rebel slave who would assert with vehemence his own human dignity and clothe it in historical terms. At the same time, it was not a metaphysical rebellion, so typical of India and the East. It was not a protest against the universal condition of man whose life is interrupted by disease, old age, or death, as was that of Buddha. It was essentially a moral rebellion, couched in the social terms of civilization, which Gandhi defined as good conduct with the entire weight on performance of duty and observance of morality. The supreme duty was to attain mastery over mind and passions in the performance of which we know ourselves, that is, knowledge accrues. The performance implied proper use of hands and feet and the process led to the limitation of indulgences, reduction of wants, and simplification of life. All these ideas formed a whole pattern of thought, beliefs, attitude and action which placed Indian civilization in sharp opposition to what he sometimes called the Western, at other times the European, but what was really modern civilization centred on material values.

Let us follow the development of Gandhi's ideas. In October 1924, soon after he had broken one of his famous fasts, he gave an interview to a student from Santiniketan, Sir Ramchandran, who questioned him on his views on the place of Art in national regeneration and on machinery. Ramchandran asked (*Mahatma*, Vol. 2, p. 212):

R. 'Are you against all machinery?'

G. 'How can I be when I know that even this body is a delicate piece of machinery? The spinning-wheel itself is a machine; a little toothpick is a machine. What I object to is the craze for machinery, not machinery as such. The craze is for what they call labour-saving machinery. Men go on 'saving labour' till thousands are without work and thrown on the streets to die of starvation. I want to save time and labour, not for a fraction of mankind, but for all. I want the concentration of wealth, not in the hands of a few, but in the hands of all. Today machinery helps a few to ride on the backs of millions. The impetus behind it is not the philanthropy to save labour, but greed. It is against this constitution of things that I am fighting with all my might.'

R. 'Then you are fighting not against machinery as such, but against its abuses, which are so much in evidence today?'

G. 'I would unhestitatingly say yes; but I would add that scientific truths and discoveries should first cease to be mere instruments of greed. Then labourers will not be overworked and machinery instead of becoming a hindrance will be a help. I am aiming not at eradication of all machinery, but limitation.'

R. 'When logically argued out, that would imply that all complicated power-driven machinery should go.'

G. 'It might have to go, but I must make one thing clear. The supreme consideration is man. The machine should not tend to keep atrophied the limbs of man. For instance, I would make intelligent exceptions. Take the case of the Singer Sewing-Machine.'

R. 'But, in that case, there would have to be a factory for making these Singer Sewing-Machines, and it would have to contain power-driven machinery of ordinary type.'

G. 'Yes, surely. But I am Socialist enough to say that such factories should be nationalized or State-controlled. They ought only to be working under the most attractive and ideal conditions, not for profit, but for the benefit of humanity, love taking on the place of greed as the motive. It is an alteration in the conditions of labour that I want. This mad rush for wealth must cease and the labourer must be assured not only of a living wage but a daily task that is not a mere drudgery. The machine will, under these conditions, be as much a help to the man working it as to the State, or the man who owns it. The present mad rush will cease and the labourer will work, as I have said, under attractive and ideal conditions. This is but one of the exceptions I have in mind. The sewing-machine had love at its back. The individual is the one supreme consideration. The saving of labour of the individual should be the object and honest humanitarian considerations, and not greed the motive . . . . Therefore, replace greed by love and everything will come right.'

Next morning the interview was continued. Ramchandran persisted:

R. 'If you make an exception of the Singer Sewing-Machine and your spindle, where would these exceptions end?'

G. 'Just where they cease to help the individual and encroach upon his individuality. The machine should not be allowed to cripple the limbs of man.'

R. 'But I was not thinking just now of the practical side. Ideally, would you not rule out all machinery? When you except the sewing-machine, you will have to make exceptions of the bicycle, the motor-car, etc.'

G. 'No, I don't, because they do not satisfy any of the primary wants of man; . . . . Ideally, however, I would rule out all machinery, even as I would reject this very body, which is not helpful to salvation and seek the absolute liberation of the soul. From that point of view, I would reject all machinery, but machines will remain because, like the body, they are inevitable. The body itself, as I told you, is the *purest piece* of mechanism; but if it is a hindrance to the highest flights of the soul, it has to be rejected.'

The quotation is important from many points of view. The views expressed in 1924 seem to mark a departure from those of 1908. Gandhi was a realist in the best sense of the term. The seeds that had been sown in the *Hind Swaraj* grew into a plant in the upturned soil of India. Gandhi had started the non-co-operation movement and the Khilafat movement, but he realized that the people of India were not yet ripe for the supreme renunciation his values demanded. Non-violence and Truth could not be the bread of the masses. That was the bitter lesson of Chauri-Chaura (1922). The masses wanted bread, and for them 'God was bread and bread was God'. A terrible famine raged in Orissa, and it haunted his dreams. In various cities of India strikes occurred; and their lesson was not lost on him. His sense of limits, a gift which every moral genius must possess, came into play. And in that process he realized a few historical truths. It was clear to him that the impetus behind the large-scale use of machinery was profit or 'greed'—which was 'in the constitution of things' as they were, and not philanthropy or love, that 'today machinery helps a few to ride on the backs of millions', that the labourer must get a living wage and a secure daily task and his labour should not be drudgery and above all, that man, that is, the labourer, was the supreme consideration. In Gandhi's view man was the producer, the bread-worker by hand, an idea which he had imbibed early in his career in South Africa from Ruskin's *Unto This Last*, which he had translated as *Sarvodaya*. Gandhi, be it underlined, would have nationalized or State-controlled factories of power-driven machinery to control the profit and produce for 'the benefit of humanity', love taking the place of greed as the motive. At this point Gandhi presumably believed that the State was, and would be, an agency for transforming greed into a love for humanity, though elsewhere he was less hopeful. All this appears to be a move away from the uncompromising position taken up in the *Hind Swaraj*. Be that as it may, it was not a sacrifice of his basic, or he called it, the 'ideal' position. 'Ideally, however, I would rule out all machinery, even as I would reject this very body (the purest piece of machinery) which is not helpful to salvation and seek the absolute liberation of the soul.' This idea of salvation and absolute liberation from the body is, in my view, the key-note of Gandhian values, or Indian values, as Gandhi and many others would interpret them. In short, Gandhi would have welcomed the 'natural destruction' of machinery and mills, together with law-courts, railways and hospitals, but not a violent destruction. By 'natural' he appeared to have meant the potential nature of the scholastics—the nature that sprang from love, purity, simplicity, and flowered in fulfilment and renunciation. His exceptions arose from the 'actual' nature of man in India, his unpreparedness. (*Young India*, January 1921, 'A World of Explanation'.) Truly could Gandhi say: 'Ripeness is all.'

These values, it is obvious, centred in renunciation and non-possession. The Hindu idea of renunciation is not *vairagya*, which is probably a Buddhist concept incorporated into Hinduism. Renunciation in the Hindu sense is *aparigraha* (non-possession) of the Geeta, as Acharaya Vinoba has pointed out more than once in the pages of the *Harijan* (10 April 1949). The concept of love, or altruism, the good of all, as opposed to the hedonistic calculus of the greatest good of the greatest number (*Autobiography*, Part iv, Chap. viii; *Young India*, 9 December 1926) was probably a mixture of Vaishnava, Christian and later Buddhist ideas. Whatever its origins, it worked very well indeed, particularly as a means of propagation of Gandhi's ideas among the masses. In other words, the 'ideal' pattern of Hindu values was never forsaken by Gandhi. It was woven round 'wantlessness'. How could technology and machines geared to the production of goods for the satisfaction of wants, which created more wants, joint wants, derived wants, the infinite hyperbola of wants, be consonant with the pattern of Indian norms? How could such norms square for that matter, with economics, grounded as it was on wants and their satisfaction? If absolute liberation of the soul from the body be the utter sum of existence, then Gandhi, and with him, every Hindu who was aware of his ancestry, would raise the eternal query: Why this craze for machinery? Why machine-civilization at all? Other problems such as machines helping a few to ride on the back of millions, the concentration of power and wealth, of justice for the labourer as man, securing attractive conditions of life for him and of giving him security of employment, etc., would be subsidiary. These latter, in Gandhi's opinion, ultimately hinged upon non-possession, *aparigraha*, wantlessness, subordination of body and bodily wants to the need of the soul's liberation from its physical encasement, which was *the* end.

These subsidiary problems, however, were far from socially insignificant. In the Gandhian view of life they were related to the means. To many 'educated' Indians they were the ends, or the primary values. Gandhi had many opportunities of discussing them with those who were more sensitive to the needs and ideas of the day. Rabindranath Tagore's objection was of a different type, but it was met by the logic of means. The poet had written in 1925 against the *charkha* (the spinning-wheel), because he felt that it would bring about a deathlike sameness in the nation. Gandhi met this argument on the highest level. Taking his cue from the Hindu philosophical conception of oneness, identity, or sameness, which Sankar had carried to its logical extreme, Gandhi held that 'behind a variety of occupations there is an indispensable sameness also of occupation'. After inveighing for a while against exploitation both by European and Indian manufacturers, Gandhi conceded: 'Machinery has its place; it has come to stay. But it must not be allowed to displace the necessary human labour. An important plough is a good thing. But if by some chance one man could plough up by some mechanical invention of his the whole of the land of India and control all the agricultural produce and if the millions had no other occupation, they would starve, and being idle, they would become dunces, as many have already become. There is hourly danger of many more being reduced to that unenviable state. I would welcome every improvement in the cottage machine but I know that it is criminal to displace the hand labour by the introduction of power-driven spindles unless one is at the same time ready to give millions of farmers some other occupation in their homes.' (*Young India*, 5 November 1925; *Mahatma*, Vol. 2, p. 283.) Here was argument on the purely economic level of means, that is, of employment and unemployment. (Also, Vol. 4, pp. 34, 238-9.) To a modern Western economist it may appear to be old-fashioned. He thinks that he has devised excellent measures against various types of unemployment, cyclical, structural, frictional, seasonal, and all that, and he is not worried if even under full employment 2 to 5 per cent are unemployed. But Gandhi was not to be deluded by such theories and measures emerging out of the practices of countries that had been wedded to industrial and technical civilization, that had colonies to exploit and accepted competitive values in production, trade and commerce. The essence of Gandhi's concession in this open letter to Tagore is, however, historical. That is to say, so long as 'some other occupation in their homes' was not available—and it was not likely to be available in that historical context, or in the near future, because imperialist exploitation would not allow India to create alternative occupations—Gandhi would stick to the spinning-wheel and be against the displacement of labour by machinery. In other words, India in her present context should have labour-intensive economy for the sake of full employment.

Gandhi was very respectful towards Tagore, and as we have seen met the poet's cultural charge with economic arguments. But he was not so soft towards the Indian Communist M.P. Mr. Saklatwala, in his reply to the latter's appeal, which he duly published in *Young India*. The differences with Tagore were not vital, but with Mr. Saklatwala they were. Gandhi wrote in *Young India* under the caption 'No and Yes':

'His facts are fiction and his deductions based upon fiction are necessarily baseless. And where these are true, my whole energy is concentrated upon nullifying their, to me, poisonous results. I am sorry, but we do stand at opposite poles. There is, however, one great thing common between us. Both claim to have the good of the country and humanity as our only goal. Though we may for the moment seem to be going in opposite directions, I expect we shall meet some day. I promise to make amends when I discover my error. Meanwhile, my error, since I do not recognize it as such, must be my child and my solace.'

Having said this in true humility—and there is not the slightest reason to doubt it—Gandhi reveals himself in the full panoply of his original, uncompromising, absolute, non-historical faith. He wrote:

'For unlike Saklatwala, I do not believe that multiplication of wants and machinery contrived to supply them is taking the world a single step nearer its goal. Comrade Saklatwala swears by the modern rush. I whole-heartedly detest this mad desire to destroy distance and time, to increase animal appetites and go to the ends of the earth in search of their satisfaction. If modern civilization stands for all this, and I have understood it to do so, I call it satanic and with it the present system of government, its best exponent.'

Then follow some sentences which would remind one of the wrath of prophets, but with a difference. 'I would destroy that system today, if I had the power. I would use the most deadly weapons, if I believed that they would destroy it. I refrain only because the use of such weapons could only perpetuate the system though it may destroy its present administration. Those who seek to destroy men rather than their manners adopt the latter and become worse than those whom they destroy under the mistaken belief that the manners will die with the men. They do not know the root of the evil.'

The last paragraph seems to retain its pertinence today in spheres wider than the Indian. The points to be noticed in Gandhi's reply to Saklatwala's appeal are Gandhi's firm faith in wantlessness as a cardinal human virtue, and his objection only to the 'modern rush', in which he included both the Western and the Indian values of the day. We may further note his association of modernism with the British Government in India. Strictly from the point of view of the propagation of an unswerving faith, this mixture of basic values with nationalism was excellent. A sociologist would not cavil at it. Technological values are usually associated with the nationalist values, particularly in the Eastern countries in the period of their anti-imperialist struggle which centres in their opposition to the obstacles that imperialism places in their economic growth, and also in the period of economic advance which is held to be possible only with the help of technology. But it is equally understandable that nationalist, anti-subjectionist motives and attitudes should be integrated with the basic values which are, or are interpreted to be, specific to the culture of the nation. While it is true that in this extract no reference is made to the Indian-ness of the objection to the modern rush and the argument appears to rest on the personal level, it is apparent, as it certainly was to the Indian of 1925, that it was a typically Indian argument securely grounded on the Indian philosophy of life, *aparigraha*, non-possession, enjoyment through giving away, *tyaktena bhunjitha*.

We must repeat that Gandhi collected other arguments round this basic objection to machines. They were mainly what we would call sociological arguments on the score of excessive population on land, of idle labour, of bad distribution of wealth, benefit to the nation, that is to say, the welfare of the people. He referred to unemployment again and again, to bad health, unwholesome food, and to the decay of art. He categorically stated that labour had a unique place in *swaraj*, or independence, and formed its content. Each argument depended on another and the whole formed a pattern of positive values. In 1935, on 23 April, he said after opening the first All-India Village Industries Exhibition at Indore: 'The reason why our average life-rate is deplorably low, the reason why we are getting more and more impoverished is that we have neglected our 100,000 villages. We have indeed thought of them, but only to the extent of exploiting them. We read thrilling accounts of the "glory that was Ind", of the land that was flowing with milk and honey; but today it is a land of starving millions. We are sitting in this fine pandal under a blaze of electric lights, but we do not know that we are burning these lights at the expense of the poor. We have no right to use the lights if we forget that we owe these to them.' Gandhi would seldom forget to remind his audience of their responsibility towards the people. The expression 'owe these to them' is an English rendering of the Hindu concept of *rina* or debts, contracted by every individual at his birth to his ancestors, his gods, sages, and to nature, the universe or society, debts which must be duly discharged in the course of existence. Hindu social organization is built on the principle of obligations which Gandhi insisted on resuscitating in all social and economic spheres of activity, *vide* his concept of rich men holding their riches in trusteeship for the poor. Only in the sphere of political struggle against foreign rule would he allow the exercise of the Western sense of rights, and these too hedged in by the sense of social obligations, which was one vital significance of non-violence. Gandhi continued: 'There is a difference between the civilization of the East—the civilization of India—and that of the West.'

Formerly he had contrasted only the modern civilization with the earlier, pre-technical one and minimized, if not ignored this distinction between the East and the West. However, this again is not quite a shift in position; in fact, he was also speaking to the West. And he was only referring to the defects of the tendencies of the Western civilization, and not to its inherent nature, as Mahadev Desai pointed out in his preface to the 1938 edition of *Hind Swaraj*:

'It is not generally realized wherein the difference lies. Our geography is different, our history is different, our ways of life are different. Our continent, though vast is a speck on the globe, but it is the most thickly populated, barring China. Well, the economics and the civilization of a country where the pressure of population on land is greatest (the conjunction "and" should not be made much of) are and must be different from those of a country where the pressure is the least. Sparsely populated America may have need of the machinery. India may not need it at all. When there are millions upon millions of units of idle labour, it is no use thinking of labour-saving devices. . . . The reason of our poverty is the extinction of [cottage] industries, and our consequent unemployment.'

There follow certain figures about the increasing dependence on land as a result of the destruction of cottage industries and the loss of health through the elimination of vitamins in grain after being ground in machines. Gandhi's context was the first exhibition of Village Industries, which he was building up as the base of his constructive programme. He was an anti-machinist with a purpose, and the language of his argument was suitable to the masses hearing him.

Gandhi seemed to have been perpetually alive to this problem of unemployment. On 22 October 1937 he inaugurated the Educational Conference at Wardha and developed his ideas of education through handicrafts. It was a new setting for his constructive programme—an integration of living in love, with efficiency and independence, without exploitation, conflict and poverty, and with education of the body and mind. In expounding his thesis, he said:

'Then, take the question of machinery. I think that machinery is not necessary for us at all. We should use *khadi* (home-spun cloth); and, therefore, we do not require mills. We should try to produce all the necessary cloth in villages, and we need not be the slaves of machines. I am afraid, by working with machines we have become machines ourselves, having lost all sense of art and handwork. If you still think that we cannot do without machines, the scheme (of new education) I have placed before you will be futile. You wish to keep our village alive by means of machines and think of imparting education to the village children through them. Machines will only help in making all the thirty-five crores of people unemployed. If you think that machines are really indispensable, you must reject the scheme and suggest a new one.' (*Mahatma*, Vol. 4, pp. 238-9.)

In 1946 India was passing through a severe food crisis. Gandhi offered advice to those who sought it. There were suggestions and counter-suggestions. Even in those dire days he would not move from his fundamental ground. In one of his replies he said:

'I regard the existence of power-wheels for the grinding of corn in thousands of villages as the limit of our helplessness. I suppose India does not produce all the engines and grinding machines.... The planting of such machinery and engines on a large scale in villages (a suggestion made by a correspondent for resolving the food crisis) is also a sign of greed. Is it proper to fill one's pockets in this manner at the expense of the poor? Such machinery puts thousands of hand *chakkis* (grindstones for corn) out of work, and takes away employment from thousands of housewives and artisans who make these *chakkis*. Moreover, the process is infective and spreads to every village industry. The decay of the latter spells too the decay of art. If it meant the replacement of the old crafts by the new ones, one might not have much to say against it. But this is not what is happening. In the thousands of villages, where power-machinery exists, one misses the sweet music in the early morning of the grinders at work. But to come to the main point. Whilst I hold that these power engines are, at present, being put to wrong use, it would be some compensation if these engines, in addition to their present use, were also used to pump water out of the rivers, tanks and wells for irrigation.' *(Mahatma,* Vol. 7, pp. 71-2.)

Probably the most comprehensive and yet succinct account of the place of machinery in the context of independence was written by Gandhi in the *Harijan* of 15 July 1946. It was a clarification for the benefit of Congressmen of his concept of independence. He painted a glorious picture of self-sufficient villages, giving free and voluntary play to mutual forces, highly cultured in the sense that there every man and woman knows what he or she wants and, what is more, knows that no one should want anything that the others cannot have with equal labour, a society based on the living force of truth and non-violence, a society not like a pyramid but like 'an oceanic circle'.[1]

On 31 July 1946 Gandhi addressed a conference of Ministers of Industries of different states in Poona. There he clarified his conception of village industries and referred to the imbalance between town and village economies and the need for establishing justice in their relation. In that connexion he came to a fairly elaborate explanation of what he meant by machines. Sir D. G. Tendulkar, the author of *Mahatma,* gives the following summary: ' "Ours has been described as the machine age," remarked Gandhi, "because the machine dominates our economy. What is a machine? One may ask. In a sense, man is the most wonderful machine in creation. It can neither be duplicated nor copied." He had, however, used the word not in its wider sense, but in the sense of an appliance that tended to displace the human or animal labour instead of supplementing it, or merely to increase its efficiency. That was the first differential characteristic of the machine. The second characteristic was that there was no limit to its growth or evolution. That could not be said of the human labour. There was a limit beyond which its capacity or mechanical efficiency could not go. Out of this circumstance arose the third characteristic of the machine. It seemed to be possessed of a will or genius of its own. Machine was antagonistic to man's labour. Thus, it tended more to displace man, one machine doing the work of a hundred, if not a thousand, who went to swell the army of unemployed and underemployed, not because that was desirable,

1. 'I may be taunted with the retort that this is all Utopian and, therefore, not worth a single thought. If Euclid's point, though incapable of being drawn by any human agency, has an imperishable value, my picture has its own for mankind to live. Let India live for this true picture, though never realizable in its completeness.... In it, there is no room for machines that would displace human labour and that would concentrate power in a few hands. Labour has its unique place in a cultured human family. Every machine that helps every individual has a place. But I must confess that I have never sat down to think out what that machine can be. I have thought of Singer's Sewing-Machine. But even that is perfunctory. I do not need it to fill in my picture.' (*Mahatma,* Vol. 7, pp. 201-2.)

but because that was its law. In America it had perhaps reached the extreme limit. He had been opposed to it not from today, but even before 1909, when he was in South Africa surrounded by machines. Their onward march had not only impressed him, but had repelled him.

' "It then dawned upon me that to suppress and exploit the millions, the machine was the device *par excellence;* it had no place in man's economy if, as social units, all men were to be equal. It is my belief that machine has not added to man's stature and it will not serve the world, but disrupt it, unless it is put in its proper place. Then I read Ruskin's *Unto This Last* . . . . I saw clearly that if mankind was to progress and to realize the idea of equality and brotherhood, it must act on the principle of *Unto This Last*."

'In the machine age, this principle had no place. Under it the fittest alone survived, to the exclusion and at the cost of the weak. "But that is not my picture of independence, in which there is room even for the weakest", observed Gandhi. "That requires that we must realize all available human labour, before we entertain the idea of employing mechanical power." ' *(Mahatma,* Vol. 17, pp. 214-15.)

We have traced the development of Gandhi's ideas on machines, and on machine-civilization and found that despite many concessions to the 'proper' use of machines his values were definitely opposed to those which make for technological civilization and are made by it. By 'proper' he meant, positively, that which was prompted by love and good for humanity, and negatively, what did not lead to concentration of wealth in a few hands and inequality, to centralization of power, to urbanization, to unemployment, to political, economic and social exploitation. These evils, which in his view, were the characteristics of the modern society, with its American apogee, were the consequences of the large-scale use of machines, and they had to be fought with vigour. To that extent he was placing Indian (Eastern) against Western (Euro-American, modern) values. It was certainly not a case of revivalism, but a clear statement of a principle of social organization which was different from the one that had succeeded in imposing itself on the strength of political suzerainty. His minimal idea was to establish co-existence of different social systems, on the basis of equality, though the prophetic strain that came to him in the course of his experiments with Truth led him to think that the values he propagated would also be good for the Western world. We will leave it to the Western sociologist to ponder over this issue. An Indian sociologist can only mention that Gandhi's protagonism of Indian values was not a manifestation of the romantic agony of nationalist historians, nor was it a reactionary, obscurantist throw-back. It is submitted here that he was a revolutionary and what a revolutionary in India should be, viz., an Indian revolutionary, that is, one who would first be steeped in Indian realities and then evaluate the nature of changes in social realities in order to create fresh norms. Gandhi did not go to the past: in fact, he was not an Indologist; he only went to the roots and the sources. And 'the deeper you go to the root the more radical you become'.

At this stage it will be relevant to note the revolutionary elements in his views. Their importance arises from the problem before us, that we here must consider the conditions under which technological change can take place without causing the various tensions and frustrations which bring about aggression, violence, and war, which lead to mental unhealth.

In other words, we must ask ourselves whether technology cannot but generate these evils; whether technology should always depend upon wants and their increase and bring about a state of culture in which material wants are king. The inner significance of Gandhi's concessions to the use of machines, that is to say, the logical meaning of the term 'proper' use, is that they do not, and need not, go together. It is perfectly possible, in Gandhi's opinion; and it is also logical to assume under stated conditions, that technology can be introduced into India without upsetting the Indian pattern of values. These conditions are non-possession, *aparigraha*, the 'oceanic' constitution of Indian independence in terms of self-sufficient villages with their group-existence fulfilled through the panchayats, bread-labour, *sharir-srama*, with its concomitant of the dignity of labour symbolized in *khadi*, *sarvodaya*, that is, total awakening or uplift, and of course, non-violence and Truth, that is *satyagraha*. Of these, *aparigraha*, non-possession, or wantlessness and *srama* or labour, alone are selected for discussion. (Gandhi would have emphasized Truth.) Now, non-possession in the context of human history has been an individual value, and at best, a value for the *élite* group, known as the Brahmin caste, to be perpetually practised by it. Others practised it, but the Brahmin was the specialist. Gandhi would institutionalize it in the State which would own, and not possess for greed or profit. To this extent he was a Socialist—or even a Communist as he called himself before Mr. Louis Fischer *(Mahatma*, Vol. 7, p. 190), but with this difference that his Socialism did not grow out of industrial civilization, technological values, class-conflict, or according to the operations of the laws of dialectics. (That it could only be social expression of Truth, non-violence and faith in God, is important, but not relevant to our selected purpose.) It was to grow out of agriculture, cottage industries, and 'oceanic' rural organization, into a non-possessive State which would be wedded to public good and be a guarantee of non-exploitation by large machinery in the hands of the rich. Meanwhile, Gandhi would ask the rich and the fortunate few to hold their fortunes in trusteeship, practising *aparigraha* themselves. Trusteeship, however, for Gandhi, was an interim measure sanctioned by Indian traditions.

A second revolutionary element in Gandhi's prescription is the concept of *srama* or manual work. So far as this writer knows *srama*, or the value of the dignity of labour, was not quite an Indian value. In a hierarchical society, types of work are defined and relegated to different strata on the two assumptions: that spiritual 'work', that is, pure contemplation, is the highest type; that each stratum, or caste, which is fixed by birth, has its own *swadharma* ('bond', 'religion') the practice of which means fulfilment of personality, and the departure of which means 'destruction' of self. But Gandhi had a different conception of labour. He writes (from *Yeravada Mandir*, Chap. IX):

'The law, that to live man must work, first came home to me upon reading Tolstoy's writing on bread-labour. But even before that I had begun to pay homage to it after reading Ruskin's *Unto This Last*. The divine law that man must earn his bread by labouring with his own hands was first stressed by a Russian writer named T. M. Boudaref. Tolstoy advertised it and gave it wider publicity. In my view, the same principle has been set forth in the third chapter of the Gita, where we are told that he who eats without offering sacrifice eats stolen food. Sacrifice here can only mean bread-labour. There is a world-wide conflict between capital and labour, and the poor envy the rich. If all worked for their bread, distinctions of rank would be obliterated; the rich would still be there, but they would deem themselves only trustees of their property, and would use it mainly in the public interest. The ideal body-labour is agriculture, but the next best would be spinning, weaving, carpentry and smithery; and the logical, common body-labour is scavenging . . . .'

Surely, this is not Indian value. The dissociation of bodily labour from mental and spiritual labour has had a long history, which Gandhi did not take into account. His attitude towards what is known as the caste-system cannot be discussed here. But on the matter of bread-labour bringing about economic equality he was anti-caste and, therefore, a revolutionary—almost a Socialist. In other words, if the Socialist gave up the usual Western assumption, i.e., no high technology, no Socialism, and remained content with the use of certain special types of machinery which would not displace labour or exploit human beings for greed or concentrate power, then Gandhi would bless him. If further, the Socialist accepted this idea of bread-labour and built on the revolutionary content of this view, the ending of the separation of physical labour—now the only duty of a whole class of people who form the majority—from mental labour which is now the monopoly of the few, then the difference between him and Gandhi would not exist, except in the matter of wantlessness. One could argue here that there was a danger in this concept of bread-labour, that it involved the possibility of lowering the impulse and the level of intellectual work by making the intellectual workers work physically for bread without raising the intellectual level and stimulating the impulse of physical workers. But Gandhi would reply that this could be averted.

Thus the Gandhian conclusion in regard to machines and technology is logical if one accepts the postulates that India has a separate norm of values—with the hidden assumption that values determine conduct—that she has a separate principle of social organization which would be disturbed and even destroyed by large-scale use of machinery for greed and profit, and that a proper use would presuppose certain attitudes, some traditional and others not, but all working in alliance, and also a type of State that would own and control large machineries, if they were indispensable for defined purposes. Otherwise, the machineries to be used would be of a special type suitable for removing the drudgery of handicraft and improving its quality, if possible. They would operate in the general context of decentralized economy, in close alliance with agriculture. Gandhi would thus remove the stings of Capitalism and Socialism alike.

In this author's opinion, Gandhi's views have to be carefully studied before any scheme of technical assistance and large-scale technological development is initiated. While it is very true that among certain strata and sections of the Indian people these views appear strange, even though lip-service is paid to them, and that such people would want to initiate rapid technological change in the name of economic advance, evolution and progress, it is also clear that an unintelligent injection of technology would so disturb the existing social pattern of human relations that work would cease to be associated with joy and workmanship, that skill would be replaced by efficiency, that 'the public identity of the job' would be lost, that scientific management and discipline would squeeze the labourer of all humaneness, and that a new instrument of social power would 'teach docility' or 'break the intransigence of workers', all the time keeping greed, profit and more profit in the background, beyond the sight of those who are to be immediately benefited by higher wages, better conditions of living, welfare measures and the like (*Social Theory and Social Structure*, R. K. Merton, pp. 318-22).

In other words, the sociologist would do well to study the sociology of the demand for technology in India and the sociology of its supply. Fortunately, the Indian masses are not yet fully taken in by the technological values. They are being acted upon by technology, and they are showing healthy, normal reactions to the injection by absenteeism, inattentiveness, a sort of lackadaisical attitude towards work in the factories, unpunctuality, the so-called absence of pride in work and workmanship, but unfortunately, quite often in accidents and ill-health. Even strikes, which are bemoaned as symptoms of industrial conflict, can be traced to the search of the soil-bound peasantry of India for mental and social peace in holiday, away from the scene of work, the din of factories and technology, to the villages where the pattern which they know and instinctively feel to be right, rules even today.

An Indian sociologist cannot thus help questioning the manner and the possible hidden motivations of a technological advance, of those who want it and those who supply it. He can, at least, categorically state, with Gandhi, that if change is inevitable, let it come in the shape of certain types of machines, at the proper time, in the proper context; and that if large-scale use of machinery is unavoidable, let it be owned and managed by the State, a new form of State. Judging from experience, he cannot share Gandhi's hope of an interim trusteeship by the fortunate few. In short, the whole problem of technological advance in India, which, let it be repeated, is undeveloped only in the purely technological sense, and, therefore, in the sense of being more socially integrated and less fragmentized, has to be studied from the points of view of both the types of machinery to be introduced and of the types of people who would accept them with due regard to the motivations of introduction. In India, human beings are not yet atomistic, so that no functional specification in the most common productive processes, which are those of agriculture, is possible. Nor has it occurred in many industries. In India, no productive section of society is 'universalistic', that is, only very few 'criteria possibly present in any segment of the population without regard to previous social relationships or membership in irrelevant groups' are available. In India, human relations are affective rather than rational and impersonal. The normative system suitable for the industrial mode of production through large-scale use of machines is thus not the normative system of India. A matter of additional importance is the fact that this normative system has combined with nationalism, anti-imperialism, and Gandhi's interpretation of independence to convince some people that it is still valuable. So change must take account of these facts in order not to produce the same evils to which the West has been an heir.[1]

1. Most of the quotations from Gandhi's writings have been taken from D. G. Tendulkar's monumental biography *Mahatma*, seven volumes of which only are available at the time of writing, the eighth being in print. The 1946 edition of Gandhi's *Hind Swaraj* has been used here, and the 1951 edition of *Sarvodoya, its Principles and Programme*. Both are published by the Navajivan Publishing House, Ahmedabad, Gujerat, India. An autobiography: *The Story of My Experiment with Truth*, translated from Gujrati by Mahadev Desai, 1939 edition, Phoenix Press, London, has also been cited.

OCCIDENTAL AND ORIENTAL
CONCEPTIONS OF ECONOMIC PROGRESS

C. GINI

In the name of economic progress the white races have developed many lands formerly closed to trade or, in their opinion, insufficiently used. Thus England conquered India; the United States ended Japan's segregation; Australia, unused and unpopulated, was annexed by England. Professor Mukerjee warns: 'Australia cannot ... remain untenanted ... a constant temptation to hundreds of millions of industrious and progressive neighbours, whose numbers are exceeding their food supply. ... The world will not tolerate much longer the spectacle of enormous potential resources left undeveloped because of a national dog-in-the-manger policy, upheld by union leaders and politicians living in a few gay cities on the fringe of a vast barren continent.'[1] Similar arguments could justify the settlement of Indians, Chinese and Japanese in various Pacific islands, Papua, Australia, and on America's Pacific Coast.[2]

Mukerjee adduced various facts which, if somewhat outdated, are still significant. Oriental land cultivation still supports a much larger population per unit area than in the West: 100 acres in England support 45 to 50 people, in Canada probably only 10, in India 100 to 110.[3] The Asians could give Australia a population of 450 millions; South America one of 2,400 millions.[4]

Such wide differences in efficiency depend only partly on the smaller needs of the Oriental peoples, because of their lower basic metabolism, and their better adaptation to hot climates. The essential reason is that they obtain a much higher yield from the land. Thus the Japanese took land abandoned or rejected by others, and made it highly productive.[5]

It is by average yield per unit area that economic progress can be measured; on this the superiority of the Oriental system depends. For even the high living standards in Western industrial areas are partly based on primary produce from overseas. Mukerjee recognizes the value of past work by Westerners in developing the East, but considers Orientals better fitted for continuing this task. Behind Mukerjee stands half of human kind, confined to some 4 per cent of the world's

---

1. See Radhkamal Mukerjee, *Migrant Asia*, Rome, 1936, p. 210.
2. ibid., p. 57.
3. ibid., pp. 12-13 and 257. Kazushi Okhawa's reprint, 'International Comparisons of Productivity in Agriculture', The National Research Institute of Agriculture, Tokyo, *Bull. No. 1*, September 1949, in substance confirms Mukerjee's conclusions.
4. ibid., p. 193.
5. ibid., p. 137.

surface. No nationalism will in the long run resist the expansionist force of these people, arising from their indisputable economic superiority.[1]

The essential reason for this superiority lies in intensive hand-cultivation of the soil, with the minimum of livestock, fertilizing with every available particle of organic matter, under the system of 'circular farming'. To obtain as many calories by raising livestock requires five times the area. Modern machinery is little used. The system is substantially large-scale horticulture. Acceptance of this view implies the paradoxical conclusion that the most progressive economic system was introduced during the night of the past.

Such a conclusion is unacceptable. E. F. Penrose considers a stronger population better than one more numerous, but enfeebled by deficient diet.[2] Bertrand Russell, discussing the so-called 'biological theory,' which considers as a supreme end the survival of the largest number of representatives of a species, particularly of humans, objects: 'I cannot see any justification for such a mechanical and arithmetical outlook . . . what human person would prefer a large population living in poverty and squalor to a smaller population living happily with a sufficiency of comfort?'[3] This last phrase reveals the Western criterion of economic progress —the individual's income on which this comfort depends.

This criterion is accepted by the optimum theory of population. The optimum population occurs when, under given conditions, the highest possible average income is reached. This theory can easily be criticized. It ignores many factors, like the aspirations of religious propagandists, politicians, and soldiers who all see strength in number; it overlooks the organizational and cultural advantages of a dense population. But such extra-economic objections leave the concept of an optimum population untouched as a measure of strictly economic progress.

Thus qualified, the above criterion correctly portrays the Western conception of economic progress. Like the Eastern, it is based on income but it differs in that average *per capita* income is the yardstick of economic progress. This leads to a radically different classification of the several countries. India and China pass from the first to the last places; Argentina from the tail to the head.

Even more striking consequences emerge from considering individual estates and not whole countries. An Argentinian estate, grazing immense flocks on vast areas, would represent an advanced stage of progress; its owner secures a very high income. Similarly, tribes like the Bantus would head economic progress, since their members often own huge herds of cattle. This idea probably reproduces a stage traversed by early society. The Western, like the Eastern notion suggests that—from prehistoric ages—humanity has achieved little economic progress.

Indeed this Western notion convinces us less than the Eastern; it runs counter to popular demands for agrarian policies to reclaim swamp-lands and break up great estates. Such works, though reducing the income of the owner and his small family, increase income per unit of land.

The weak point in both arguments lies in the underlying notion of income. This is admittedly the current one, being based on output, net of all costs except, in the case of a free producer, for his maintenance and amortization. I have long

1. ibid., p. 11.
2. E. F. Penrose, *Population Theories and their Application, with special reference to Japan*, Food Research Institute, Stanford University, California, 1934.
3. Bertrand Russell, *Authority and the Individual*, The Reith Lectures for 1948-49, London, Allen & Unwin, pp. 117-18.

protested against this exception and pointed to some drawbacks.[1] We now consider another drawback.

The current notion of income is illogical, first, because it treats differently two workers, one free the other a slave, who differ only in extra-economic characteristics. This makes it impossible to compare the income of a country before and after slave-emancipation. Maintenance and amortization costs, previously deducted from slave-owners' incomes, are still deducted from the individual entrepreneurs' production, but they increase global national income, being income for the workers. Second, it is illogical to deduct the wear and tear of machines but not the expenses of maintaining and amortizing men. If a country loses x men by emigration, replacing them by machines producing an identical product at the same cost, the country will figure as having a lower income. The expenses of operating and amortizing the machines are then deducted from income; maintenance and amortization of the men were not.

The objection is raised that men are both producers and consumers. But national income calculations attempt to estimate, though imperfectly, national economic welfare. One cannot speak of welfare until essential needs are satisfied. Only goods in excess of such needs can be included in an index of welfare. Admittedly, satisfaction is greater when needs are keenly felt, but this satisfaction merely compensates for pain previously felt.

This conclusion is supported by modern fiscal practices. Not only are minimum incomes exempted, but all earners receive tax-free allowances based on the subsistence minimum for themselves and their dependents. As this exemption ceases for children at a certain age, it is clearly intended to cover the expenses of upbringing and training.

If one allowed for such costs of maintenance and amortization of human beings one would need a new word referring to the remainder of income, which would then supply an index of welfare, establishing reliable comparisons in space and time. Such an amended measurement of income gives plausible conclusions. Let us assume that $10 represent the individual's maintenance and amortization costs (here, to save space, called 'subsistence').

1. If 1,000 persons on 100 hectares give an average output of $10, total output will be 10,000 units. Income will be nil, 10,000 units only covering the 'subsistence' of the workers. Such is the case in overpopulated countries with intensive cultivation, like India.

2. If only 3 people live on 100 hectares, with an average output of $1,000, total output will $3,000. Income, net of 'subsistence', is 2,970 units. This is the case for example in the Argentine pampas.

3. If 100 people on 100 hectares give an average output of $80, total output is $8,000, leaving an income net of 'subsistence' of 7,000 units, far more than in 2. Such is the usual position in Western countries.

The Oriental criterion of economic progress seems well-founded provided we deduct 'subsistence' from income. Agrarian policy that reduces estate-owners' incomes but increases global income from the land seems justified. But the common intuition of Westerners, who believe their economic system to be more progressive, is also well-founded, because income per acre, after deducting 'subsistence', is higher in the West.

---

[1]. See, for example, *Report on the Content and Use of the Estimates of National Income, Studi sul reddito nazionale, Annali di Statistica*, Series VIII, Vol. III, 1950, and (in English) *Banca Nazionale Del Lavoro, Quarterly Review*, No. 5, April 1948.

MONEY, WORK AND SOCIAL CHANGE
IN INDO-PACIFIC ECONOMIC SYSTEMS

R. Firth

My main object in this paper is to examine the social effects of the introduction or expansion of monetary exchange in a peasant economic system. An alteration of this kind in the technical media of exchange, need not, *a priori*, have of itself any social concomitants. It is theoretically possible for the appearance of a novel type of exchange medium such as money, or for an enlargement of the amounts of money available and of its uses, to have effect in economic terms alone, facilitating the circulation of goods and their production without making any substantial changes in the social position of the people involved. In fact, however, this is very unlikely—social values usually tend to be attached to the new income or consumption effects. And even if income and consumption effects are not large, the new experiences acquired in the production and exchange processes, in gaining and using the money units concerned, become matters of social evaluation, and tend to emerge in differences of social status.

Three points must be made at the outset.

First, the aim of this paper is analytical, not ethnographic. I am taking my examples from the Indo-Pacific region, because that is the one I know best. But I am not trying to cover the whole range of phenomena presented by these diverse societies. What I hope to do is to set out some of the main considerations involved when money is introduced to an economy in which it has formerly not been known, or when there is a sudden expansion of the uses to which it can be put. This may indicate a framework of propositions for argument and research. The presentation is helped by the great variations found in the region. On the one hand there are relatively simple economic systems such as those of Tikopia or of the central highlands of New Guinea, to which money is just being introduced; on the other, there is the relatively sophisticated economy of peasant Malays or Indonesians, in which money of various types has been known and used for centuries in some transactions.

Second, at this stage it would be imprudent to pretend to have achieved a clear isolation of factors. In talking of social change it is necessary also to talk of economic change, since the social elements are so often mediated through the economic. It would be superficial to argue, as is sometimes done, that the peasant producer has no interest in a new production technology as such, but only in the income effects to be derived from it. Just as conservatism in retention of traditional tools may be in part a compound of aesthetic and psycho-physical elements involved in rhythmic use and quality of results, and of status interest in skill of manipulation, so the welcome given to a new tool or to a machine may be partly a recognition of its better technical quality, the novel skills which can be developed with it, and the social esteem which its control may bring. But on the whole, though these elements may influence the adoption of a new technical device, they are marginal to its permanent establishment. In the long run, it is the effects upon incomes and consumption levels, both experienced and anticipated, that seem to be of major importance. In a peasant economy technological progress is not conceived as a normal desirable end, towards which special sectors of economic effort should be regularly directed. So it is with the use of money. Since social changes associated with a new or expanded technology emerge through economic changes and the social evaluation of them, it is difficult if not impossible at this stage of analysis to disentangle the changes due to the introduction or wider adoption of money in an economy from those due to other aspects of a development process. When young men go out from the village to work for wages, the important social changes that come about may be due as much to the patterns and results of their new type of work as to the fact that they get money for it.

Third, the primary purpose of this paper is social theory, not social application. Already, in some cases, the accumulation and interpretation of data may have been ample and acute enough to allow a counselling programme or advisory service to be of use. But on the whole we are still working out the implications of data which are much too inadequate for solid generalization. Our main task is first of all to call attention to the nature of the problems and the means required for studying them.

CHARACTERISTICS AND EXCHANGE VARIANTS IN PEASANT ECONOMY

Before discussing the social changes associated with the intervention of a money economy in the wide sense, the major characteristics of an Indo-Pacific peasant economy may be outlined.[1] There is a simple equipment and technology, with little use of machinery and no ideology of mechanization. There is no high differentiation of technical training. Market relations are of a limited character, with a relatively small range of goods and services involved. In prices, conventional estimations are apt to play a large part, and a 'price' is often not given monetary expression. Control of the means of production is non-capitalistic, i.e., capital exists but the owner of it does not control the productive process; there is no clear separation of capitalist-rentier from worker-management in the persons contributing to production, or sometimes even in function when the person is the same. This merging of factor-control is seen also in the merging of rewards of production —the lack of separation of interest, wages and management rewards, for example. The scale of producing units and the volume of product for any single unit are comparatively small. The scheme of economic relations thus tends naturally to be of a more personalized order than in a Western economy. This kind of economic system is closely geared to a type of society in which the social units over much of the field of operation are small with a local community emphasis; in which leadership and authority are largely produced from within the local group, and are often kinship-based or kinship-linked; and in which local religious cults tend to strengthen the community in many of its operations. Despite the great

---

1. Further details are given in my *Malay Fishermen*, London, 1946, pp. 22-5 *et passim*. See also the distinctions made by J. H. Boeke, *The Structure of Netherlands Indian Economy*, New York, 1942, p. 57 *et seq.*

variation in scale and in sophistication, such characteristics are common throughout the region.

Such a system is conservative in the sense that there is rarely a wish to reject radically any of its major institutional elements[1] and substitute others. But there may be no stubborn refusal to adopt new items. There may be indeed an enthusiastic acceptance of them, with the implication that they are additions to the economic and cultural stock of a system which retains its basic familiar character. So subtly have new crops entered the economy of Indo-Pacific communities that it is almost impossible to reconstruct any 'indigenous' production scheme for agriculture. The adoption in recent times of the drought-resisting manioc in Tikopia, for instance, has made significant changes in the crop cycle and is likely to alter correspondingly the system of land use and tenure. The substitution of steel axe for stone axe in the interior of New Guinea—a process now almost complete—seems to have led to greatly increased felling of primary forest, with alteration of the balance in the provision of natural soil cover, and increase in danger of soil erosion and loss of fertility. Thus while the impetus to social change may be said to be given by a technological change, this in itself has only been possible by an acceptance or 'committal'—to use a fashionable term—which has welcomed the possibility of increased income in at least some limited spheres. To put the point another way, the real impetus lies not in technology as such, but in seeing the possibility of alternative uses for labour and other resources which will yield the increased income. But apart from realizing the efficiency of the new instruments or processes, one must be willing to subject oneself (or others, if one has command over their labour) to a new discipline. In order to obtain the benefits, one must forego some types of satisfaction hitherto enjoyed. Change is the implication of human choices. When we speak of the social implications of technological change, we do not mean that the total process is inevitable; we mean only that an initial acceptance or committal in the technological field is likely to be followed by certain results. Some of these may be foreseen, but others may not. Yet it is these unforeseen results which are often of greatest importance, because they are often undesired. Being unexpected, no provision has been made against them, and being often long-term rather than short-term, they may eventuate long after there is any ordinary possibility of reversing the trend.

Now turn to the monetary aspects of Indo-Pacific peasant economic systems. Several kinds of system may be crudely distinguished here according to the degree to which money of Western type is current. There are those few systems where money is not used, and purchasing power is provided by bark-cloth, mats, and shell goods.[2] There are those systems, still common in the Pacific, where Western money is used for a limited range of transactions, but where other articles of more traditional type also still have purchasing power. Here again there is variation. Some systems, as on the south coast of New Guinea, using money for most exchanges of goods and services, reserve shell armlets, necklets and other treasures for certain particularly important transactions, especially those affecting the status of human beings, in which they may play a symbolic as well as an economic role. Others, as on the Gazelle peninsula, may add the complication of dual or

1. Cases are known in which this appears, as the communities of the Purari Delta under the influence of Tomu Kabu, or the Manus of the Admiralty Islands. But it is a question how far the implications of such a rejection were fully perceived by the people.
2. I leave out of account here the arguments of Paul Einzig (*Primitive Money*, London, 1949) as to how far such indigenous valuables can be termed 'money'. In my view he pushes this category beyond the point of usefulness, in not distinguishing those which serve as general media of exchange from those which do not.

multiple exchange media. So in the Rabaul market one may see fruit and vegetables sold indifferently for tobacco, for cowrie shells, or for cash.[1] Again, there
are the systems common in Indonesia, the Philippines, Malaya, where money is
the general medium for a range of transactions comparable with those of a Western
rural economy. The points of significance in these distinctions are the types of
services and goods for the purchase of which money can be employed; and the
level or range of purchase which can be undertaken. Every society has its conventions about which kinds of goods and services are proper for calculation and exchange in monetary terms, and which are not. One of the important implications
of the introduction or enlargement of a money system in an economy is the re-
estimation of goods, and particularly of services which is likely to follow. This
may mean in effect a reorientation of the moral values of the society. One of the
most meaningful aspects of the coming of a money economy may be said to be
the introduction of a medium of exchange with external as well as internal purchasing power. Reference to an external standard is likely to tend at once to a revision
of internal estimations, and by offering hitherto unknown or unrealizable alternatives, to alter conventional placings of resources. Similar results are likely to
follow from a rapid expansion of the moentary medium, as by the opening up of
new markets for labour or commodities.

EFFECTS OF INTRODUCTION TO A WAGE ECONOMY

Let us now examine in more detail what the economic and social results are likely
to be in a community where money with an external purchasing power has not
previously operated, or has operated at only a very low volume of transactions.
For simplicity take first situations of money acquistion through wage payments,
as in a plantation economy. What money may do in such circumstances is as
follows.

It may introduce an element of uncertainty into the socio-economic operations of some people, and reduce the relative level of skill and knowledge of those
not regularly handling it. In Tikopia in 1929, the use of money was not understood, and the relative values of British coins were unknown. In 1952 there was a
spread of knowledge, but unevenly. Some men who had been outside the community to work owned and handled money with reasonable fluency and aptitude.
Others, usually older men, might own some money, but handled it with caution
and an admittedly imperfect knowledge of its relations, and the price levels of commodities within their economic universe. They had to rely on others to undertake
transactions for them. For a few old men, and many women, there was still no real
understanding of the nature of money and its operations. This situation can be
paralleled by the observations of Kunio Odaka and his colleagues on the Li of
Hainan during the war. These people had to supply labour for the Shih-Lu iron
mines, according to quotas set by the authorities. They were paid in military
currency, which was new to them, whatever their acquaintance had been with
other money before. They were allowed to buy some ordinary consumption goods
with it from stores, and they used it in trading among themselves, though the
sums involved were small and their interest in it limited. But they were not able
to figure out the values with ease; many women, and even some of the elders,
could not distinguish 5 sen from 10 sen, and they confused sen and yen. All this

---

1. Similar to those eastern Nigerian markets in which cowries, cash and *manilas* (brass armlets) serve equally as
media.

obviously gives an economic advantage, and probably a status advantage too, to those who take on an interpretative or middleman's role.[1]

The introduction of money from wage labour may result in a temporary inflation or pseudo-inflation, in that the amounts of goods and services for which it is regarded as suitable equivalent may be relatively small, and knowledge of the market imperfect. Hence prices may be uneven as regards alternatives, rise erratically, and give 'windfall' profits to some people in positions of temporary advantage.

Money wages may reduce margins of skill, ability and responsibility between workers in respect of traditional types of tasks. For example, on a plantation, or in similar types of work where there is little differentiation made, the common payment of flat rates per month means that all workers of the same classification get the same income, irrespective of skill. (Steadiness and energy may lead to retention in employment, however.) In the traditional economy, principles of equal sharing in teamwork often operate; but there respect for the work and traditional sanctions often tend to keep up the level of production. Differential treatment, by giving wages for individual or team piece-work, or by payment of bonuses for higher output, or by having a graded scheme of jobs, can all tend to give expression to elements of skill and ability. But in all such work there is a general tendency to reduce the level of economic responsibility, of interest in the relation between ends and means, as compared, say, with traditional agriculture. There the worker is always faced by problems of decision about timing and quantity in planting, culling, harvesting, and this gives variety to the occupation.

On the other hand, the creation of new working roles, especially those associated with mechanical operations, may give some workers margins of income greatly in excess of any they might get in the traditional economy, and greatly in excess also of incomes obtained by their fellows in the new working scheme. A Papuan carpenter or electrician in New Guinea, for instance, may get four or five times as much in real wages as his fellow-villager working on a plantation or the roads.

Yet the introduction of a money economy may also tend to remove from the labour market some marginal categories of labour which were absorbed and active, as far as their limited capacity went, in the traditional economy. The physically weak, the deformed, and many young persons who are not regarded as worth the flat rate of pay, tend to be excluded from wage employment.

The advent of money in wage labour form tends also to alter the economic contribution of women. If a plantation system which handles migrant labour is in operation, the women may be left behind, in which case they may have to put in extra agricultural work. If the women are taken with their menfolk in families then the reverse may be the case—there may be no place for them in the economic structure. Alternatively women may find other paid work outside the men's economic scheme.

The income effects of these operations have repercussions in the wider economic and social spheres.

The wage labour pattern tends to provide income in relatively large sums, as against the small increments of local marketing in the more unsophisticated systems, and this may affect consumption patterns. With the advent of a monetary economy there is also usually an enlargement of consumption patterns by taking in goods not purchasable by the traditional circulating media. This involves the possibility of greater differentiation in property-holding, diversification of cul-

---

1. K. Odaka, *Economic Organization of the Li Tribes of Hainan Island* (*Yale Southeast Asian Studies*), Yale, 1950.

tural interests owing to differences in taste, to a wider range of personal incomes.

On the other hand, while the substitution of money for the traditional means of remuneration may enlarge the economic field, it will not necessarily do so, or do so to the extent expected. In the scheme of preferences, the attractions of traditional, non-wage employment may still be high, either subsistence agriculture, etc., or cash-cropping. The Li of Hainan worked in the iron mines because they were drafted, not for the money. To the question as to which type of work they preferred, they all answered farming. And when asked if their mine pay were increased greatly, to two or three or even twelve times what they were receiving, in addition to their food, they still stated a preference for farm work. Again, while the conventional notion about earning money is that one gets as much of it as one can, the backward sloping supply curve of labour is often found with the advent of a monetary reward for work. The worker is used to having a certain level of consumption goods as his target, and so long as he can reach this, he is satisfied. So an increase in the rates of wages may result not in an increase of the amount of work done, but in a decrease, since the target is reached sooner. For the Melanau of Sarawak, for instance, the only permanent form of investment is in land, and they are used to preparing sago, their main work, to procure a certain level of income, to meet family obligations, to build a house, to arrange a marriage. Otherwise, they do not produce sago. If the price of sago is high, and cash is therefore easy to obtain, the women tend to reduce the time they spend in trampling the sago pith. If a young man has earned enough money for clothes, and customary presents to girls, he stops felling and rasping sago palms. The hardest workers are married men with young families, or landless orphans approaching marriageable age.[1] For them the marginal value of the product is higher.

The cumulative effects may also mean a modification in the general income structure of the community. In particular, they make available to young able-bodied men a source of wealth inaccessible to their elders, in quantities far greater than the traditional economic organization can usually afford. But the effects must not be overestimated. Hogbin and C. S. Belshaw have pointed out how for the Solomons, in the traditional agricultural scheme, the accumulation of wealth likewise depended upon the energy of young men, who thereby obtained wives and authority. Today, when the young man works for money, this only provides the initial impetus in dynamic situations. Moreover, as Hogbin points out, proximity to a market may make a great difference to the situation. In Busama, which is near the small market town of Lae, older men can earn small sums themselves and this mitigates the challenge of the young men.[2]

This alteration in income structure again may not necessarily involve a corresponding alteration in the wealth structure of the community. This depends on how far three elements operate:

1. Traditional arrangements for control of income may still be recognized, which secure to the senior members of the community the major handling of what income is obtained. In many Pacific societies, returning plantation labourers hand over to their father or other senior kinsman a considerable portion of their wages. Hogbin notes that among Busama men, on the north coast of New Guinea, it was the usual practice to give to the guardian (father

1. H. S. Morris, *Report on a Melanau Sago Producing Community in Sarawak* (*Col. Research Studies*, No. 9), London, 1953, *passim*.
2. H. I. Hogbin, *Experiments in Civilization*, London, 1939, pp. 166-72 and op. cit.; C. S. Belshaw, 'Trends in Motives and Organization in Solomon Islands Agriculture', *Proc. 7th Pacific Science Congress*, 1953, pp. 171-89.

or uncle) about half the wages brought back, about one-quarter to another uncle, and to divide about one-eighth among other members of the community, thus leaving only about one-eighth to the man himself[1]. In 1952 Tikopia labourers abroad followed a conventional practice of making up a 'box' for each of their chiefs, with lengths of calico, tools, fish-hooks, etc. Every man of the group contributed to each of these—to the boxes of other chiefs as well as that of his own clan chief—and they amounted to a substantial tribute.

2. New forms of arrangement may still retain the general control by the senior members of the community, or the community interest in the use of the new wealth. A case of this is the collection of funds by Toaripi people (of southern New Guinea) working for wages in Port Moresby, to help finance the purchase and transport of a trading schooner to carry their copra.[2]

3. Competing attractions for the use of income may tend to drain off some of the accumulated income. In some societies the pressure of the demands of young women results in large-scale spending on female consumption goods, which reduce the amounts of money taken back home. Or again, if savings banks or savings societies have managed to be established, the accumulation of capital there may mean that the alteration of the wealth structure takes a long time to become visible, or to have its effect on production or consumption.

Other effects of a wage labour system may include a reduction in the independence of women, whose incomes now may be comparatively reduced, or who may have to rely more directly on their menfolk for cash to buy what they want. It may mean also the creation of more vulnerable categories of persons—invalids, old folk, deformed, etc. Since they cannot be enlisted for labour, they are thrown more on the resources of others, especially if there is a reduction in the traditional forms of employment, or if monetary standards tend also to be applied to employment within the society.

COMMODITY PRODUCTION AND TRADE

Wage labour by itself, especially at the rates generally prevailing in Indo-Pacific conditions, does not offer much prospect of building up capital resources on any scale, and of making major developmental changes in the economic and social structure. Commodity production and marketing, on the other hand, offer more scope. If we consider commodity marketing for cash, such as occurs in many parts of the region, we are at once confronted with a different range of magnitudes than for wage labour. The vegetable marketing of the Malay or Bornean peasant woman may bring in only a few cents per day—an income which, however, does allow of independent subsistence by many members of vulnerable social categories, such as widows or divorcees. At the other end of the scale a Malay or Chinese master fisherman or vegetable grower or rubber producer, or a New Guinea or Gazella Peninsula copra producer, may reckon his annual earnings in thousands of dollars or hundreds of pounds. In such areas in the Pacific, at least, a marked change in the size of income has been the concomitant of the transition of many

1. H. I. Hogbin, *Transformation Scene*, London, 1951. The figures refer to a few years ago, but Dr. Hogbin tells me that the same system certainly still applies.
2. Raymond Firth, 'Social Changes in the Western Pacific', *Journal Royal Society of Arts*, 1953, p. 810 *et seq.*

of the people from wage labour to commodity production and marketing.[1]

The same general effects on the income and wealth structure, with similar social repercussions, are observable as with wage earnings. But there are certain significant differences.

There is a different kind of risk that has to be taken. Among the economic attractions of plantation labour, for instance, is the regularity of the income. With commodity production the more incalculable elements of drought, flood and pests enter more directly. Again, while fluctuations of raw material prices affect both, they are likely to be more sudden and more severe with the commodity producer than for the labourer, since wages tend to have a distinct lag in response to changes in raw material prices. This tends then to involve a different type of selectivity in the economic process. The entrepreneur in commodity production or marketing tends to emerge as an individual with more distinct economic responsibilities, sharper in perception of economic advantage, often impatient of claims of his communal obligations. On the other hand, his need for initial capital may make him continue in close relation with others of the community on whom he may draw. And the need for equable relations with labour may lead him to continue in working association with kinsfolk and others in traditional patterns. There is also the tendency for the general social values of his community to weigh heavily with him, especially if there be added to them additional elements resulting from interracial competition or conflict.

Hence there is the common tendency for the entrepreneur in such conditions to operate within a local social milieu. The complex interchange of goods and services involved in the production or marketing scheme until the time when the goods reach the alien buyer takes place in ways which are neither according to the traditional forms, nor according to ordinary Western practice. In the blending of individual and community interest, it may be hard to identify the shares which go to economic functions rather than to persons. As has been often discovered, book-keeping in such circumstances may be a difficult task. Too literal adherence to the rules of accountancy may rob the operations of much of their spontaneity. Yet a good index of the extent to which the advent of a monetary economy has brought with it Western economic notions is the effective accounting system practised, for example, by some of the co-operative societies in New Guinea and elsewhere. One of the useful functions of the new entrepreneur, however, is to act as stimulus and example to his fellows.

One of the great problems in this whole field is that of capital formation. While commodity production and marketing offers possibilities of building up considerable wealth, they may also lead to great difficulties. The operation of a monetary system, with access to external consumer's markets, can lead to high rates of expenditure, and to the contraction of debts at a level virtually impossible in a traditional non-monetary system. If there is a depression in the commodity market, then the situation becomes parlous for many producers. In Malaya, in 1934, an inquiry among coconut smallholders showed that they were practically all in debt, at levels of from $100 to $1,500 per holding of 10 acres or less in the largest coconut area. The debts were mainly to Chinese

---

1. An interesting description of the processes involved in Indonesia has been given by J. H. Boeke, op. cit., pp. 104-10. C. S. Belshaw has drawn attention to the differences in the proportion between plantation labour and peasant agriculture as a function of the type of market organization available. In the Solomons, where no good price was available for village products, natives preferred to sell their labour to Europeans rather than produce themselves, in contrast to the New Hebrides where the balance was about equal, and to New Caledonia, where few natives worked away from the village (op. cit., p. 181).

and Chettiar money-lenders, contracted in times of high prices, and there was little prospect of their ever being repaid. Indebtedness is of course a great bane of the peasant everywhere, and its effects are if anything increased the more the economy is related to external markets. And since so much of the indebtedness is contracted not for the financing or production, but to meet consumption requirements, there is little opportunity of building up capital thereby, in any general fashion. When individuals enrich themselves by lending, there is little of the 'multiplier' effect produced, in that the loans have a very small income-generating influence. Moreover, the social implications of this type of indebtedness are commonly those of friction and strain in the community.

On the other hand, organizations which both meet the need for capital greater than that which any individual entrepreneur can provide, and yet peg the enterprise to some kind of community interest, have been devised in a number of areas. Among the Maori of New Zealand co-operative organizations are of many years' standing. Some establish the communal title holders of land as incorporated owners of land, and give them the legal right of borrowing funds with which to develop the land in the interest of them all. Under the leadership of the late Sir Apirana Ngata, a former Minister for Maori Affairs, State aid was obtained for these organizations in various ways, and pastoral and agricultural undertakings of some magnitude have been the result. To meet the needs of these and other tribal enterprises, a new set of men has emerged, the business managers, who can lay down policy and administer affairs like a Western business man.

Reference to land-holding raises another aspect of this problem. In many of the unsophisticated economic systems there is no free market in land. As the systems become transmuted by the advent of a money economy, a market in land may develop, with relative freedom of transfer, often only with deference to community or kin group approval. In some systems, for instance Tonga, the State early took over all final titles to land, allowing to individuals only very restricted titles, with very limited rights of transfer and transmission. In others, the final titles still lay with specific social groups, but some limitations were placed on transfer, while rights of transmission were regulated by the courts. In such conditions, where the growth of a commodity market gives a fillip to the use of land, changes in the social structure may be stimulated. In the attempt to gain an income from land, either by personal production or by sale or lease, there have been among the Maori of New Zealand and the Cook Islands, for example, an intensified interest in kin ties as giving title to lands; disputes over land, with much litigation in the courts; and a tendency in some cases for departure from traditional customs of land inheritance in favour of testamentary disposition. Apart from this there has in New Zealand been fragmentation of land, and much subsequent consolidation. There are also many landless Maori and some Maori landlords—with European tenants in a number of cases. In less than a century-and-a-half the transition from a simple non-monetary peasant economy to an economy of practically Western type, with commodity markets and markets for labour, greatly increased the differentiation in the status of people and has affected the Maori social system deeply in other ways.

As another example of how a change in market conditions, with expansion of a price economy, can affect social conditions, consider the results of rubber production in Negri Sembilan, in Malaya. Here is a society of relatively small-scale producers, with a strongly matrilineal system of lineage groups and lineage leadership, and with a traditional interest in the cultivation of valley rice. The advent of rubber has made for substantial changes. In summary, they are these.

There was of old a distinction between the ancestral lands, the rice plots in the valleys, worked generation after generation, largely by women, and the new lands, cleared from the jungle by men, and retained by them as the product of their labour. The latter they could transmit to their sons, the former were transmitted through their sisters in their own lineage, and through their wives. No man could pass ancestral lands on to his son. In the clearings were grown fruit and vegetables, essentially secondary in economic importance to the staple, rice. Then, less than half a century ago, came the cultivation of rubber. Soon the economic balance of production tended to be upset. It was far more profitable to produce rubber than rice, and some people even turned their rice lands into rubber land. Some of the upland areas were sold or leased to aliens. The lineages, seeing valuable assets tending to pass out of their grasp, often debated the issue whether the rule of control and inheritance of these cleared rubber lands was through females, as in the case of the ancestral lands, or should be through males, especially from father to son. On the whole the tendency has been for the interest of the men to be strengthened in the control of such lands.

Moreover, the more general tendency has been to promote a change in the inheritance system, from matrilineal to patrilineal. This has not been so in the lands classed definitely as ancestral (*tanah pesaka*), but the pressure has tended to become manifested in land of other types, and also other property. In this struggle —for the issue was often keenly, even bitterly fought—powerful support was given to the patrilineal interests by the leaders of Islamic orthodoxy, who were in conflict on other grounds as well with the local *adat* (customary rules). Furthermore, these forces together were in support of, and to some degree assisted by, the interest of the ruler and his kinsfolk, a group of patrilineal descent rules, and opposed in some respect to the matrilineal descent leaders by whom they were surrounded and on whom they had to rely in the body politic as a whole. Though opposition between them was not overt, it was clearly to the interest of the ruler that the power of leaders deriving their status from a customary base alien to his own should be diminished. Thus a simple technological change, represented by the different processes involved in the production of rubber, meant also important changes in the social structure.

Finally, one may characterize the subject in more general terms again. As the influence of a monetary economy grows, there is a tendency for the scale of social relations to widen, as new contacts are formed. On the other hand, there is fragmentation and realignment of some social units. Lineage and other kin groups often cease to be effective land-holding units; joint family and allied units tend te break up economically and disperse residentially into simple families. Even the simple, elementary family organization is seen to be vulnerable—changes occur in relations of husband and wife through labour or differential production; there is exaggeration or reversal of the economic differences between generations, and different frames of reference for social experience appear; the authority structure may alter. As the processes continue, new structural arrangements may be formed, with new class alignments and new patterns of leadership. The requirements of new legal norms, and the new ethics of business involve different behavioural sequences. There may be a shift of symbols not only of wealth but also of social status and political authority. At the same time, consciousness of the changes in so many spheres may lead, as in Polynesian societies, to a renewed emphasis on traditional or modified (pseudo-) traditional forms, which are as it were obtruded as evidence of a social solidarity which may in fact be threatened or lost in other fields.

The resultant of all these forces is likely to be an economy and a society not in equilibrium but with conflicts of ends, and conflict about means to secure agreed ends. These processes of social and economic change are not novel. But the diversification of technical skills is growing; technical processes are for the most part apparently irreversible; and the pace of technical advance is increasing. The widening of the gap between the skilled and unskilled, and the growing differences in experience, would seem to suggest that it is not in the realm of shared empirical knowledge and skill that common factors of unity are likely to be found. But to think that the future co-ordinating elements may lie in non-empirical systems of ideas suggests also reliance on fairly short-term solutions.

CAPITALIST DEVELOPMENT
IN INDONESIA AND IN UGANDA:
A CONTRAST

J. H. BOEKE

Since 1870 Western entrepreneurs have had ample opportunity to invest and exploit their capital in Indonesia. The extent to which they have availed themselves of this opportunity—especially after the beginning of the twentieth century —has since then completely determined the economic development of the colony. As early as 1827 the highest authorities in the Netherlands Indian Government had strongly advocated this policy which they described as 'colonization by capital'. Their main argument was that the Western enterprises should be a convincing example to the population of the opportunities for profit afforded by market and export crops, an example all the more indispensable because without it the Javanese farmer could not be weaned from his traditional rice culture and subsistence economy.

His Majesty's Government in the Netherlands recognized the validity of this argument and shared the expectations of its promoters. But it considered inopportune any long-range policy which would not in the near future provide the profits which the mother country and the king needed urgently. For this reason King William I preferred another scheme that had been put before him, according to which the native rural population of Java should be compelled to grow, by order of the Netherlands Indian Government, certain profitable or at least promising export crops such as, for instance, indigo, sugar-cane and coffee. They were to use either their own fields or waste lands allocated for that purpose, and the produce had to be sold for the benefit of the mother country. This was the well-known culture system which from 1830 on, dominated Java, in particular. For sugar-cane cultivation, it lasted almost to the end of the nineteenth century and, for the other important forced crop, coffee, even till 1915, although the end came almost unnoticed, the system having collapsed decades earlier.

Under the culture system the Javanese peasant was a forced entrepreneur: he had to bear the risk and perform all the labour, but under such adverse conditions that he conceived a thorough dislike for the compulsory crops and could not be induced, after the termination of the system, to continue of his own free will. In another respect also the culture system was a bad, demoralizing influence. Diverted from his subsistence farming, the peasant had only one aim, to get through his imposed duties with the least trouble and exertion. He worked slowly and carelessly; he neglected and destroyed rather than cultivated—when he was given the chance; he acquired no new skills, merely new vices.

This false conception of his labour obligations, on the part of the farmer subject to forced cultivation, induced the sugar mill owners to extend their activities from cane crushing to cane raising on fields hired from the native owners. Consequently, the part taken by the village people in the production of this important crop shrank considerably, although it still had a serious effect on all village life. There was in the first place the leasing out of irrigated fields by owners and part-owners, none of whom had land to spare and all of whom therefore in so doing deprived themselves of their main source of subsistence. Secondly, there was wage-labour in the fields as well as in the mill—occasional labour mostly, irregular, unskilled, seasonal at best owing to the seasonal character of the sugar industry itself. For both categories of participants, the lessors of land as well as the occasional labourers, the sole motive of their contact with the sugar mill is and always has been the need to acquire cash to meet their most urgent financial obligations, their taxes above all.

The Western enterprises in Java other than the sugar plantations and the estates in the outer provinces were started without connexion with the culture system and most of them not before the present century. Their beginning meant the realization of the proposals of 1827. For this reason the prediction of their advocates, that private Western estates would prove to be indispensable incitements to the population to raise market and export crops, may be questioned. The answer will be only partly and conditionally affirmative, for reasons which are different in Java and the outer provinces.

In Java the density of the rural population so reduces the field area per farmer that the more extensive methods of cultivation become impracticable, whereas when intensive methods are used the increase of production costs jeopardizes the profitability of the market crop. The value of the Western example is recognized by the small native landowners but they find themselves incapable of following it. Moreover, an imitation covering hardly one thousandth of the area of the example and attempted without capital differs so widely from the example as to become an original experiment. These experiments were made but remained exceptions, more often born of emergency than from the conviction that this change to market crops meant profit. In this way native sugar-cane cultivation was undertaken on land which the decrease of irrigation water made useless for the rice crop, and the native tea gardens were originally confined to impoverished land where food crops no longer thrived.

Sometimes, and this also applies to the outer provinces, there was another impediment to the adoption of plantation crop cultivation. When a crop required further important mechanical manipulation of the raw material to make it marketable, the native producer owing to lack of capital, technique and commercial ability was unable to start his own plant. This put white sugar or palm oil production entirely beyond his means, unless he could obtain the co-operation of a Western manufacturer. But in that case the economic strength of the two parties was so unequal that there was great danger that the interests of the native supplier of raw materials would suffer. This explains why the Netherlands Indian Government as a rule forbade the buying up of native cane by Western sugar mills, and why it hedged in by all kinds of protective measures the native tea planters who had to sell their wet leaves to a tea factory.

Under these circumstances it is all too obvious why export crop cultivation in Java never became important and why in the outer provinces only native rubber and coconut production attained any volume. Native rubber, moreover, had to compete with estate rubber, and here another difficulty arose which never fails to appear in similar circumstances. The large plantations which are amply capitalized and scientifically managed have a production capacity and a productivity many times that of the native gardens, and by direct and close contacts they are able to adapt their product to the continually changing demands of the international markets. In all these aspects the native producers lag behind. Their strength lies in their low production costs, in their extreme parsimony which borders on actual neglect. Such production methods do not make for quality in the product. This low quality standard may not matter so long as the market is a seller's market and the buyer accepts any offer. But as soon as the buyer gains the upper hand, he raises his standard and becomes selective. Then the native product falls short, fetches very low prices or becomes unsaleable.

It is typical of agriculture that wherever climate and soil conditions are favourable for a certain crop, mass cultivation is to be expected, because little capital is needed in the production process. This mass character of native export crop production may be an advantage when specific natural requirements of the crop restrict its potential area, otherwise it easily leads to overproduction and a fall in prices, jeopardizing all profit. Further, when child labour is profitable, as in cotton picking, this mass character may lead to a rapid increase of population, neutralizing the advantages of the new crop (Egypt).

One other threat to native cultures, especially those of perennial crops, must be mentioned in connexion with the general neglect and lack of renewal. The greater part of the native plantations date from the first world war. This means they have reached an age when the replacement of old trees by young ones becomes a necessity. But the large majority of the garden owners can no longer afford to abandon for years a large part or the whole of their accustomed revenues; they prefer to await the exhaustion of their plantation.

All these features of native export crop production in Indonesia have resulted in a state of affairs in which the native planters are unable to take over production from the Western estates, to oust them or even to compete with them successfully.

There seems to be one exception to this rule—native rubber growing in Sumatra and Borneo. Here the expansion of native export reduced the part of estate rubber to 28 per cent in 1951. This, however, was only possible by excessive tapping and an undiscriminating seller's market. Now that conditions have changed, the native rubber exporters are rapidly losing ground. In a single year, 1952, the part of estate rubber in the export volume rose from 28 to 40 per cent. Many native planters have returned to food crop growing and I venture to prophesy that this regression in native rubber growing will continue indefinitely and that the Western estates will recapture most of the market, unless the policy of the Indonesian Government and of the trade unions compels them to liquidate. But in that case, what will take their place? Here I come to the core of my argument.

The relations between the Western estates and the rural population have become static, incapable of any development. The position of native labour on these large plantations is subordinate and must remain so. For the masses of the Javanese countryside the importance of the estates was the opportunity they offered to earn a modest supplementary money income. The wages were low and remained so, in spite of the endeavours of the Netherlands Indian Government, in the second half of the thirties, to induce the employers to raise the native wage scale. In general only unskilled and simple labour was asked of the labourers, for whom their wages in most cases did not form their exclusive means of support. Much of the labour was performed by women and children whose home ties were not broken as they could usually find work in the neighbourhood of their village. The fact that these occasional and irregular workers supplied the main part of the labour was also owing to the seasonal character of many plantations and plants. The whole organization of the plantations was based on the circumstance that most of the labour came from cheap occasional workers: in the fields and gardens there was very little mechanization; much task work was done by free groups, enabling the employer to restrict his dealings to the foreman of the group; the individual labourers had freedom to come and go; an elastic wage scale was continually adapted to changing conditions.

In the outer provinces these occasional and irregular labourers were unknown. Here dualism, the separation between the capitalist estate or plant and the surrounding pre-capitalist society, was much greater. Here the labourers were recruited from Java or China, whereas the autochthonous population had only incidental contact with the Western plantation and, for the rest, benefited by the modernization of their society, brought about and paid for by the Westerners, and the lively trade and traffic arising from the indirect influence of Western capital on the whole region.

These two aspects of Indonesian society must be considered more closely; first, the fact that in Western economic development, in the capitalist production process, the labour of the native population was only important for its mass character, not for the value of individual performances, so that the tie which bound the main body of workers, as producers, to modern Western business was extremely loose, tenuous and weak. Secondly, the native population had a much larger share in Western development as consumers through the benefit derived from the Western superstructure of society, a superstructure which was due to the financial strength and the indirect economic influence of Western business. This benefit had to compensate for the shortcomings of Western business in the direct remuneration of native manual labour.

In this state of affairs, the sovereign Indonesian Government brought about two fundamental changes. It has considerably reduced the significance of the rural population as collaborators in Western production and it has furthered a great increase in the demands of the labourers as consumers. By this policy the economic balance between the various production factors has been radically disturbed, the life of numerous Western enterprises has been jeopardized, and the foundation of the modern superstructure of the entire Indonesian society has been undermined or at least severely weakened.

These statements require some further explanation. First, as to the way the Indonesian Government has encroached upon the value of the population as collaborators, as co-producers, in Western business. As early as 1948, in the revolutionary period of the 'Indonesian Republic' at Jogjakarta, a labour law was promulgated proclaiming a 7-hour working day and a 40-hour working week. Later on, 16 official national holidays were proclaimed.

In agriculture, where the pace of the labourer cannot be checked or fixed with any degree of precision, a 7-hour working day is certainly far too short. An official report on small-scale agriculture in the Netherlands declares the normal working day to be 10 standard working hours. In its annual report for the year 1950 the Amsterdam Trading Company states that after the war 70 per cent of its oil palm plantations have been reopened, that the oil production from this area has declined to 40 per cent of pre-war output, but that to obtain this reduced quantity 150 per cent of the pre-war labour force was required. This may serve as an illustration of a phenomenon general throughout the business world in Indonesia.

As to the present demands of the labourers in their capacity of consumers

I have in mind the wage increases for which constant pressure is exerted by the trade unions. They have convinced the employers' syndicates of the necessity of collective labour contracts which *inter alia* bind them to minimum wages for their labourers, to be paid partly in cash, partly in kind (rice). This minimum wage is 30 times the pre-war minimum wage paid to regular adult male labourers. It is supplemented by bonuses, premiums and social charges, for the most part dictated by the government.

The official exchange rate of the rupiah has declined to one-third of the pre-war Indonesian guilder, but the real value of the rupiah in the interior is so much lower that this 30-fold minimum wage may indeed be considered as no more than a living wage, that is a wage providing a living for a family of husband, wife and two children, completely dependent on the wage-earnings of the bread-winner. Before the war the large majority of wage-earners were occasional labourers, people who, as families, still found their main living within the village communities, supplemented only by earnings on the estate. Now suddenly every one of them, male or female, has become a regular labourer and, in the case of the adult male, a bread-winner of a family. This has caused a revolutionary change in the labour structure of the Western enterprises and completely upset their business calculations.

From a social point of view there is a still more serious consequence. The employer who has to pay his labourers as regular labourers wants them to behave as such, wants them to work six days a week and seven hours a day. He, therefore, is no longer prepared to allow them to come and leave at their convenience or to form free groups of task workers. The employer has to contract with each worker individually, to register every one of them. In this way the Javanese villagers have lost an important, for many even the most important, source of cash income; and the connexion between the Western enterprise and the village household has been broken. The regular estate labourers are proletarians, without social standing in the village community. Even if they continue to live in the village, they take no part in its life, they are outsiders. The social dualism, the separation between the two domains, that of the village and that of the estate, becomes more rigorous.

Another reaction of the Western estates should be stated. It is natural that every concern tries to escape utter ruin. Some only prolong their existence by exhausting their real capital, some liquidate without further struggle. None of these are replaced by Indonesian estates or small native gardens. To Indonesian society their disappearance is a total loss. But the larger, stronger concerns who realize that this course of events cannot go on much longer, that Indonesia in the long run cannot do without them, that the present situation is a transition period, and who can persuade their shareholders to foot the bill, follow another course. By every means they try to reduce their unsatisfactory labour force, they mechanize. For the very reason that before the war the abundance of cheap labour checked this policy there are still great possibilities in this direction. The labour supply is still superabundant, it increases, relatively and absolutely, with the increase in population. Nevertheless the demand is shrinking rapidly and continually for the simple reason that the wage-level has been artificially raised and maintained far above the equation point of supply and demand. This makes mechanization and the dismissal of labourers, wherever possible, a vital necessity.[1]

1. In the foregoing paragraph mining in Indonesia was left out of account because it lies outside the problem of human implications as analysed in this paper. The mining plants use only regular labourers, recruited in Java or abroad, and relatively few in numbers. They are pure enclaves in the region where they work and only indirectly influence the society which they have helped to open.

On balance of the state of affairs in Indonesia it seems that the economic dualism has penetrated too far into Indonesian society to be denied. If the Western estates were to abandon the unequal struggle nothing could be brought forward to take their place and economic collapse and serious overpopulation would threaten. Neither Indonesianization of management staffs nor nationalization of the principal concerns can help here. Indonesianization would not alter the dualistic situation or even appease the class rancour of the trade unions. Nationalization is a slogan without real meaning in a country lacking native capital, producing for export and dependent on the vagaries of foreign economic policy.

The problems implicit in the economic development of Indonesia, the social implications of technical progress in that country cannot be more clearly elucidated than by comparing them to a contrasting development in another country. For purposes of comparison, then, a brief review of the course of economic development in the British Protectorate of Uganda follows.[1]

The contrast is not to be explained by the fact that in Uganda a policy of indirect rule was applied; the same policy was followed much earlier in Indonesia also. Neither was it of direct importance that Lord Lugard deemed it necessary to amplify this policy by furthering native industry and attempting to preserve as far as possible traditional village life rather than leaving the adult male population to seek wage labour in remote Western estates and plants. At the outset it formed no part of the British scheme to apply these principles to the Protectorate of Uganda. England needed raw materials for its industries and it was for the British colonies to procure them. The quickest way was to further export production by Western plantations. Therefore, in Uganda, too, a policy was adopted of promoting white settlement, offering wide areas to settlers, and encouraging the population to perform labour services on the newly opened estates and earn in this way the money needed to pay taxes. The spreading of cotton culture among the native population formed no part of the official programme and was readily left to the Anglican Mission, which initiated the project.

Therefore, in Uganda too, the Western estate system would have formed the basis of export crop cultivation but for the accident that the land assigned to the white settlers proved unsuitable for growing cotton and because both the first world war and the world-wide depression of the thirties interfered with further experiments with other export crops. Thanks to these adversities, native cotton growing got its chance to determine the economic future of the Protectorate. However, it must be said in favour of the British administration that it shifted the helm when it saw that native cotton growing promised to become a success. For the estates this change of direction meant new difficulties because from now on the recruitment of workers for the white plantations was no longer backed by the authorities.

It is sometimes pointed out as an advantage of economic development by means of small native export cultures, that this welfare policy guarantees a wholesome gradualness. 'Economic development, if properly guided, can be integrated into the structure of African society instead of remaining an external disintegrating force' (L. Mair, *Native Policies*, p. 13). This statement seems only partly correct. I am rather inclined to endorse the theory that development from below also may cause a revolutionary change and that in Africa in any case it has done so. The male has replaced the female as principal agriculturalist; production for subsistence has been ousted from the first place by production for the market and

---

1. The factual data for this description are borrowed from a thesis in preparation by J. P. van Dooren, drs Indology.

for profit; occupation has become business; the family provider has become entrepreneur; new money needs have been created; with the appearance of import commodities a new type of distributive retail trade has grown up; in short the African's whole world has been transformed, and with might and main the authorities seek to awaken a new capitalist mentality in a pre-capitalist society. A revolutionary process of this kind cannot be prevented from having a disintegrating influence on communal traditions.

It was undoubtedly a favourable circumstance that the introduction at least of this radical social change was left to a missionary organization. Both its means and its standing permitted only a moderate pace at the start of the movement. This changed when, once it was under way, the administration interfered and government machinery was switched on. In accordance with the system of indirect rule the tribal chiefs had to serve as intermediaries, and the first thing the authorities tried was to awaken the emulation of the chiefs: 'Look at the Eastern Province and be ashamed' became the slogan in Buganda, otherwise the foremost province. But coercive measures also were applied, albeit in an Eastern sense only. The administration officers limited themselves to addressing exhortations and recommendations to the chiefs, but they were fully aware that for the chiefs every recommendation was an injunction—an injunction followed all the more readily since the chiefs, being also landlords, found it to their interest to have their farmers try the new culture.[1]

In the same style, the chief secretary (by wire) put it up to the people of the Western Province: 'Natives to be informed that three courses are open, cotton, labour for government, labour for planters, but no attempt is to be made to induce them to choose any one in preference to the others. Only one thing to be made clear, that they cannot be permitted to do nothing and be of no use to themselves or to the country' (Report, East Africa Commission, 1925, p. 143). Also the chief secretary will have been conscious and confident that the 'free' choice would fall on cotton which at least allowed the producer to stay at home.

It is a strange fate for the colonial welfare policy to have the government assume the role of revolution maker. Or is it not a revolutionary act to supplant by a single rule the pre-capitalist ideal of life: repose above all ('to do nothing') by the capitalist law of life: time is money and work is man's vocation?

Once the profits of the new crop became tangible to the producers, further encouragement was unnecessary. 'The sale of his produce enables [the native cultivator] to buy imported goods and stimulates the desire for individual gain. Once this has been liberated from the control of custom, he needs little further inducement to concentrate on export crops, and wants more money so as to clear or buy land and hire labour' (J. S. Furnivall, Colonial Policy and Practice, p. 293).

The two world wars and their aftermath were favourable to native cotton cultivation in Uganda and it spread rapidly. They demonstrated England's dependence on Empire cotton and forced up prices. In 1950 a population of less than 5 million earned an income of more than £30 million from cotton export, that is, from a crop introduced less than fifty years before in the pioneer cotton area in the Eastern Provinces. The area which in 1910 hardly covered 6,000 hectares in that part of Uganda by 1938 had already increased to 250,000 hectares. In Buganda the growth of cotton culture was still more striking; it had started later, but within a generation it was in the lead.

---

1. As a rule these farmers were crop-sharers: a share of the cotton crop also had to be delivered to the landlord. In this way the cotton culture formed a kind of forced culture in miniature.

The rapidity of this penetration of money economy into a pre-capitalist society intensifies the revolutionary character of the change. This revolutionary change necessitated a radical government policy which could, however, as soon as the first world war was over, assume the paternalistic character typical of welfare policies in most colonial countries. In 1922 a valorization policy was applied; about the same time plough culture was introduced with cattle as the tractive power; during the years of depression and overproduction of cotton other export crops (coffee, tobacco, etc.) were produced in addition to cotton; a licence system was established for buyers and payment in money adopted; prices were controlled and regulations passed to protect quality. For the cotton culture especially, these government measures were further supplemented by cost-free supply of cotton seed; interdiction of certain specified methods of sowing, harvesting and ginning; interdiction of a second planting on the same field in the same year; interdiction to stock seeds or plants; prescription to apply rotation with food crops; authorization to the governor to prohibit cotton cultivation in specified tracts and to destroy the whole crop without compensation in case of pests.

In the war years of the forties this paternal interference by the government increased still further. A government monopoly was set up for the buying up of the two main native export crops, cotton and coffee, and this government agency also acted as single seller to foreign countries. A fixed minimum price was guaranteed to the producers. The surpluses received by the selling agencies were paid into two price stabilization funds, which in a few years could put several million pounds at the disposal of the authorities.

As described above, part of the revolutionary government policy was to instil an entirely new conception of labour. But so to remould the African mind is easier said than done. Thus far, the average man only sees the new market crop as a source of money income, which does not require too much exertion, and enables him to make purchases beyond his daily needs. He does not yet feel dependent on these new crops nor does he love their culture as such. If ever the economic situation permits him to acquire the same extra revenue with less labour, he would prefer the same income with less exertion to a higher income at the cost of his sweat. Exertion as such has no merit: labour remains a necessary evil, the less necessary the more evil. No one believes work to be the purpose of life, no one has pledged his heart to the cultivation of cotton.

Under these circumstances the task the government has set itself is to change a people of consumers into a people of producers; into a society which will give its whole attention to performing its part in the production process and to the productivity of its labour, instead of to the question of how to enjoy life to the full; to educate the people to see labour as man's vocation on earth and repose as a preparation for fresh exertions. It may be that this alteration in the conception of life is ultimately unavoidable since without it there remains the danger of irregular production, of insufficient care of the crop, decline in quality exhausting cultivation, of adulteration, etc.

Up to the present the government has succeeded in conjuring the serious symptoms of this threat by its paternal economic policy, which in all probability is not justified, and already led to disturbances in 1949. Apparently the government is going on the theory that when a certain wholesome tradition or custom can be developed these are a sufficient substitute for rational insight and love for the crop in the individual producer.

Nevertheless, the consequences of the capitalist change of mentality are bound to appear. Thus, the increasing influence of self interest on social and economic activities is one of the first expressions of growing individualism. 'A common complaint among the black people is that hospitality has disappeared and instead the travelling man has to pay for food and shelter even with his relatives' (R. C. Thurnwald, *Black and White in East Africa*, p. 133). Mutual help in the village community is also disappearing. The easy earning of money has become a sport and a game. Even the children became conscious of the charm of making money; boys and girls in Buganda have laid out their own small cotton fields and convert the produce into money for their own use.

A more important consequence of the social trend towards capitalism has been the appearance of the 'kulak', the rural exploiter. As has been said, the new capitalist mentality is by no means a universal phenomenon. Only a few become imbued with it and are thus able to dominate their weaker brethren: they increase their landed property; they change agriculture into a business undertaking based on capital: they enter into crop-sharing contracts or farm out their lands; they act as money-lenders and buy up the native market crops, they are traders rather than peasants and they shirk manual labour. They form the capitalist counterpart of the tribal or clan chiefs, whose landed property, wealth and power are not founded on personal qualities but on status and tradition. They are, however, also gradually usurping the place of the Indians in retail trade. It makes an essential difference whether the agriculturalists they exploit are subsistence farmers or growers of cash crops. In the latter case they do not disturb a closed pre-capitalist household economy, but rather introduce an element of social differentiation into the agrarian community; they have, therefore, a much more positive social function and may be considered and accepted as pioneers on the road to modern conditions.

The authorities have less reason to take action against the 'kulak' because they have found a powerful and efficient weapon for the protection of the ordinary farmer in the co-operative society. It is a promising feature of the co-operative movement in Uganda that the first co-operative societies were organized without government interference and before co-operative legislation had been enacted; in the countryside and among farmers; not for credit purposes, but for the marketing of produce. For the time being the authorities had best overlook the fact that the most active of these co-operative societies have somewhat the character of closed companies and that the democratic principle of individual equality of all the members is not strictly adhered to in practice. On the other hand the co-operative organization can and should also be used, on behalf of the ordinary village people for other than strictly economic purposes: in the first place to develop a consciousness of social responsibility and the sense of solidarity with a community. If this succeeds the co-operative society may replace the traditional village or tribal community which is doomed.

THE IMPACT OF MODERN TECHNOLOGY
ON THE SOCIAL STRUCTURES
OF SOUTH ASIA

K. Motwani

In the long story of the cultural relationship between the East and the West, there has never been a greater need of accurate recording and evaluation of scientific and historical material than today, for on this depends the possibility of authentic cultural and spiritual commerce between the two great sections of humanity. Researches in the fields of archaeology, linguistics, literature, religion and culture-patterns of both the East and the West have yielded a considerable body of material, but much depends on its interpretation. A brief statement from the standpoint of an Asian student of the subject is all that can be attempted here.[1]

Asia is one, and in Asia it was India that set the seal of her social and cultural attainments on the various Asian countries and gave a certain homogeneity to their cultures. Her earliest contributions to various sciences—medicine, music and dancing, archery, military science, mathematics, architecture, grammar, phonetics, etymology, ritual, astronomy and astrology—recorded in her early Sanskrit literature, such as the *Vedas*, *Upa Vedas* and *Vedangas*, all now available in English translations,[2] were woven into her psychological, philosophical and sociological thought. On the foundation of this knowledge, India raised a superstructure of social institutions. All this knowledge of sciences and arts, of religious and philosophical thought, and of social ideals and organization, India shared generously with the various countries of Asia and Europe. Every country of Asia, excepting Russia, but including ancient Sumeria, Babylon, Ninevah, Crete, Egypt, Greece and Rome came under India's cultural influence.[3] The vitriolic touch of modern science has no doubt erased the marks of India's cultural contribution to the West,[4] but the evidence of her impact on the whole of Asia is abundant.

1. The countries dealt with in this paper are India, including the country now known as Pakistan, Burma, Siam, Malaya, Indonesia, Indochina and Ceylon.
2. For references on this subject, see standard works such as *Sciences of Ancient India*, by Sir B. N. Seal, *History of Hindu Chemistry*, by Sir P. C. Ray, *Positive Background of Hindu Sociology*, by B. K. Sarkar. The author of this paper has dealt with the sociological implications of these scientific contributions of India in his *Science and Society in India*, a series of lectures delivered to the various universities of India under the auspices of the Indian Science Congress Association, in 1944.
3. The publications of the Greater India Society, organized under the patronage of the late Rabindranath Tagore, deal exhaustively with India's impact on the East and South-East Asia. Professor R. C. Mazumdar, former Vice-Chancellor of Dacca University, has summarized the available material in a compact, interesting manner in the course of his Sain Das Memorial Lectures, 1940. Sir James Tennent gives an interesting account of the knowledge of sciences and arts existing in ancient Ceylon, taken from India, see his *Ceylon*, 1860.
4. A fuller treatment of this subject will be found in *Message of Plato*, by Professor E. J. Urwich, former Chairman of Sir Ratan Tata Chair of Social Sciences in London University, *Our Oriental Heritage*, by Dr. Will Durant and in *Eastern Religions and Western Thought*, by Sir S. Radhakrishnan.

This all-pervasive influence of India established through the spread of her institutions, ideologies and people, sometimes reinforced by political predominance, imparted homogeneity to the cultural pattern of this region. To be sure, there were variations due to environmental and ethnological factors and historical influences but, in the main, there was one homogeneous culture-pattern in all these countries before modern technology entered the arena. It is in terms of this common cultural ancestry and view of life that changes brought about by modern technology have to be assessed and understood.

The earliest creations of modern technology, which initiated the era of social change in South-East Asia, were the means of communication, such as railways, ships and telegraph; telephone, wireless, radio, cinema, newspaper and literature came later. These mechanisms of rapid communication and locomotion offered facilities for travel and opened up a two-way traffic, commercial and cultural, between the West and Asia. The European countries, such as Britain, France, Holland and Germany, which were already engaged in traffic with the East since the sixteenth century, fought among themselves for mastery of the seas and control of trade, and with the exception of Germany, succeeded in carving out empires in South-East Asia (excepting Siam, whose independence was more apparent than real since it was intended to serve as a buffer between the conflicting interests established in Burma and Malaya on one side and Indochina on the other). The railways, for instance, started an unending series of social changes in every country. The steel tracks cut across the countryside, disturbed the agrarian configuration, caused water-logging which, in turn, gave birth to malaria and other diseases. The railways introduced machine-made goods from the West, which pushed out local products from the market, crushing indigenous industries, robbing the peasant proprietors and hereditary craftsmen of their work and sources of livelihood, reducing them to the status of wage-earners. The railways accelerated the tempo of travel and social contacts; the various castes and classes travelled together on equal terms and the social distances between them maintained by tradition and custom began to diminish. The isolated, static societies of Asia were confronted with a challenge and their crystallized attitudes and stratification began to take wing. Thus, the railway alone may be said to have brought about a social revolution in this region affecting their modes of travel, agricultural setting, industries, employment, health, social attitudes and structures. The spatial and social distances began to disappear; the process of communication which, as Professor Cooley says, is the heart and soul of social change, became accelerated. But the various technological inventions, mentioned above, reinforced each other, giving a scientific temper to the minds and thought of the South-East Asian people, affecting vitally every phase of their lives.

The birth of technology in the Western countries had produced similar changes in their social structures. Their agricultural self-sufficient economy was quickly transformed into an industrial, commercial and exporting economy. The gaping jaws of the machine had to be continuously fed with the raw materials imported from outside; therefore, the major interest of the Western rulers in their tropical possessions was economic. Natural resources and agricultural and animal products of certain types became their main concern. Mining of coal, iron, silver, gold, mica, tin, petroleum, etc., commenced on a large scale. These 'robber industries', which took from the earth but gave back nothing, became highly organized. In the field of agriculture, emphasis was placed on production and export, not local consumption. Coffee, copra, cotton, rice, rubber, sugar, tea and wool became the major agricultural industries of South-East Asia, resulting in unbalanced, undiversified economies. A considerably enhanced demand for these commodities resulted in feverish haste of production. Millions of acres of jungle were cleared; steadily expanding industrialization at home and in the metropolitan countries, development of railways which required timber for tracks and for steam-power, laid a heavy toll on forest reserves. Deforestation resulted in soil erosion, silting of rivers, interference with the hydrological cycle, the lowering of the fertility of the soil and deterioration of the health of the people.

Production for export and profit substituted competition for co-operation, individual ownership for communal and village ownership, money economy for barter and created the money-lender and the so-called 'economic man'. The impersonal and uncontrolled forces released by technology sucked both the proprietor and the producer into their orbit and affected the attitudes and relationships of both towards each other. Instead of being joint owners of means of production and producers and consumers of goods themselves, they became agents of competitive production for foreign markets, and since payment was made in money, everything came to have a money value. Taxes and wages were now paid with money, while formerly service for taxes and food and shelter in place of wages had sufficed. But now, land revenue for a top-heavy alien administration forced the producer to resort to the money-lender who kept him pressed down to the starvation level.

The village which was the basic economic and cultural unit of these people came under the disrupting forces of technology. Its self-sufficiency disappeared and it became tied up with the city, the nation and the outside world. Village industries, such as spinning and weaving, pottery, brassware, oil pressing, vegetable dyes, lacquer work, etc., languished; machine-made goods, such as aluminium wares, kerosene, textiles and synthetic dyes took their place. A superfluity of cheap manufactures displaced the craftsman, depriving the group of his hereditary skill. The rooting of the farmer to his soil and of the craftsman to his hereditary calling had produced a sense of social solidarity, an *esprit de corps*. But with the disruption of the ecological balance, all this disappeared, rendering the populace mobile, restless, shiftless. The village, which was formerly a family, became transformed into an adjunct of factory, a mob.

The economic development of South-East Asia through native and Western enterprise was accomplished by the crushing out of the rural, agricultural, non-profit, collective economy and the simultaneous emergence of highly organized capital, the breaking up of the populace into two hostile camps of capital and labour. The banking barons of the West had their counterparts in Tatas, Birlas, Dalmais, Thappars of India, Chettys in Burma and South Asia. Labour, unaccustomed to work for wages, became conscious of its powers and organized itself. The workers in the major industries, such as mining, steel, textiles, jute, railways, posts and telegraphs, sugar, rubber and shipping organized trade unions on a national scale, while workers in cities engaged in tailoring, hotels and restaurants, trams and buses, tobacco and match industries organized their city-wide unions. Strikes, lock-outs and sabotage involving considerable loss of life, property and output, became a recurrent phenomenon, as in the West.

One of the significant phases of the impact of technology on this region has been the phenomenal rise in population. Industrialization encouraged large families, since every member was a wage-earner, and Western medical science and sanitation had stamped out various diseases and cut down the rate of mortality which, because of nutritional deficiency, nevertheless continued to be high. The traditional knowledge of how to keep down the birth rate was lost, while early marriage and high fecundity resulting from a preoccupation with sexual matters, added to the numbers. In 1800, the whole of South-East Asia contained about 10 million people; by 1916-20, it had shot up to 80 million! The population of India is said to have stood at 280 million in the 1880s; it is approximately 500 million now, if we include Pakistan. The life expectancy and the average weight and height have steadily declined. This heavy pressure of population has resulted in impoverishment of the soil, has lowered the standard of living and hastened the biological degeneracy of the people.

In the pre-industrial era, the stability of the social organization was maintained by custom and status; these together regulated prices, wages, rents and land taxes, thus holding individualism and exploitation under leash. Now free competition has replaced custom and status, has torn the villager from his family, caste and craft, and made him a physical, emotional and spiritual nomad. Corporate life was weakened; the family and caste lost control over him and no longer determined his status; self-interest and pursuit of wealth became the mainsprings of his action. Labour became mobile, wages and profits became elastic; they were all linked up with the fluctuating fortunes of the stock exchange and commodity markets of London, Paris and The Hague.

This process of liberating the individual affected the family institution. With the upsetting of the rural life and the land-man ratio, the cityward migration became rapidly augmented. The joint family system started breaking down. The social virtues fostered by the family began to disappear, while neglect of the unfortunate members, such as the aged, the widows, orphans and disabled, made organized social welfare and security legislation an urgent necessity. Science has affected sanctity of marriage; pre-marital relations, abortions and divorce have made their appearance. The modern cinema, a creation of science, has put virtue on the defence; its glorification of glamour and seductive arts have entered every home and the models of virtue and character are no longer heroes and heroines of the ancient religious epics, but actors and actresses of the modern screen.

The impact of technology brought about a complete change in the special organization of these countries. The idea and the institution of *varba-ashrama-dharma* of the Hindus spread to all these countries, while spatial isolation, long distances and absence of quick means of communication fixed the 'caste system' into their social structure. Sociologically and historically considered, this much maligned but little understood institution was not such an unmitigated curse in the life of the Eastern people as it has been made out to be. Preservation of skill in craft and industry, division of labour and a just distribution of rewards, welding together of the heterozygous populations and reconciliation of their conflicting claims, transmission of their cultural heritage to the succeeding generations, evolution of the national spirit; protection from anarchy due to the shifting fortunes of ruling dynasties, and synthesis of cultures were some of the contributions that this institution made to the social stability of the people of this region.[1] But, with the passage of time, it had become a 'cake of custom' to use Professor Keller's well-known expression, and technology started the era of its liquidation. The multiplicity of contacts in the various aspects of the life of the individual and the group, in work and play, rubbed off the caste distinctions, facilitating inter-caste marriages, even against the wishes of the parents. Vocation was no longer an index of the caste. Science accelerated mobility, both horizontal and vertical, enabling the people to move freely and quickly from one place to another, from one profes-

---

[1]. For a full description and analysis of this institution, see the author's *Manu: a Study in Hindu Social Thought*, 1934, and *India: a Synthesis of Cultures*, 1946.

sion to another and from one caste and status to another. Society, with a common cultural tradition but plural features, now became a plural society, its distinguishing marks being aggregation of individuals without being a corporate or organic whole, racial and communal segregation, and an incomplete, counterfeit life for the individual. To be sure, the various sections of people intermingled in each country, but only as individuals, by force of economic circumstances, and a dissolution of their union can easily precipitate a relapse into anarchy. Indeed, signs of it are not wanting in most of the South-East Asian countries.

We see this plural society everywhere. The city is a creation of technology; urbanization and industrialization must go hand in hand. The ships needed harbours, warehouses, customs offices, railways to bring raw materials for export and take the imports from abroad into the interior. Financial corporations were established, and factories and mills grew up round them. These were followed by educational institutions, hospitals and law courts. This centralization of transport, finance, industry, education, government and legal functions gave birth to cities. Also, specialized centres of industry such as textile mills, engineering workshops, leather, sugar, jute, copra and other industries grew up in other places. Thus arose the great cities of South-East Asia, huge mausoleums of coal, smoke, iron and steel, of dirt and squalor, of over-crowding, of cooly lines and human warehouses. Long hours, low wages, bad housing, woman and child labour, infant mortality, accidents, high rents, poor sanitation, prostitution, gambling, racing, dope dealing, dance halls, cabarets and night clubs were features of all the cities. The noise corroded the nerves of the city dwellers, while absence of neighbourhood restricted their social contacts and made them strangers to each other. The city governments were invariably run on communal lines, in addition to being inefficient and corrupt. Cities are parasites on the rural areas—they draw the food products and send back manufactured commodities, they suck out the sturdy, healthy stock from the villages and sterilize it into a race of weak, neurotic dregs. Cities are dysgenic.

Development of ports has also been responsible for split of interests in South-East Asian countries. Ceylon has a cultural focus at Anurudhapura and a commercial-administrative focus in Colombo; Burma in Mandalay and Rangoon; Siam in Bangkok and Mekong; Malay in Kuala Lumpur and Singapore; Indonesia in Jakarta and Batavia; Indochina in Hanoi and Saigon, while India has a plurality of foci round Calcutta, Madras, Bombay and New Delhi. These dual foci in each political unit represent a split, a conflicting pull of national interest and sentiment in one direction and commercial needs in the other.

The story of the impact of technology on education makes dismal reading. The demands of technology showed scant regard for the spiritual and cultural attainments of these people; Macaulay did not consider all the religious, philosophical and scientific literature of India worth one shelf of books of European literature. The whole upbringing of the subject peoples was supposed to prepare them for the next world, while the rulers wanted to train them to live here and now, to produce more, to adopt Western ways of life, to learn their business techniques. The integral character of their knowledge and culture was ignored and one-sided education, reflecting the economic, political and industrial needs and evolution of Europe, was imposed on them. The rulers devised various ways to gain their objects and technology came to their aid. The printing press made it easy for them to produce at low prices and for extensive use books dealing with their countries. In this literature, they went in for wholesale glorification of their countries and their culture and vilification of those of their subjects. Western geography, history, literature and economic, political and religious doctrines, quite unrelated to the needs and experience of the student, were pushed down his throat, involving considerable effort of memorization. Demand for mastery of the rulers' languages added to the strain and education degenerated into propaganda, a powerful instrument in the hands of the rulers to effect and reinforce social changes that accompanied the advent of technology.

The rulers put a premium on education received in their metropolitan countries. Thousand of young men and women went from this region to the West, costing their countries thousands of millions of rupees and, on their return, they became cultural outposts or salesmen of the products of their rulers' countries. Reared in a technological milieu, they became enthusiastic about the Western institutions and ideologies *en bloc* and, on entering public administration, carried out policies of their rulers, introducing the Western outlook into education, medicine, law, arts and sciences, far more effectively influencing their own people in the direction of new ways of life than their Western colleagues.

Since Western education came to be the *sine qua non* for employment in government service, great emphasis was placed on examinations. The system of examination in all South-East Asia is cruel and wasteful. According to figures collected by the writer for 1936-40, approximately 500,000 students failed every year in all the post-secondary examinations in India. If the parent of each student spent approximately Rs.500 on his child during the year, the Indian parents lost Rs.250 million. To this should be added an equal amount spent by the governments and public agencies on salaries of teachers, libraries, laboratories and administrative machinery. This colossal waste of funds and of the best years of the lives of young men and women, makes a mockery of all much-publicized adult education schemes and only succeeds in swelling the numbers of educated, discontented unemployed, a malleable substance for subversive activities.

The most harmful features of education, for which quick means of communication and transport are undoubtedly responsible, were centralization of administration and a rigid curriculum admitting of no scope for experimentation. While these two features were probably innocuous in the countries of the rulers where distances were short and there was homogeneity among the people, they were very harmful in tropical countries, which had much larger territories and varied histories and needs. This centralization gave rise to slow, cumbersome, elaborate machinery, with a plethora of academic bodies and committees that do not promote educational progress. In recent years, every political unit of this region has established a university of its own; India has added six to her former twenty or so. But it is doubtful if the authorities will be able to shake off alien influences, mental and spiritual, and it seems certain that they will succumb to internal dissensions, communal controversies, nepotism and administrative mismanagement.

Some of the defects which have become visible in recent years in these institutions of higher learning are admission of students and appointments of members of faculties to schools, colleges and universities on a communal basis, in contravention of civil rights guaranteed by their constitutions; corrupt practices in public examinations, futile language controversies, and the mistaking of instruction for education. Perhaps, the worst, and yet an inevitable feature of the impact of technology on education, has been the separation of the sciences from the liberal arts and humanities and the introduction of an exclusively rational, empirical, secular philosophy of life. A careful analysis of the educational philosophy current in these countries in ancient times reveals a remarkable synthesis of the arts and sciences of both matter and spirit. But the separation of these two branches of human knowledge, initiated by Aristotle in the West and culminating in the supremacy of the age of technology, has had its repercussions on the educational philosophy of these South-East Asian countries, resulting in the emasculation of liberal arts and the humanities and in the glorification of the natural and applied sciences dedicated exclusively to the problems of physical existence.

According to this scientific, secular view of man and the universe, the world of the senses alone is real. Matter is a mass of molecules, life a movement of mechanical forces, the human psyche a bundle of conditioned responses, a few complexes and glands; values are what society makes them at different times and places. Religion is an escape and death draws a veil over the whole drama. Therefore, all sciences pertaining to the problem of existence became rationalized, and when they were offered to students in these countries invariably resulted in the disintegration of personalities which had thrived on the spiritual view of life. The consequences have been fatal indeed. It would not be an exaggeration to say there is not a handful of men in Asia who are fully aware of the formidable impact of this rational view of life and who can safely pilot their careers. To be sure, dim outlines of this spiritual view of man and the universe begin to be discernible in the writings and researches of leading thinkers and scientists of both the East and the West, but it will be a long time before their impact on Asian life and thought will be perceptible.

The impact of technology on the political life and institutions of the South-East Asian people has been equally strong and destructive. The direct rule of the native chieftain or king, who was governed by local traditions and needs, became supplanted by the indirect, impersonal and 'efficient' rule of the official, an agent of the alien power, who showed scant regard for public opinion or local needs. Frequent transfers from one district to another and periodic furloughs to his mother country for change of climate made him a bird of passage; he was not long enough in any place to 'belong' and be one with the people.

The highly centralized administration, facilitated by technology, struck a death-blow at the self-sufficient village republics of the East. The educational, judicial, police, revenue, sanitation and other minor functions discharged by the small committees of village men and women, elected by the entire adult population of the village, ensured freedom from control of the central government, preservation of the cultural institutions and traditions of the people, securing their rights from encroachment of the ruling powers.[1]

Thus, the normal life of the masses flowed on smoothly, unaffected by changes in the destinies of the ruling dynasties. The village institutions were the bedrock of Asian nations. Kingdoms and empires came and went in quick succession, but the villages remained undisturbed, secure from sudden upheavals. But the indirect rule introduced by technology changed the situation. The strong, invisible arm of the government reached out to the furthest corner of the country, snatched away the self-governing tasks from these committees and handed them over to their official agents. This *politicized* the social life of the people, depriving them of the best opportunity for exercising their talents for planning their lives under natural leaders. Now, they became subservient to official agents of whom they were mortally afraid.

With the diminishing of physical distance the multiplication of intellectual and cultural contacts with the technologically advanced countries of the West,

---

1. The village committees were known as *Panchayats* in India and *Gamasabhas* in Ceylon and had similar names in all the Asian countries. Writings of Sir Henry Maine, Sir Baden Powell and Professors Radhakamal and Radha Kumud Mukerjee deal with this subject at great length.

the subject peoples of this region demanded democratic institutions and began to assert their right to self-government. Now, democracy is essentially a Western institution. It is born of the conflict between the ruler and the ruled. Its success depends upon existence of two well-organized parties,[1] intelligent public opinion, a fair level of education and a national spirit, a sense of psychic unity in which the conflicting demands of race and religion, caste and creed, strain continuously towards a self equilibrium and in which the demands of the whole, and not of the parts, receive a universal assent. This might be a far-off ideal even for the West, but conditions were more favourable there than in the Eastern countries whose social and political evolution has lain along different lines. The transplantation of this alien institution has spelt disaster for the people. They have begun to believe in the hallucination of numbers; the magic of the vote has gripped their imagination. They want large electorates and large legislative bodies. Parties shoot up overnight like mushrooms. Raucous political campaigns of blatant self-advertisements, slogans and shibboleths, sale and purchase of votes and impersonation of voters have become common phenomena. Quantity reigns supreme; quality is at a discount; a mob psychology prevails. The politicians have picked up the art of lobbying and jobbery. The capitals, both provincial and central, of these countries are crowded with representatives of high-pressure groups who are eager to purchase monopoly in the form of 'protection'.

Technology has helped to draw various castes, communities, ethnic groups and administrative units into close *physical* proximity but, by a strange paradox of life, it has accentuated their *psychological* distances. Provincial jealousies are dissolving such modicum of national unity as was attained during the colonial era. India's geographical unity has been cut asunder due to communal cleavages, but she is broken up internally into ten or twelve major linguistic groups that are ferociously hostile to each other. Cabinets are constituted on a communal and provincial basis, with the addition of representatives of pressure groups. Talent is sacrificed to provincial and communal preferences; sordid nepotism at all levels, high and low, is undermining the solidarity of these nations.

The philosophy of rights, aggressive and assertive, is a creation of the mechanical milieu. The possessed and the dispossessed are always engaged in mutual war. The newly-freed peoples of South-East Asia are accepting this philosophy of rights; the logic of the situation compels them, even when they know that rights, easily enshrined in constitutions and guaranteed by charters, are easily abrogated by parties in power and in times of emergencies.[2] Dharma, duty, an intelligent adaptation to the demands of social life, with one's feet fixed firmly in the eternal verities of life, finds no place in their lives today.

Fragmentation and specialization are inevitable concomitants of technology: atomization of knowledge, of the individual, of the processes of industry. When this process becomes entrenched in public administration, its influence is fatal. The specialized education and interests of the administrators have become reinforced by departmental blinkers. The home department, for instance, would like to promote rural welfare; the department of industries would like to attract the people to the cities to enter industries and increase production, while the police, irritated by the nightmares caused by urbanization, can guarantee security by seeing the whole population behind prison bars! Utter ignorance of the art and

---

1. See presidential address delivered by Professor Quincy Wright to the first session of the International Political Science Association at Zürich, September 1950.
2. See Rositer's *Constitutional Dictatorship*, Princeton University Press, Princeton, N.J., U.S.A. To the best of my knowledge, there is no word for rights in Sanskrit and its off-shoots.

science of co-ordination is precipitating a rapid derangement of the entire administrative machinery in the South-East Asian countries.

Notwithstanding the adoption of the Western political institutions and ideologies—the latter comprising socialism, syndicalism, nazism, fascism and communism—the knowledge of the impact of technology on society in general and on the constitutional processes in particular is utterly absent. For instance, no South-East Asian country has realized that governmental control of broadcasting and propaganda is bound to result in muzzling public opinion and in giving unlimited, extra-constitutional powers to the party in power. 'Gœbelism' is likely to receive a new lease of life in this part of the world. The knowledge that society is larger than the State, one of the basic facts of their social existence, has been completely forgotten.

Technology has changed the old forms and mechanisms of entertainment. In place of old folk-songs and dances on the village green at religious festivals, there are movie houses by the hundred in cities, and by the dozen travelling in the rural areas. People now see movies, screened abroad, based on alien canons of ethics and æsthetics. Formerly, they were active participants in the entertainment which gave them emotional release; now, they are passive observers, their imagination fired by the counterfeit picture of life. The profit motive has taken possession of their arts and entertainment. The daily metropolitan papers, owned by powerful financial interests, give more space to sports, stocks and shares, races, sex and cinema than to actual news. There is abundance of newsprint available for them, while school-children go without notebooks!

Crime is on the increase. The depersonalized individual of the mechanical milieu has no moorings and easily resorts to crime. Train and bank robberies, rape, murder, kidnapping, poisoning, traffic in women and children are on the increase. The Eastern criminal now emulates his colleagues of the West; the cinema gives him visual demonstration of the latter's exploits. Hatchets and daggers have now given place to the pistol and the gun; armoured car and machine gun are not far off. The dividing line between the gangster and the political boss is pretty thin among these people today.

Religion as experience and guide for individual and social life, as distinct from the doctrine and the institution, has lost its significance for these people. Religion which helps the individual to find his niche in the social cosmos, softens the blows of fate, sustains him in his sorrows, imparts enthusiasm for the service of fellow-men and gives depths and heights to his inner life, is now non-existent. While all the major religions of the world—Hinduism, Buddhism, Jainism, Sikhism, Taoism, Confucianism, Shintoism, Christianity and Islam—had their birth in Asia, their influence on the lives of the people has dwindled to nothing. The secular philosophy of life, drilled into the minds of these people for nearly two centuries, has made them strangers to the teachings of their prophets, seers and sages, and now makes them turn, with fatal facility, towards a philosophy of dialectical materialism. Today, Marxism occupies their minds and thoughts more than their own spiritual philosophies and religions.

Religions were considered as various dialects of religion. Therefore, religious tolerance came easy to these people. But with the break-up of their culture and with the intensification of struggle for existence, religion took on a political hue and the votaries of various faiths were engaged in mutual warfare. Hindus, Buddhists and Moslems, the three major communities of this region, are at war with each other and among themselves. The advent of the Christian Church coincided with the coming of Western technology and power and it became identified with the rulers. Therefore, all the attempts of the Church to improve education and health of the people were suspected of being inspired by commercial and political considerations. To the more enlightened, the Christian Church of the nation-State was not a living faith but a part of the technological culture, since its financial investments in making converts were heavy indeed, and the social and political patronage dispensed by it inspired allegiance to the national capitals from which power and finance flowed freely.

But there is a bright side to this sombre picture. Life fulfils itself even through failures. The evil effects of the impact of technology have been offset, to some extent, by bands of eminent scholars and scientists in the metropolitan countries who have organized Royal or National Societies and Academies for the study of various phases of culture of their dependencies. They mastered Asian languages, ancient and modern, wrote their grammars and compiled their dictionaries, translated the sacred books of the East in European languages and published them, thus interpreting the best of Asia to its inheritors and their own people. Some highly-placed officials, stung by the injustices of their governments, resigned their positions, embraced poverty and dedicated their lives to the educational, social, political and spiritual uplift of the people. The Indian National Congress was organized and nurtured into maturity by the indefatigable labours of Englishmen. The dynamic, spiritual awakening of Asia is mainly due to the Theosophical Society, headed by two non-Asians: Colonel Henry Steele Olcott, an American, and Mrs. H. P. Blavatsky, a Russian. Their scientific exposition of occult truths of Asian religions put life and courage in faint hearts and equipped the people not only to meet the challenge of the Christian missionaries but to take the offensive against the Christian Church. Colonel Olcott, single-handed, brought about renaissance of Buddhism in Asia; there are about 250 primary and secondary institutions in Ceylon alone associated with his name and a grateful government allows his birthday to be declared a holiday.

Technology has brought world-view to these South-East Asian nations. They are members of numerous world organizations, partners in a world fellowship. This association in the world drama is helping them to cut down trial-and-error method in the various phases of their development. Reconstruction of ancient tanks, preservation of ancient monuments, reclamation of land long forgotten or abandoned to the jungle, sublime interpretation of art and literature, restoration of national traditions through schools of art and above all the language of the rulers in place of their dialects are some of the contributions made possible by the industrious and unselfish application of thousands of officials and non-officials from the West. Technology has brought rich treasures of the Western culture within easy reach of the common man here. The best of Europe's literature, drama, music, painting, sculpture, architecture and science is at his disposal and he is now the inheritor, not of the life of his village, district or nation, but of the world.

Technology has brought the soul of Asia face to face with the soul of the West and in the acknowledgment of their complemental character lies the hope and salvation of mankind.

BIBLIOGRAPHY

BOEKE, J. H. *The evolution of Netherlands Indies economy.*

CHRISTIAN, J. R. *Modern Burma.*

CORNELL UNIVERSITY. *Studies of technology and cultural change in Burma, Thailand, India.* (In preparation.)

EMERSON; MILLS; THOMPSON. *Government and nationalism in South-East Asia.*

FURNIVAL, J. S. *A comparative study of Burma and Netherland India.*

——. *Educational Progress in South-East Asia.*

TER HAAR, B. *Adat law in Indonesia.*

HUSSAU, HUDA *et al. Problems of economic reform and development in Pakistan.*

KENNEDY, R. *Indonesia in crisis.*

LASKER, Bruno. *Human bondage in South-East Asia.*

——. *Peoples of South-East Asia.*

MOTWANI, Clara. *Ceylon, the paradise isle.* (In preparation.)

MOTWANI, Kewal. *India: A conflict of cultures.*

——. *University of Ceylon.*

PANIKKAR, K. M. *The future of South-East Asia.*

REES WILLIAMS *et al. Three reports on Malaya problem.*

ROBEQUAIN, Ch. *The economic development of French Indochina.*

THOMPSON, V. *Labour problems in South-East Asia.*

——. *Post mortem on Malaya.*

THOMPSON; ADLOFF. *Cultural institutions and educational policy in South-East Asia.*

——. *The left wing in South-East Asia.*

WERTHEIM, W. F. *Effects of Western civilization on Indonesia.*

WICKIZER; BENNET. *The rice economy of monsoon Asia.*

ZINKIN, Maurice. *Asia and the West.*

THE ECONOMICS OF THE INDIAN VILLAGE AND ITS IMPLICATIONS IN SOCIAL STRUCTURE

B. K. Madan

The converse of the above, 'The social structure of the Indian village and its economic implications', might form an equally appropriate theme of discussion in studying the role and significance of the Indian village in the developing economic pattern of the country. But perhaps the social structure of the village represents the static element, and its economics—or broadly speaking the amalgam of influences that go to make modern material development, viz., the spirit of change—represents dynamics of village economy, and is at present the more instructive subject to pursue. Indeed, the interaction of economic and social factors in the complex and varied life of the Indian village is everywhere evident.

THE TYPICAL VILLAGE

The village is the pivot of the old economic order, the unit of the economy, and it is to the village that we must go to study the conditions in which the vast majority of Indians live and work. Six out of seven Indians live in villages, and they had acquired at an early stage a fullness of life, a vitality and continuity which have helped their survival through the ages. The persistence of the village organization in the face of successive political vicissitudes has time and again attracted notice by foreign observers, and the following passage from Sir Charles Malcafe's minute of 1830 is often recalled: 'The village communities are little republics having nearly everything they want within themselves; and almost independent of foreign relations. They seem to last where nothing else lasts. Dynasty after dynasty tumbles down; revolution succeeds revolution . . . but the village communities remain the same.'

The typical Indian village is an aggregate of cultivated holdings, without fence or enclosure, with or without some waste area attached to it, and usually there is a central site where the dwelling houses are clustered together; in some cases small homesteads and farm buildings are found separately located on the holdings. It is this characteristic of a common dwelling area centrally located amidst the open village lands which gives the Indian rural landscape a somewhat unique physical appearance.

The village was traditionally a predominantly self-sufficient economic unit containing within its bounds all the labour, capital and skill necessary for its agricultural and industrial activities. The village inhabitants may be divided broadly into three groups: (a) the agriculturists; (b) the village officers; and (c) the village artisans and menials. In India caste and occupation have traditionally been closely allied, and the alliance has produced a division of labour which is seen at its simplest in the village. Broadly, the *zamindars*, or village 'masters', own and cultivate the land, and the *kamin*, or menials, do everything else. The agriculturists themselves may consist of peasant proprietors (owner-cultivators), landowners or tenants of various grades, the relative importance of any class of agriculturist varying according to the system of land tenure; together they form the most important section of the village community. The small capital required for agriculture—chiefly on a small scale and using the most elementary tools and implements—is provided from the savings of the agriculturist or the landlord, if the cultivator is a tenant, supplemented by borrowing from the village money-lender. The agriculturists 'are themselves the managers, organizers and experts of their petty farms'.

Each village has its own officers and, in fact, the village was and remains the unit of administration in India. The first village officer is the headman, or *patel*, or *zaildar*, a hereditary office combining responsibility for peace and order with the collection of revenue and petty magisterial duties. The *patwari*, or village accountant, is the official in most intimate touch with the agriculturists, who maintains land records, makes reports on the state of crops on which remissions of land revenue are partly based, as well as actually receiving the revenues. These village officials are given plots of land in payment for their services.

The village servants—artisans and menials—constitute the third group of village inhabitants. They are an integral part of the village community and form a considerable proportion of the population. The artisan group is composed of the carpenter, blacksmith, potter, shoemaker, oil-presser, weaver, tailor, dyer and, perhaps, the goldsmith. The servants are the barber, waterman, washerman, drummer or bard, leather-worker or tanner, watchman and sweeper. Finally there is the holy man—mullah, astrologer or temple priest. All who serve the village and its needs from Brahmin (highest in the caste hierarchy) to Chamar (reckoned as one of the 'lowest' castes) have their regular clients. Indeed, such is the respect for equity in the village community that, when any servant dies, his clients are divided amongst his sons as surely as is a *zamindar's* land amongst his sons. The number and type of servants depend upon the size and situation of a village. To quote the Census Report of 1901: '. . . the feature of Indian rural life is the way in which each village is provided with a complete equipment of artisans and menials, so that, until the recent introduction of Western commodities . . . it was almost self-supporting and independent excepting in the matter of salt and a few other luxuries purchased at the village fair or brought in by the lamans or caravans'.

Village custom is so variable that generalizations about village servants can have only the broadest application and this applies particularly to their remuneration. Technically the true (attached) servant is one who performs certain fixed services periodically in return for a share of the patron's harvest. The share is a matter of custom and record, and is either a specific measure of grain or a fixed proportion of the harvest, or a combination of both. There are various perquisites, and more recently even cash payments in addition, in combinations differing according to place—wage payments in cash have become more and more common—time and class of servant. Owing to the various methods of late payment for service of this kind, it is more open to exploitation than labour paid for in cash. Relationships between the *zamindar* and the servant are, however, far different from those of employer and employee in an urban commercial establishment or factory. 'If the *zamindar* is master, he is also patron, and if he stands above, he also stands behind his servant. He will help him when he comes into conflict with others and may even make his cause his own . . . as a rule there is a friendly spirit of give and take.'[1] 'There is an underlying equity in unsophisticated village life which the modern industrial town might envy.'[2]

CASTE

The economic aspects of the caste system are an important feature of the old Indian society. The chief basis of the caste system, though by no means its sole one, is traced to function or occupation. At one time or another, professions in most countries were hereditary in practice, if not in theory. There were obvious advantages attaching to the hereditary system under which the son naturally learned the secrets of the family occupation and acquired proficiency in it with the minimum of effort in the congenial atmosphere of home, and under the affectionate care of the father. This was especially important when there was no organized system of public instruction and when a high premium was placed on manual dexterity. So long as this principle worked naturally and rationally it was open to no objection. But this ceased to be the case and, with time, the comparative fluidity of the caste system in the earlier stages gave place to rigidity.

'PANCHAYAT'

The *panchayat* is an ancient and once vital village institution the survival of which in its indigenous form in parts of the country is at once a testimony to the enduring quality of the village community and of hope for the future of democratic institutions. The *panchayat* was a council, not formally elected, but appointed by the general assent of the community, which ran the affairs of the village. In olden days, it collected the land revenue and represented the villages in their dealings with the royal tax-collectors (and occasionally even refused to pay revenue to government); it settles village disputes (except those concerning a breach of caste rules), supervises communal activities, such as the building of roads, the repair of tanks, etc., and performs many of the functions of government.

A noted observer, Sir Malcolm Darling, records his conversation on the role of the *panchayat* with a *zaildan*:

'Do people always tell the truth before the *panchayat*?' I asked. 'Always', said the *zaildar* (headman) with immense emphasis.

'And do they in *kachhery* (court)?'

'No, there falsehood is spoken.'

'And when *you* go to *kachhery*, do you speak falsehood too?'

'When I am an assessor, never', he exclaimed proudly, throwing back a solemn face.

'But what if you have to give evidence?'

'Oh then', and the wrinkled face broke into a beaming smile, 'I make the lower the higher (*niche upar karlen*).' There was general laughter at this,

---

1. The exchange of services, which is the condition of all friendly human relationships, is most evident at a wedding. If the wedding is in a patron's house, the servant may have to work hard in ministering to a large gathering of guests, but there will be generous feasting, in which he has his part, though (like the women) he must wait until the *zamindars* have had their fill. And if the wedding is in his own house, his patron will lend him beds and gear; possibly, too, money without interest.' Sir Malcolm Darling, *Wisdom and Waste in the Punjab Village*, 1934, p. 272.
2. op. cit. p. 274.

broken by a Brahmin saying in earnest tones: 'In the *panchayat* there is justice, but in the court there is none'—a sentiment which won general assent.

'But why do men fear to speak falsehood in the *panchayat* and not in court?'

'In court it is an affair of parties, but in the *panchayat* two lines are drawn on the ground, one for the Ganjes and the other for the Jamna, and no one dare speak falsehood in the presence of the holy water.'

All I ask agree that the truth is as surely told before the *panchayat* as the contrary in *kachhery*. 'How could a man venture to tell a lie before his brotherhood?' said one of yesterday's *jats* (peasants); and another added: 'It is a Hindu belief that where five sit together God himself is present and no one would dare to lie in His presence.'[1] Here was an indigenous institution 'in miniature the ideal form of government, democracy at the base and aristocracy at the head'.

JOINT FAMILY SYSTEM

Another institution, the joint and undivided family system, characteristic of Hindu society and its social structure, has greatly influenced the economics of the village, and has in turn been modified under the impact of new economic influences. Under this, as many as three generations may live together at any time in the same hive. It is a kind of patriarchal organization where the eldest male member of the family is invested with supreme authority in the conduct of family affairs. Correspondingly, the senior female member, the mother or wife of the male head, is the female head, with corresponding authority in matters of internal household management, and often with a considerable influence in general family matters as well. The earnings of every member flow into the common pool, on which drafts to meet the needs of all are regulated by the family head—everyone earning according to his capacity and receiving according to need. The joint family has its merits as well as defects. It takes the place of national social insurance, guaranteeing bare subsistence to all, to orphans, the disabled, the infirm, the aged, the unfortunate widows as well as the temporarily unemployed. It makes possible the most economical use of the limited resources of the family, avoiding reduplication of household equipment and establishment as well as the economic consequences of excessive sub-division and fragmentation of land which result from the laws of inheritance. The system, however, discourages individuality, initiative and enterprise and tends to act as a drag on economic progress.

LAWS OF INHERITANCE

It is difficult to dissociate the economics of the village, again, from the laws of inheritance of property which are themselves largely governed by the institution of the joint family. Under these laws, every male child is entitled to an equal share of the property, in contrast to the law of primogeniture. The most important economic effect of the laws of inheritance is the widespread distribution of property which results in the sub-division and extreme fragmentation of agricultural holdings and is an obstacle to efficient and economical agriculture. The laws conform to the principle of equality and distributive justice and, like the joint family system, met the requirements of an order of society where the emphasis

---

1 op. cit., p. 141.

was on status and economic stability. They are not conducive, however, to that spirit of fierce endeavour which underlay the Industrial Revolution.

All this has been changing. With the growth of international commerce and the rise of internal markets, assisted by the extension of railways and roads, the old self-sufficiency of the village has been progressively worn down; the rigidity of the old village division of labour has been softening; the old caste barriers to economic mobility are slowly yielding and cash increasingly replaces kind or barter in the village. At the same time, the expansion of towns and the diversification of employment opportunities, the rise of new trades and the decline of old ones, have been breaking the hold of the joint family system. The spread of education and the general trend of the times works in the same direction. Two world wars in which hundreds of thousands of soldiers were exposed to a new outlook in distant theatres have added a new ferment to the countryside. The advent of freedom, with accelerated economic and social reform in the abolition of large landed estates and the increase of the rights of the tenants, with elections and adult suffrage, further widens the village horizon and complicates the problems of adjustment and of devising a new stable order in place of the old.

Significant among the effects on the social order already manifest are the rise in the age of marriage, the improved status of woman, the decline in the despotism of the joint family ruler as well as the mother-in-law, and the lesser vogue of purdah or the veil and, in general, the increasing reorientation of the alignment of family relations from mother and son to husband and wife.

LAND TENURE

Fundamental to an understanding of the shifting economics of the Indian village is some knowledge of the land tenure and taxation systems. The extent of village communism before British rule is a matter for controversy, but 'either in a feudal or an imperial scheme there never was any notion of the ownership of the land vesting in anybody excepting the peasantry'.[1] When the British first drew up their land settlements in Bengal they placed the *zamindars* and *jagirdars*, the revenue farmers and the territorial chiefs, on an equal footing and, partly as a matter of convenience, partly because of a misunderstanding of their status, recognized them as owners of the land with all the rights of selling the land, etc., of the English landlord. The cultivator was thus dispossessed of his land and deprived of nearly all his old rights. The system failed in its original intention of producing a class of educated landlords who would utilize their wealth and education to improve the land (and who would also be loyal to the government). Instead, sub-infeudation—which has even been known to reach the fantastic length of over fifty intermediaries between landowner and cultivator—has prevented the *zamindars* from fulfilling the functions which provide the economic justification for a landlord and tenant system. 'The land is nobody's concern.' It has now been decided to abolish *zamindari* and, in most of the states of India where the system prevails (Madras, Bihar, U.P., Madhya Pradesh and Assam), the state legislatures

---

1. Radhakamal Mukerjee, *Land Problems of India*, 1937.

have passed laws under which the land is to be taken over from the landlords by the government on payment of compensation. If the *Zamindari* Abolition Acts become effective, over 170 million acres of land (out of over 180 million acres under *zamindari*) will be taken over from the landlords, and the peasant will hold them directly from the government.[1] The cost of compensating the *zamindars* is estimated at several hundred crores and presents a difficult financial problem to the states governments.[2]

'RURALIZATION' AND PRESSURE OF POPULATION

The position of the village artisans has undergone the greatest change. With the ousting of custom by commerce, they have lost several of their old rights— thus, the tanner no longer obtains as a right the hides of dead animals, for the farmer has discovered that these have a lucrative market. And as a result of the improvement of transport and the competition of cheap machine-made goods they have often lost, not only their former perquisites, but their actual employment. Since industrialization in the cities did not proceed rapidly enough to absorb those deprived of their customary occupations, they were driven to agricultural work. From 1891 to 1921 there was a steady increase in the proportion of persons engaged in agriculture and a corresponding decline in the proportion of industrial workers. Unfortunately the rapid growth of population has been accompanied neither by a corresponding increase in industrialization nor by a sufficient extension of the land under cultivation. In consequence, as seen in the following table, there has been a steady decline in the *per capita* area sown.

Net *per capita* area sown (British India)

Year	Population (millions)	Average net area sown[1] (million acres)	Per capita area sown (acres)
1911	231.6	208	0.90
1921	233.6	205	0.88
1931	256.8	211	0.82
1941	295.8	215	0.72

1. Represents the average for five years with the census year as the central one (Famine Enquiry Commission Report, page 78). These trends have continued since 1941: an increase in the absolute acreage sown, with a greater increase in the population.

The decline of rural handicrafts has also impoverished the farmer to the extent that he and his family have abandoned many of the occupations subsidiary to agriculture and have not found substitutes.

1. Over 70 per cent of the assessed land is under various forms of the *zamindari* or *mahalwari* (joint-ownership) systems; in the remaining 30 per cent the *ryotwari* system prevails under which the individual *ryot* or peasant is separately assessed for revenue and is held directly responsible to the state for it. He has the right to sell or transfer his land, a right which has, as we shall see later, often worked to his disadvantage in his dealings with the money-lender.
2. The increase in land revenue is expected to bring in about Rs. 200 million per annum, about five per cent o the costs of compensation.

As a result of the growth of population, the increase in the proportion dependent on agriculture, and the laws of inheritance, the average holding grew steadily smaller. The Famine Enquiry Commission found in 1945 that, in most of the provinces investigated (Bengal, U.P., Punjab, Bombay and Madras), the average holding could produce roughly two tons of cereals, the size of the average holding varying from 4.4 acres in Bengal to 11.7 acres in Bombay. These figures conceal the fact that the majority of holdings are much smaller than the averages suggest. The unit of cultivation in India is often too small to be operated with efficiency or to occupy fully either the cultivator or his bullocks. His efficiency is further reduced by the fragmentation of his holding into strips separated from each other. Attempts have been made in some provinces to induce the farmers to consolidate their holdings by exchanging their strips of land, but progress is slow and only in the Punjab has some success been achieved.

The minute and scattered nature of the average holding is only one cause of the inefficiency of Indian agriculture. Other causes of these miserable yields include the poverty of the soil; the inadequacy of good seed, livestock and other equipment; irregular rainfall and insufficient irrigation; and the ill-health, ignorance and apathy of the cultivator. The Indian farmer is not inherently inefficient; but, in general, the inefficiency and lack of initiative of the farmer proceed from his poverty and bondage to the landlord or the money-lender.

THE MONEY-LENDER

The money-lender provides a neat illustration of the vicious circle of the peasant's poverty. His indigence forces him to borrow from the money-lender—whether for the purchase of equipment or land or for the expenses of marriages, funerals or other social needs—and the exorbitant charges coupled with his own miserable income make him increasingly unable to repay the loan. With the commercialization of agriculture his needs for cash increased, while his ignorance of market conditions and ineptness at selling prevented him from realizing the full cash value of his crops. The village money-lender found himself, upon the advent of Western ideas and law, free from the old customary restraints, such as the rule of Damdupat by which he was prohibited from receiving as repayment more than double the sum lent. Under the new laws of contract and transfer of property his loans (which were now issued on the security of land and not, as formerly, on personal security) could be recorded, his claims were backed by the law, and in case of default the debtor's possession could be attached and the debtor himself arrested or imprisoned. Small wonder, then, that from 1880 onwards the money-lender flourished as the green bay tree. Not only were thousands of farmers dispossessed of their land, but several rural classes borrowed themselves into virtual serfdom.

The problem of reducing this burden has engaged the attention of the provincial governments. Numerous laws have been passed restraining the money-lender from alienating the peasant's land, regulating his accounts, forcing him to register and obtain a licence, limiting his rates of interest, setting up Debt Conciliation Boards to bring about voluntary adjustments of debt, providing for the compulsory scaling down of debts, etc. A better remedy was the provision of alternative and controlled sources of credit. The government provides loans, both for emergencies such as floods or famines, and for the permanent improvement of agriculture, and a number of agricultural credit societies, co-operative banks, etc., have been set up. These agencies together are still not an adequate substitute for the money-lender.

LANDLESS LABOUR

The small peasant dispossessed of his land and the artisan deprived of his occupation have both become agricultural labourers. The 1882 census recorded 7.5 million 'landless day labourers'; the 1931 census showed over 33 million or about one-third of those engaged in agriculture and about one-fifth of the total working population. The proportion does not appear to have changed much since. The rise of this enormous class has naturally brought a great change in the social structure and not one for the better.

THE DECLINE AND REVIVAL OF THE 'PANCHAYAT'

The impairment of the self-sufficiency of the Indian village has been accompanied by the decay of the age-old institutions which satisfied the social and human needs of the village in a hundred ways and have not been adequately replaced. Mention has been made above of the village *panchayat*. It did not merely narrow its sphere of activities—in many, perhaps most, parts of India it vanished altogether. This was partly because of the introduction of the *zamindari* system, partly because the government took over many of its functions, partly because of the gradual and partial commercialization of society. Once again an attempt was made to rebuild this institution—from 1904 onwards laws were passed in most provinces and states establishing *panchayats* and conferring on them limited judicial powers (in Bengal the *panchayats* also have some police powers), granting sources of finance (e.g., a portion of the land tax), and providing for their control by government agencies. But once again legislation was not enough: by 1941 hardly 9 per cent of the villages had *panchayats*. The existing *panchayats*, emasculated or artificial though they often are, perform useful services, but it will take a long time for them to regain anything like their former organic place in the village community.

SOME CONCLUSIONS

Since the advent of independence, indeed since the setting up of congress governments in the provinces (now states) in 1937, there has been considerable increase in expenditure for the encouragement of village handicrafts, the expansion of large-scale industries, the starting of large multi-purpose river projects as well as the intensification of agricultural improvements. There is hope that a successful stand will be made against the forces that are exerting relentless pressure on an already low standard of living. A slow advance would, however, seem to be the best that is possible. Talk of a rapid rise in the standard of living is wide of the mark, unless the rapid growth of population can be checked. The whole question of controlling the increase in population needs to be carefully considered by experts and a positive policy evolved.

In the organization of the economics of the village, the biggest problem is to find a new principle to meet the requirements of organization in an age when commercial society is breaking down the isolation of the village and old customs

and modes of organization are suffering disintegration and decay. 'The disintegration of the village community, once the peasant's strongest bulwark, is the greatest
disservice that the modern world has done him, and the spread of education is
doing nothing to arrest the process. The education we have introduced into the
country is too individualistic for that. It tends to make people more conscious of
their rights than of their obligations, and of what separates them from their neighbours than of what binds them together. It encourages the competitive, if not the
acquisitive spirit, and where comparatively few are educated, it tempts them to
scorn and even exploit those who are not. These tendencies may be accepted
features of town life, but in the village they are like white ants eating their way
unseen into the fabric of village life, for men live so closely together there that they
cannot live happily without a strong sense of mutual obligation.'[1] The answer
to the challenge of organization is furnished by the co-operative principle which,
even more than the *panchayat*, offers the best hope of the future. Wherever agriculture is the predominant industry, co-operation is coming to be regarded as the
natural basis for economic, social and educational development, and India is no
exception. Co-operation is, indeed, a method of approach, a form of organization
and a technique; as such it is capable of much wider application than merely
in the field of credit. It is a powerful means of solving many of the problems of
the rural population. The great difficulty is how to substitute for what is often the
inspiration of modern business: 'Each man for himself and the devil take the
hindmost', the motto of co-operation: 'Each for all and all for each.'

SUGGESTIONS FOR FURTHER STUDY

BADEN-POWELL, B. H. *Land systems of British India.* 1892
KEATINGE, G. *Rural economy in Bombay Deccan.* 1912.
MATHAI, John. *Village government in British India.* 1915.
MANN, Harold. *Land and labour in a Deccan village—Pipla Saudagar.* 1917.
MANN, Harold; KANITKAR. *Land and labour in a Deccan village—Jategaon Budruk.* 1921.
KEATINGE, G. *Agricultural progress in Western India.* 1921.
Royal Commission on Agriculture in India. 1928.
DARLING, M. L. *Rusticus Loquitur—The old light and the new in the Punjab village.* 1930.
MUKERJEE, R. K. *Land problems of India.* 1933.
BRAYNE, F. L. *Rural reconstruction.* 1934.
DARLING. M. L. *Wisdom and waste in the Punjab village.* 1934.
CALVERT, H. *Wealth and welfare of the Punjab.* 1936.
Report of the Land Revenue Commission, Bengal. 1940.
Report of the Agricultural Finance Sub-Committee. 1945.
TARLOK SINGH. *Poverty and social change.* 1945.
The Famine Enquiry Commission. Vols. I and II. 1945.
Report of the Co-operative Planning Committee. 1946.
NANAVATI, M. B; ANJARIA, J. J. *The Indian rural problem.* 1947.
PUNJAB BOARD OF ECONOMIC ENQUIRY. *Economic and village surveys and farm accounts and
family budgets of cultivators.*
INDIAN SOCIETY OF AGRICULTURAL ECONOMICS. *Socio-economic survey of a village—Bhuvel.*
1949.
Report of the Congress Agrarian Reforms Committee. 1949.
Report of the Rural Banking Enquiry Committee. 1950.
AGRICULTURAL CREDIT DEPARTMENT OF THE RESERVE BANK OF INDIA. *Bulletins and
reviews of co-operative movement in India.*

---

1. Sir Malcolm Darling, 'The Indian Peasant and the Modern World', *Asiatic Review*, January 1942.

TRIBAL REHABILITATION IN INDIA

D. N. Majumdar

I

The various categories into which the people of India are ethnographically classified, for census purposes and also in sociological literature, are 'tribe', 'caste', 'sect', and 'class'. The first two were originally mutually exclusive, while caste, sect and class do not represent rigid 'water-tight' compartments. Generally speaking, a tribe is a socio-political organization, territorially integrated, while caste is a social group without political function. In recent years, however, a political complexion can be traced in the various All-India caste *sabhas* or associations in their demand for political rights and their feverish activities to secure them. A sect is often a segment of a caste regrouped on a new religious basis, as represented by the Ramayats, Lingayats, and Vaishnavites, while a class has a political character emerging as it does, as a direct result of industrialization.

The minimum definition of a tribe is an ethnic group speaking a common dialect and inhabiting a common territory. Some anthropologists do not regard a tribe as a territorial unit, as all tribes were originally nomadic, but admit its political character—intertribal warfare and vendetta being common methods of settling disputes and satisfying aggressive designs, found even today among the tribes of the north-western frontier of India before partition. Nomadism, particularly in the earlier stages, was certainly a distinct trait of tribal life, but since nomadism has been superseded by settled life, a territorial affiliation can be admitted. Nomadism is also limited by regional ties and ecological considerations. A more plausible definition of a tribe given by the *Imperial Gazeteer* is commonly adopted in ethnographical literature on India. A tribe, according to this definition, is a collection of families bearing a common name, speaking a common dialect, occupying or professing to occupy a common territory and is ordinarily, but not necessarily, endogamous. Here we need to distinguish 'caste' from 'tribe'. A caste, in its simple form, is a collection of families, bearing a common name, following or professing to follow a particular occupation, observing a standard code of rules and taboos regarding marriage, food and ceremonial purification. Although a caste is merely a social group, the territorial affiliations of the castes have placed them in regional groups. When the same caste, speaking different languages, is found in two states or geographical areas, there is no social relationship or intermarriage, and each caste is a distinct social unit in its own territory. Endogamy is vital to a caste, as for a territorial group, though in the case of the former, endogamy may have been dictated by the desire for ceremonial purity, racial pride, cultural homogeneity, or even isolation. In the case of a tribe, endogamy is probably a consequence of cultural and dialectical differences, beliefs in *mana* and taboos. A caste is split up into smaller sections or sub-castes, the latter also observing endogamy, as for example, among the Kayasthas of Uttar Pradesh, of whom there are twelve divisions, each endogamous and, for practical purposes, independent castes. Similar is the case among the various sections of the Brahmins, and even the agricultural Kurmis are split up into Biyahuts and Sagahuts—originally mutually hypergamous, but now endogamous; the former prohibit widow marriage, the latter still practise it. As we pass from the higher to lower castes in an area, the solidarity of the caste increases and is maintained by a caste organization, caste *panchayat*, which is now being replaced in northern India, for the present, by the *Gaon Hukumat*, or village self-government.

The numerical strength of the tribal people in India approximated to 25 million, according to the census of 1941. Since then, the total population of India has increased by nearly 13 per cent. As the various tribes in India represent many levels of progress and decay, we are not sure whether this increase may be credited to the tribal people as well. Tribal demography in India, today, as before, is characterized by three trends: (a) a progressive decline of many tribal groups; (b) a slow increase among many tribes; and (c) a rapid increase among tribes living in certain parts of the country, specially protected by legislation and catered for by the administration. In the decade 1941-51, there has been a good deal of assimilation of the tribal groups into Hinduism, so that the figures of tribal strength in the different states may not be accurate. The Uttar Pradesh has had to liquidate all tribes, except the criminal groups, owing to rapid change and the claims of the tribes for higher cultural status. In many parts contacts with civilization have undermined tribal solidarity, have invaded tribal security, introduced discomforts, diseases and vices. Many have failed to maintain their tribal structures, and have been partially or wholly assimilated into the lower strata of the Hindu caste system. Some have left their settlements and are scattered over wider areas. Where the tribes live in a compact territory, as do the Santhal Parganas or the Chota Nagpur in Bihar, the tribal cultures have not faced much disorganization and there is not so much detribalization. However, tribes which live in the neighbourhood of organized and more advanced groups have either become assimilated with the castes or have developed a symbiotic relationship, or 'acculturated' to the advanced cultures, though in some areas, a process of contra-acculturation is manifest.

The tribal returns as recorded in the census, decade to decade, reveal a heterogeneous category including Moslem tribes of Pathans, Baluchis, Brahuis, Afghans, Mapillas, comparatively primitive tribes like the Todas and the Kotas who still worship their own tribal deities, those who have become partially Hinduized—like most of the Bhils and Gonds among whom the tribal name is on the way to becoming a caste name; those largely Christianized, like the Oraons, the Mundas and the Khasis; and others who are wholly Hinduized, like the Bhumij of Bihar, the Rajhwar of Sarguja, the Patela of the Panchmahals, or the Manipuris of Assam. All these tribes can be territorially grouped into: (a) tribes of the north-western frontier; (b) those of the north-eastern frontier; and (c) of interior India; the last can be subdivided into: (i) Munda group; (ii) Dravidian speaking. The former speak dialects of the Munda group of the Austro-Asiatic sub-family of the Austric family of languages, the latter, i.e., the peninsular tribes, speak the various Dravidian languages or their patois. The Mongoloid tribes speak Tibeto-Burmese, though the Indo-Aryan languages have influenced the vocabulary and pattern of all tribal languages.

Racially, the tribal population of India, both of interior India and of the north-eastern frontier, belongs either to the Indo-Australoid (Pre-Dravidian) or the Mongoloid stock. The Nagas and the Kukis of Assem are of Mongoloid origin, and other tribes, like the Garo and the Rajbanshi, have a mixed Mongoloid-Australoid descent. The Mongolian strain has entered Assam and outlying parts of eastern Bengal (eastern Pakistan), and even high-caste people in these parts show unmistakable Mongolian traits. The Indo-Australoids are scattered over the whole country. In peninsular India they have mixed with the Mediterranean type, and in central India they have been assimilated here and there by an Alpine element which forms the apex of the racial structure in Gujarat and Bengal. In one or two tribes of the south there is evidence of a 'negrito' strain, which some anthropologists claim to be the 'basic racial stratum' in the Indian population, but the 'negrito' has never been indigenous to India, though the woolly hair, short stature and a mesocephalic head (not broad) among the Kadirs may be due to 'negroid' mixture. In fact there is ample evidence of infiltration in coastal parts of India of western 'negroids', and some anthropologists think that the Mediterranean race has had a 'negroid' association before they spread out. Even if there was a 'negrito' element in the Indian population, its contribution to the making of Indian ethnic types must have been negligible. The Mongolian race has not influenced the population of interior India, though the Scythian branch of this race has left its impression on the Kathis of cultural Gujarat and probably among the Mehrs, Rajputs and Oswal Jains of Cutch. From the evidence of blood-groups, it appears that the Indo-Australoids show more of O and A than B, the A percentage, 60 per cent, among the Paniyans of Malabar being the highest.

Briefly, the majority of the tribes belong to the Indo-Australoid ethnic type, which probably represents the substratum of the Indian population today. There is plenty of support for this view, as the Austric language has had a very wide distribution in India. Even the tribes of the south, who speak the dialects of the Dravidian family of languages, were once speakers of the Austric family of languages. The general features of the Indo-Australoids are a dark skin, a longish head, a broad flat nose, coarse features and short stature. These tribes were probably assimilated by a race who must have spoken Dravidian languages, and the Indus Valley civilization was probably Dravidian in origin, according to competent prehistorians. Of course, waves of immigration have disturbed the ethnic structure of the Indian population and it is difficult to say with any degree of certainty what constitutes the race elements in any particular type, tribe or caste.

In a racial and serological survey of the Uttar Pradesh which was undertaken in 1941 in connexion with the census operations, a gradual transition was found of ethnic types among the 22 castes and tribes measured. They could be divided into three basic *groups*: (a) the Brahmins, both of the eastern and western districts; (b) the artisan castes; and (c) the tribal group—with many intermediate types. The tribal groups of the U.P., both Mongoloid and Indo-Australoid, can be readily differentiated from the Brahmins and the artisans on anthropometric evidence, while the serological status of the castes and tribes follow more or less the accepted social precedence. This is significant, indicating ethnic differences; the Brahmins are at the apex of the ethnic pyramid of the province, then follow the Chattriyas and the Khattris, then the Artisans, ending with the Kahars, a menial caste whose affiliation with the tribes is more intimate than that of the other artisan castes, while the tribes behave as distinct units with varying degrees of relationship among them. When we compare the somatology and serology of specific castes like the Chamar or the Dom we find a good deal of intermixture, so that, in some anthropo-metric characters, the Dom resemble the higher castes, in others, they affiliate themselves with the tribes, indicating the extent of miscegenation among the lower castes, all or most of them having had originally tribal, particularly Indo-Australoid, origin. The results of the U.P. anthropometric survey which have been put forward in a joint publication by P. C. Mahalanobis, D. N. Majumdar and C. R. Rao (*Sankhva*, Vol. IX, Parts 2 and 3, 1949), throw light on the question of tribal dynamics and cultural change. The same kind of results were obtained in the Gujarat anthropometric survey,[1] in which we found a grouping of tribes and a hierarchy based on ethnic considerations, with the Brahmins at one end of the racial scale and the tribal Kolis and the Bhils at the other. It is, therefore, a fact that the tribes of a particular region are more intimate ethnically to the lower castes of the region, and in one province, viz., the Uttar Pradesh, the differences are such as to support the view of their ethnic homogeneity, the basis on which earlier ethnographers have treated the castes of the U.P. as racially similar but functionally distinct. Thus the functional theory of caste is a plausible and mini-mum explanation of caste origins in the province.

The kaleidoscopic account of race origins given above indicates, very super-ficially, the extent of fusion and fission of races in India, and everywhere in tribal India we find institutions and practices which have resulted from culture contacts. It is not possible to map out the zonal distribution of a specific culture or cultures— as may still be possible in Africa and the Oceanic areas inhabited by 'native peoples'—except perhaps in the outlying parts, for example, in the Naga Hills in Assam or in the Agency tracts of Orissa and Madras, in Bastar, Hyderabad, and in tribal Mysore. From the tribe to caste, social distance has followed the order of racial precedence.

III

Culturally, the tribes have distinct patterns of life; some matriarchal, like the Garos and the Khasis of Assam, others patriarchal, while many show signs of transition or have a matriarchal matrix. A tribe is ordinarily split up into sections, septs or clans—these clans in some cases were organized on the basis of a dual structure, divided into two distinct moieties or marriage-classes, as among the Gonds of the Satpura hills and the Garos of Assam. A tribe may have a number of clans, which are named after animals, plants or material objects found within the common area owned by the tribe. Totemic ties, territorial contiguity, or mythical origin from a common ancestor, determine inter-group and intra-group affili-ations, every clan being a kinship group, though the political role exercised by the clan, as evidenced in the *Parha* organization of the Mundas, may be a function of common residence within a territorial limit. In the majority of cases, clans and tribes recognize both territorial and kinship ties. Where political ties are more important, as among the Naga *khels*, exogamy is patterned on the territorial frame. Where totemic beliefs and practices underlie bonds of kinship, as among the Munda-speaking tribes, exogamy is determined on the totemic principle. Where feudal ties exist, they may also ban intra-clan or even intra-village marriages, as among the Indo-Aryan Khasis of the Cis-Himalayan region.

---

1. *Race Realities in Moha Gujarat* (Genj., Rec. Soc. Publication, 1950).

The tribal people of India are both aristocratically and democratically organized. The Naga chiefs represent a predominantly aristocratic organization, the *Parha* system of the Munda tribes, a democratic organization where annual *yatras* or festivals cement bonds of territorial kinship. Each tribe or section of it, besides its hereditary or elected chief, has a council of elders who assist the headman or the chief in the maintenance of the tribal code, law and morality, and there is a spontaneous conformity to traditional ways of life with only occasional lapses, owing to contacts with civilization or disintegration forced either from within or without.

Of all the factors that impinge on and influence cultural progress, economy is probably the major one, and in any scheme of tribal rehabilitation, an emphasis on tribal economy is natural. The various methods by which the primitive people of India eke out their subsistence can be understood only in the context of their environment, for it is the natural resources of their habitat that provide the bulwark of defence against starvation, squalor, and destitution, particularly so as technological aids are so limited and crude, if available. The economic activities of the primitive tribes are the collection of edible fruits and roots, herbs, and plants from the forests; hunting; fishing; bird-catching; honey-gathering; domestication of sheep and cattle; crude cultivation, such as shifting, terraced, or semi-permanent agriculture; spinning; weaving; basket-making and minor arts and crafts. Even today, the primitive tribes spend the major part of their working hours in the procurement of food, and they are constantly faced with the food problem. The scope for their food supply has been considerably narrowed owing to non-availability of fruits and roots, restriction on the use of forests, lack of knowledge about efficient agriculture, and changed ideas about their diet, the last resulting entirely from their cultural contacts with the plains people.

Hunting is no longer a major occupation of the tribes, and *jhum* cultivation and terraced farming are no longer efficient substitutes for hunting. The fertility of the fields was in the past believed to be secured by sacrifices and prayers based on the belief in 'soul-substance' and the observance of fertility cults. Today, however, there is a disintegration of tribal life, and beliefs and practices which aided the struggle for adaptation and secured the food supply have been dropped, while the phenomenal increase of population among certain tribes has made heavy inroads into their primitive economy. Where the tribes live near the plains people, they have learnt permanent agriculture—the Khond, the Munda, the Santhal, the Garo, the Khasi, and the Angami Nage cultivate their lands in the same way as the plains people, and irrigation and use of manure as a fertilizer have become essential aids to agriculture. The use of the plough has become popular, if not universal, and cattle have replaced human labour, which often used to be yoked to the plough to make the field yield a bumper harvest; artificial irrigation is now resorted to by most of the tribes mentioned above, but the vagaries of rainfall, the inefficient and crude tools and equipment, lack of foresight and lazy habits impede their economic efforts. Some of the tribes have little artistic taste; their arts and crafts are crude, and in no way serve to help them to earn a living, while there are tribes like the Angami Naga and the Lushai whose artistic enterprises can yield a rich dividend if properly handled.

On the basis of tribal economy, the tribes can be grouped into several clusters or categories. There are tribes who live in the hills and fastnesses and cling to their simple collection or hunting economy. In some parts, they live by shifting or *jhum* cultivation, supplementing the meagre produce from their fields by lumbering, simple barter of forest products, and occasional or permanent labour in mines, factories and plantations. Some settled tribes live on permanent agriculture, but with only rudimentary knowledge of the farming practices that give security to the agricultural communities of the plains; they keep poultry and cattle, know weaving, spinning and pottery. Terraced farming, associated with *jhum* or independent of it, is practised by various tribes, such as the Khasi, the Khond and the Saora, who use every available slope whose declivity is not too steep for agriculture, and sow seeds broadcast, sacrifice animals, raise *menhirs* or stone structures in their fields (perhaps as the source of 'soul-substance'), and even drench themselves in the monsoon rains to make a bargain with nature for their food; their needs can be met only if all dances are danced, all rites performed and none omitted, and if the gods are satisfied by the prayers and sacrifices traditionally prescribed.[1]

IV

From time to time, the primitive and backward conditions of the aboriginal population of India had received some attention from the British administration, but they followed, as far as practicable, a policy of *laisser faire* with regard to these people, with the result that occasional but violent revolts were reported from tribal areas, caused by expropriation of the tribes from their tribal lands, exploitation of tribal labour, and exactions of the money-lenders and the alien vendors of toys and trinkets. It is not possible here to deal at any length with the various efforts of the administration to give relief and work out schemes for the rehabilitation of the primitive hill and jungle tribes, but a few instances might be put forward to illustrate the solicitude of the administration for tribal welfare. It must be pointed out, however, that the absence of a definite policy with regard to the tribal people left them at the mercy of the advanced cultural groups, economically more organized. Missionary activities received the full approval and active support of the then administration of the country, and the government was lulled to a sense of security on the assumption that what was necessary was being done through missionary activities. It was thought that the long-range policy of converting the tribes to Christianity should be viewed with tolerance on the part of the administration.

Yet, some legislation had to be passed to reduce the discomforts of the aboriginal people. The Paharia came into conflict with the Hindu *zamindars* quite early, and British interference took the form of attempts at pacification and military operations, while the leaders of the revolt were granted land and *sanads*. To neutralize such violent outbursts the Paharia were surrounded by a ring of disabled and retired soldiers, who were encouraged to settle in and around the Paharia tract to keep the peace. Gradually the leaders of the tribe had to be vested with civil and criminal jurisdiction in the villages, till the improved state of law and order earned for them special treatment and the withdrawal in 1782 of the Rajmahal Hills from the jurisdiction of the ordinary courts. In 1796, the code drafted for

---

1. The first group includes tribes like the Rajis of Ascot, Almora district, U.P., the jungle Birhor and the Kharia of the Ranchi district of Bihar, the Darlung Kuki of Tripura state, the hill Maria of Bastar, Madhya Pradesh, the Koya, the Kadar, the hill Pantanam of Hyderabad and Mysore states, and probably the Juang of Orissa state. The second group includes the Korwa of Mirzapur in U.P., the Garo, and the Malpaharia of Assam and Bengal respectively, the Naga tribes, the Muria and the Dandami Maria of Bastar, the Khond and the Saora of the Ganjam Agency tracts in Orissa, and the Kamar of Chattisgarh. The advanced tribes who can be ill-distinguished from the lower agricultural castes of the plains, except in the social structure and tribal beliefs and practices, are the Tharus of Tarai, U.P., the Munda-speaking tribes of Bihar, the Oraon of the Ranchi district, the Khasi of Assam, the Parja, the Bhatra and the Gond tribes of Madhya Pradesh and Orissa, the Badaga, and probably the Kota of Madras, the Bhils and the Koli of Gujarat.

the administration of the Daman-i-Koh, the new name for the Paharia tract, became Regulation I, and the tract was thenceforth administered by the collector without regard to any of the laws in force in British India, according to his own rules.

Chota Nagpur and the Santhal Parganas were seething with tribal discontent, and armed intervention by the government was frequently sought by the *zamindars* to restore peace. The 1855 Santhal revolt made necessary the creation of Daman-i-Koh, and the Santhal Parganas, as a separate district, was declared a non-regulated area by Regulation XXXVII of 1855. All this was done on the ground that the complicated machinery of 'civilized' laws was unsuited to the genius of the aboriginals, a subject on which S. C. Roy, the pioneer anthropologist of India, had made pertinent observations. Several bits of legislation were passed under the authority of the Executive Council of Fort William, Fort St. George, and Bombay. By the Indian Councils Act of 1861, the British Parliament validated rules and regulations made by the Governor-General-in-Council and by certain local authorities for non-regulated tracts. The Government of India Act of 1870 further empowered the Governor-General-in-Council to issue laws and regulations for the administration of areas where the operation of the Civil and Criminal Procedure Acts in force in British India was restricted. In 1874, the Indian Legislature passed the Scheduled Districts Act or Act XIV of 1874, whereby the 'local' government was empowered to declare in respect of the tracts specified in the Act what enactments were or were not in force, and to notify the extension, with modifications or restrictions if necessary, of any enactments in force at that time in any part of British India.

The scheduled tracts which were created to give effect to the Government of India Act of 1870 were as follows: in Assam—Ajmer-Merwara, Coorg, Andaman Islands; in Bengal—Jalpaiguri, Darjeeling, and Chittagong Hill tracts, the Santhal Parganas, Chota Nagpur division, and Angul Mahal; in Bombay—Aden, Sindh, Panchmahal and estates of Mewasi chiefs in West Khandesh; in the C.P.—Chanda Zamindaris, Chindwara Jagirdaris; in Madras—14 Mallhas in Vizagapatam, some areas in Godawari district, and Laccadive including Minicoy; in the Punjab—Hazara, Peshawar, Kohat, Bannu, Dera Ismail-Khan, Dera Ghazi-Khan, Lahaul and Spiti; in the U.P.—Jhansi division, Kumaon and Gardhwal, Tarai Pargana, few areas in the Mirzapur district, family domains of the Maharaja of Benaras, Jaunsar-Bawar in Dehradun district, and Manpur Pargana of the Central India Agency. The last was removed from the list in 1938. Most of these areas were exempt in revenue and civil matters from the ordinary laws, except where operation was extended to their territories by special notification.

Despite the protective measures for these areas, many hardships had been felt by the primitive and aboriginal inhabitants of the tracts, particularly as a result of the alienation of their tribal lands and the exactions and exploitation of the people by the *mahajans* and alien landlords. In 1917, Madras enacted a law by which it sought to regulate the rate of interest that could be charged on loans advanced to members of hill tribes, and to check expropriation from their lands by the Uriyas, and other money-lending classes, in the Agency tracts in Ganjam, Vizagapatam and Godawari. As early as 1876, in the Santhal Parganas, the government had prohibited the sale and transfer of land, either privately or by the orders of the Court. The Montague-Chelmsford Reforms accepted the position with regard to the backward tribes, and these areas, the list of which was occasionally revised, were to be administered by the Governors of Provinces. But the Government of India, in their proposals under section 52-A of the Act of

1919, proposed a division of the backward and scheduled areas into areas (a) wholly excluded, and (b) partially excluded, though 'opinions were not unanimous with regard to the demarcation of areas under the latter category', and the advisability of treating areas as partially excluded. The tracts declared backward for the purpose of the Government of India Act of 1919 were as follows: (1) Laccadive Islands and Minicoy; (2) Chittagong Hill tracts; (3) Spitti; (4) Angul district; (5) Darjeeling district; (6) Lahaul; (7) Ganjam Agency; (8) Vizagapatam Agency; (9) Godawari Agency; (10) Chota Nagpur division; (11) Sambalpur disctrict; (12) Santhal Parganas district; (13) Garo Hills district; (14) British Pulia of Khasi and Jaintia Hills, excluding Shillong municipality and cantonment; (15) Mikir Hills; (16) North Cacher Hills; (17) Naga Hills; (18) Lushai Hills and Sadiya, Balupari and Lakhimpur frontier tracts.

Protective measures were also adopted in 1935 when the list of areas to be considered as excluded and partially excluded was revised and regulations were drawn up to give relief to the aboriginal population and save them from exploitation and alienation of their lands. The reports subitted by the various provincial governments on the subject of tribal welfare and rehabilitation leave the impression that even if the desire to ameliorate the condition of the tribals existed, nothing significant could be done by the administration because the resources at its disposal were not sufficient. The missionary activities, the only real rehabilitation measures in many parts of tribal India, became suspect as the contacts of the tribal people with the plains increased owing to a phenomenal increase of population in the plains and the need for opening up the areas inhabited by backward and primitive peoples. At the same time expanded communications and the need to exploit the natural resources of the tribal areas brought the problems of the tribal peoples to the fore, and anthropological studies of the remote, inaccessible people described the woes of tribal life. As the demographic facts of tribal areas came to be known, as the knowledge of tribal depopulation and distress increased, opinions began to be crystallized on the need for a new policy with regard to the tribal areas. Nevertheless a policy of segregation was still the watchword of some missionaries and British administrative officers.

With the transfer of power and the formation of the Indian Republic, a greater awareness of tribal distress forced the tribal problems into the open and the avowed policy of the Indian Government has become one of contact and understanding rather than *laisser faire* and segregation. The Constitution of the Indian Union, therefore, has adopted articles expressing the solicitude of the people for the tribal elements and, if the provisions are observed, this will constitute a great step forward for the tribes. In the short period of 10 years, it has been proposed to bring the tribal peoples into line with the rural population of the countryside, and to make them feel that they belong to the land they live in, with common goals, common ideologies and national aspirations. To effect this transition of tribes, the Constitution of India has specifically provided safeguards and directions for tribal rehabilitation. Article 46 of the Constitution, for example, lays down that states shall promote with special care the educational and economic interests of the weaker sections of the people, and shall protect them from social injustice and exploitation. Schemes of development are to be financed out of the Consolidated Fund of India, by grants-in-aid from the revenues of the State, for promoting the welfare of the scheduled tribes (a. 275-i). Under Articles 330 and 332, seats for scheduled castes and tribes have been reserved both in the House of the People, and on the Legislative Assembly of the state in which the tribes live. Article 335 provides for special consideration of members of the scheduled castes and tribes for appointment to posts in the Union and the states. Article 338 provides for appointment of a special officer for scheduled castes and tribes, and Article 340 envisages the appointment of a commission for the welfare of the backward section of the people. The fifth and sixth schedules specifically refer to the administration of tribal areas in Parts A and B states and in Assam, respectively. In view of the fact that the special treatment of the backward peoples has been contested in the courts as 'discrimination', it has been found necessary to incorporate some amendments to the Constitution validating such treatment, which are now on the legislative anvil.

V

The various states with tribal and backward population have recognized the urgent need of social service and welfare activities, but most of the measures so far adopted have been on the economic plane, and are therefore in a sense half-measures. The need for a total approach has not yet been fully recognized and much effort is being wasted on publicity and propaganda which have a limited fuction and are of doubtful expediency. A brief résumé of the activities of the various states is given below.

A five-year plan of tribal welfare work for nearly 50 lakhs of tribal population in Madhya Pradesh (C.P.) was drawn up by the late A. V. Thakkar as early as 1946, and the state government has initiated a number of welfare schemes. Stress has been laid on education, economic improvement, medical relief, water supply and extension of communications, and both state and private enterprises are taking part in the work. Some of the state-aided welfare societies own vans, cinema and radio equipment, and popular lectures and entertainments figure prominently in their rehabilitation efforts. An equal number of the tribal population in Bihar, concentrated in Chota Nagpur and Santhal Parganas, are being catered for by the state and private organizations. The initiative that was in the hands of the missionaries seems to have passed into those of the administration, and a number of benefit schemes with regard to education, sanitation, health, irrigation, cottage industries, co-operative societies of the multi-purpose type, have been launched. The system of indirect rule is being slowly replaced by direct administration, for example by the *Thana* system which has as its ostensible object welfare work, but which is gradually being vested with other responsibilities. The tribal attitude to the *Thana* system has, however, been more misinformed than hostile, for suspicion and distrust of aliens are on the increase among the tribal peoples, and tribal leadership appears to have passed to the Christians among them whose education and awareness have put them in the vanguard of tribal movements. In Orissa tribal welfare is under a Minister, in view of the political unrest of the tribal elements and the need for a positive approach to tribal problems.

Bombay has a record of tribal welfare work initiated by the former government. A Backward Classes Department had introduced a number of measures for relief among the Bhils, the Katkaris and the Warlis. Madras had a large tribal population, at various levels of progress, a large section of which has already been assimilated into the caste structure of the province. A Backward Classes Advisory Committee is now looking after the interests of the tribes, and state and private organization are working to rehabilitate them. In Andhra, Kerala and Tamilnad, a good deal of activity is reported and the Malabar centre of the Servants of India Society has put forward a scheme to help the dying Todas to recover lost ground. The state of Hyderabad has had a long start in tribal welfare activities, thanks to numerous sympathetic and competent administrative officers, mostly British, and today a Social Service Department is initiating large and costly schemes to ameliorate the conditions of the tribals with particular emphasis on educational, medical and economic benefits. Tribal lands have been protected, money-lending has been controlled, agricultural loans are provided free of interest, co-operative societies function for multi-purpose benefits, irrigation works have brought large acreage under the plough, and tribal dialects have found a place in the educational curricula.

Assam has a unique status, with 28 lakhs of tribal people fringing the north-eastern frontier of India. The tribal people were allies of the British army in the war, and their sufferings as a result of the Japanese invasion have earned them a priority in matters of redress and relocation. Assam's problems being different and the tribal population of strategic importance, the responsibility for rehabilitation is being shared by the central government, and a three-crore plan has been drawn up by the Central Planning Commission, with particular reference to Assam's specific needs.

The Rajasthan government which has a strong tribal element, there being eight lakhs of Bhils alone, has organized a Backward Class Welfare Department, and tribal problems have received adequate attention as indicated by provisions already announced. The Bhil Seva Mandal, founded by Shri A. V. Thakkar, has done much valuable work among the Bhils and is now a key organization for social welfare in the Bombay state and other parts of the country. A significant achievement of the Mandal has been the successful reorientation of the Bhil's attitude to his tribal culture. In spite of contacts with civilization and the force impinging on the Bhil culture, there is hardly any detribalization, and even educated boys and girls take to their indigenous culture pattern without misgivings or suspicion. In this way the Bhil dances and songs have been preserved and are inspiring the Bhils to greater activity. Western Bengal, which even after partition has a significant tribal population—nearly two million—has created a separate ministry for aboriginal and backward classes, and a cadre of special officers has been trained to tackle tribal problems on the administrative level. From a recent report of a speech by I. I. Chundrigar, Governor of North-West Frontier Province in West Pakistan, it appears that a scheme to make the tribal areas self-sufficient is being worked out. The Assistant Director of Public Instruction of the State and the Inspector-General of Civil Hospitals, North-West Frontier Province, have, in fact, been asked to give a detailed report on the educational and medical facilities to be provided for the tribal people.

All these measures are good so far as they go, but a total approach to tribal problems is perhaps the greatest present need. After centuries of apathy and neglect, a *malaise* has set in among many tribes and backward groups, and mere economic improvement may not be the solution for tribal ills today. The Munda tribes are passing through a difficult period of change, and their contacts with civilization have introduced problems. The bride-price, which formerly was paid in kind—particularly cattle—is now demanded in cash and—the cost of marriage has increased so much that it has become impossible for an average man to secure a wife. With an excess of female population and a social etiquette that forbids parents to settle the marriage of their daughters without being approached by the parents of the bridegroom or by the latter himself, marriage is a distant prospect for the young women. Marriage by capture, celibacy, late marriage, pre-marital and extra-marital licence have brought the Munda tribes to the verge of a major cultural crisis. The conflict of ideologies brought about by missionary activities has put the matriarchal Garos in a desperate position in which all the tribal values are being challenged. The potato cultivation among the Khasis has precipitated an economic crisis; the self-sufficient social economy of the Khasis is being replaced by a dependent economy, in which the Khasis are subject to the whims and caprices of alien traders and their neighbours, while the contacts with soldiers have disorganized family life. The shifting or *Podu* cultivation of the Saoras and the Khonds of the Agency tracts, Orissa, no longer secure them against starvation and squalor; sexual promiscuity and disease are on the increase and are hastening the complete cultural collapse of the Bhotiyas. Contacts with aliens have affected the culture-pattern of the polyandrous Khasis of the Cis-Himalayas, and the traditional ways of life are no longer sacrosanct. The status of joint marriage is on the decline, divorce is on the increase, and wealthy families indulge in polygamy so that the acute shortage of women is widening the gulf between the rich and the poor. These problems which the tribal societies are facing today cannot be solved by mere economic rehabilitation.

The problems of tribal rehabilitation must be viewed in the context of tribal dynamics. Under the prevailing economic conditions, disintegration of tribal life is as real today as the lack of social solidarity in community life in the villages. The war brought the tribes in many parts of the country into close contact with the fighting forces, and war economy forced the tribes into the arms of alien agencies so suddenly that there was no time for adjustment. The process of disintegration has set in and, often, the material conditions of tribal life have rapidly changed without corresponding changes in the cultural life. The pattern of tribal life everywhere has been disturbed, and unless tribal cultures can be readapted to tribal dynamics, the future of the tribal people cannot be assured.

Vigilant administration has at no time been more needed than it is today, for the very centres of tribal life have been infected and, in some cases, even atrophied. The lack of patience on the part of tribal leaders has contributed to upsetting the balance of tribal life. However, planned rehabilitation must take into account the hopes and aspirations of the people, misconceived though they may be. The two axioms of cultural rehabilitation should be: (a) we cannot be civilized unless every one of us is civilized, and (b) every people, however primitive or civilized, has a right to its own way of life, and to the development of its traditional culture. To reconcile these two requires a complete grasp of the details, and a sympathetic understanding of the realities of tribal aims and aspirations.

SELECTED BIBLIOGRAPHY

AIAPPAN, A. *Socio-economic survey of tribal and backward classes in Madras State* (Madras).
ELWIN, V. *The aboriginals* (O.U.P.).
FURER-HAIMENDORF, C. von. *Tribal Hyderabad* (Hyderabad Deccan).
GHUREY, G. S. *The aboriginese, so-called and their future* (Gokhale Institute, Poona).
GRIGSON, W. V. *The challenge of backwardness* (Hyderabad Deccan).
HUTTON, T. H. *Census report of India*, Vol. I, Pt. I, 1931.
MAJUMDAR, D. N. (1) *Fortunes of primitive tribes*: (11) *Matrix of Indian culture* (Lucknow).
THAKKAR, A. V. *Adim Jati* (Hindi); (Delhi).

THREE INDIAN COMMUNITIES IN PERU

J. Matos Mar

Peru, like most of the Latin American countries, is considered to be 'under-developed'.[1] A third of its 9 million inhabitants eke out a precarious existence and take practically no part in the life of the nation. Owing to their racial and cultural characteristics, this great body of people, commonly known as the Indian population, is only slowly being absorbed into the Peruvian culture, giving rise to a series of cultural adjustments and disadjustments and finally to 'acculturation', a phenomenon which has been characteristic of the country for the last four hundred years but which is taking place in unpropitious circumstances. This process is leading to the development of a mixed, or mestizo, population (both culturally and physically) which is at present predominant in the country, its members belonging to several different cultural levels. Most of the 3 million people who make up the lower social classes live in 'Indian communities', which are relics of the old 'ayllus' surviving in spite of the disappearance of the institution which brought them into existence and made them vital entities. They are now recognized by the law and, for the past thirty years and more, have been placed under special protection to prevent their disintegration, so that they are no longer in danger from the greed of neighbouring landowners. They are social units which can and should be revivified, for, generally speaking, their present level of production is scarcely sufficient to meet local consumer needs. These communities are at present being studied by Peruvian ethnologists who are preparing a plan for converting them into active centres of production, by taking advantage of the latent energies which in the past helped them to lay the foundations of the old Peruvian culture. If such a plan is to be prepared, it is essential to have the co-operation of teams of specialists in various branches of study—anthropologists, economists, sociologists, agricultural experts, doctors, teachers, psychologists, town planners, engineers, etc.—working closely together in the central government departments and in the villages themselves. The Huarochiri project (in an Indian community in the department of Lima) is the first experiment along these lines, undertaken partly as a pilot project.

In order to show how far these communities have an organized structure and are prepared for modern life, we shall describe the position in three of them, Muquiyauyo, Tupe and Taquile. Muquiyauyo is considered to be one of the

---

1. This expression is used in the sense in which it is employed by the United Nations—'Measures for the Economic Development of Underdeveloped Countries'. Report by a group of experts appointed by the Secretary-General of the United Nations, May 1951.

most highly developed communities in Peru. Tupe is the surviving remnant of an old ethno-linguistic group, the Kauke. Taquile, on Lake Titicaca, is the least advanced of the three communities and may be regarded as being still, in 1954, at the stage characteristic of the old Indian communities.

THE ISLAND OF TAQUILE[1]

Taquile is a homogeneous community of 650 people living on one of the islands on Lake Titicaca, at an altitude of nearly 12,600 feet. Only two adults and six children speak Spanish, the remainder of the population speaking only Kechua. The native economy is agricultural and the main crop is the potato; for centuries past the people have had the subsistence economy typical of Indian communities. They have only one harvest a year as they have no water for irrigation; the rains are therefore a determining factor in the annual rhythm of their life. The change in the system of landownership which has been going on over the last twenty-five years determines their entire attitude and conduct. Until 1930 all the Indians were simply *colonos* (peons) of absentee mestizo landlords. Since then, as a result of various favourable circumstances, the *colonos* have begun to purchase their own land.

The island, which is about three miles long and one and a quarter wide at the widest part was, in 1580, awarded to a Spaniard, who became its first owner under Spanish law. During the seventeenth and eighteenth centuries, it passed into the hands of a series of different owners, and thereafter was transmitted by inheritance until, in 1930, it was divided between eight owners who habitually referred to their estates on the island as 'haciendas'. Until that date, small as the estates were, the landlords still received a proportion of the crops. Throughout this long period, the Indians, being treated as *colonos*, were really serfs bound to the soil; they were transferred, with the land and animals, from one owner to another and, even away from the island, were obliged to perform a series of compulsory tasks without payment; *kipu, mitani, pongo* and *watache* were some of the names given to them according to the work they did. As the estates were split up into units hardly adequate to maintain the Indians themselves, the landowners lost their authority.

The journey to Puno, the nearest town, which was then made on rafts of *totora* (known as *balsas*) was very tiring; it took 15 hours to cover the 30-mile stretch of water. This was one of the main reasons for the isolation of the island and the lack of interest shown by the landowners after a certain time, especially as they derived no great profit from their lands there. This situation encouraged a group of Indians to form a company which, by formal deed, purchased three of the properties on credit; this action was subsequently repeated until there are now only two small properties not belonging to the Indians. Until then the head of each family was simply entitled to a limited area of arable land in each of the four *suyos* into which the island is divided, a house (accompanied by a small *canchon* or vegetable plot) on the estate of which he was a *colono*, and a few animals for his own needs. After the purchase of the land, these traditional rights were maintained and further plots of land were allotted according to the contribution made by each individual. An Indian of exceptional ability was the prime mover in this

1. José Matos, *La Propriété dans l'Ile Taquile*, extracts from the *Travaux de l'Institut Français d'Études Andines*, Vol. III, Paris-Lima, 1951; Rosalia A. Matos, *L'Organisation Sociale dans l'Ile de Taquile*, idem.

action and so became the largest landowner on Taquile. This began to make the other Indians distrustful of him and as a result they no longer presented a united front.

Lake Titicaca is subject to periodic fluctuations, its level rising and falling in regular sequence; one of the great falls in its level (16 feet in five years) began in 1944, leading to the almost complete disappearance of the *totora*, a species of typha growing on the banks and in the shallows of the lake, which is an extremely important raw material in native industries. At the outset, the disappearance of the *totora* was a calamity. Owing to the shortage of raw material for building their rafts, the Indians were in danger of being left with no means of communication. This problem, which also affected the inhabitants of the other islands and peninsulas in the lake, led to the use of sailing boats. In this way, the journey from Taquile to Puno was reduced from 15 to four or five hours. The first boat was bought but the others were built on the island by the Indians, who now have five of them. The growth of landownership and the change in communications have quite altered conditions in the island. The closely-knit community has come safely through a stage of crucial importance. Although the Indians have become the owners of almost the whole island and although the performance of services, without payment, for the former owners has been abolished, the importance of the island in the life of the country has not increased and scarcely any progress has been made with its assimilation. Ownership of land is now in the hands of individuals, but the land lying fallow is used for common pasturage; the system of cultivation follows the traditional pattern, the same crops are grown and the same implements used for tilling the land—the *taklla* (a primitive foot plough) and the ox-drawn plough. The work is done both individually and collectively: the systems of *ayni* (mutual help), *minka* (communal work), *yanaparikuy* (mutual help among people not related to one another) and independent co-operative groups for the conduct of specific activities are all working perfectly satisfactorily.

The Indians make their own clothing and weave their own cloth. Their harvests are sufficient for them to engage in a little trade, partly barter and partly sale for money. They gradually collect the necessary amounts for the purchase of land, the building of boats and the buying of the commodities they need for their own consumption, such as matches, lamp oil, wool, alcohol (for celebrations) and miscellaneous goods. They supply the outside market with potatoes, wood for fuel, and a few carved stone objects.

The presence of a school, which has been in existence for eight years, has so far brought about no improvement, mainly because it has not taken due account of the special requirements of the community.

The struggle for the ownership of land and the change in the means of communication and transport are thus the two main factors conducive to economic development and the introduction of modern technology. The Indians living on the island are now in close and constant touch with Puno which, in its way, is the most advanced centre on the Peruvian plateau. The other Indian communities look up to them and quote them as an example, as being the first to acquire ownership of the land they cultivate. It is interesting to note, however, that the people of Taquile, from all other points of view, are still the most conservative group to be found on the islands in the lake. Their traditional institutions are still marked by the Western influence to which they were subjected in the seventeenth and eighteenth centuries. The people are skilful at weaving and stone-working. As the possibilities of agricultural development will always be limited, even in the most favourable circumstances, the increase in the population will make it more and more difficult for the land to support the people. This problem cannot be solved on Taquile; the necessity of leaving the island to find another means of livelihood is beginning to be felt, and a few of the inhabitants have gone as far away as Arequipa to work on the land, taking the places of peasants who have become industrial workers.

If, therefore, agriculture and cottage industries were organized along new lines on the island with the help of modern technology, it might be possible to raise the standard of living of people who have no option but to find work as agricultural labourers or in industry as the country's industrial development proceeds.

THE INDIAN COMMUNITY OF TUPE

Tupe is a mestizo community in which the Indian influence is predominant. It is today a survival of the Kauke ethno-linguistic group, which is akin to Aymara, although it differs both from this and from the Kechua. It is a conservative group which is also represented, in another part of Peru (the mountainous region of the department of Lima), by a series of surviving communities that have not lost their vitality. It consists of about a thousand people, living in four 'centres of population,' all of whom, without exception, speak Spanish and Kauke. This community is in direct touch with more advanced centres such as Cañete, Chincha and Lima. Until the last thirty years, the men used to make long journeys on foot for the sheep and cattle trade. As a consequence of the development of communications, they have given up this practice and now scarcely ever leave their own part of the country, where they carry on agriculture, their principal form of activity, and stock-rearing. The main road linking them with the large towns is four or five hours' walk away and, like the neighbouring communities, they are trying to build themselves a connecting road. The community lives at an altitude of about 9,300 feet in a mountainous gorge in the Andes. Like most of the communities in the department of Lima, it leads an isolated life; the ground is so broken that the villages have very little contact with one another. The greatest concentration of these communities is at Huarochiri, where there are 12 of them. Generally speaking, communication with the outside world is by way of the nearest valley to the neighbouring coastal towns and, by way of the latter, with Lima.

There have never been large estates owned by outsiders at Tupe; the land has always been the property of the local peasants. Up to a hundred years ago, or rather less, the land was collectively owned, but today it is in individual ownership. The main crops are potatoes and maize, both of which are used for local consumption; money income is derived from the sale of animals (cattle, sheep and goats) and from the sale of wool and cheese. The *puna* (plateau), at an altitude of about 13,000 to 16,000 feet, is the only land still held in common, and there the flocks are reared. The community itself has a capital fund which was established a long time ago and is increased year by year by the contributions of the members of the community and the interest on investments in the shape of annual loans. Women, on an equal footing with men, play a very active part in the life of the community; the work and responsibilities they undertake (the agricultural work is entirely in their hands) give them prestige and the men are thus left free to engage in trade. The preservation of the old traditions is very largely due to the women's influence.

Unlike the school at Taquile, that at Tupe, which was established fifty years ago, has already achieved much, the members of the community themselves being responsible for its success. It is now, however, going through a period of crisis. (Because of the past history of the place, there are still a few people in Lima who originally came from Tupe and are interested in the welfare of the community, although, as things are at present, they can take no effective action on its behalf.)

For administrative purposes, the village comes under three institutions—the government, the municipality and the community council. The field of the first is purely political; the municipality is short of money and of very little importance; the community council in fact carries out the necessary improvements and development work. Without any encouragement from the authorities of the department and province, the Indians have been carrying out the projects they consider most desirable or accepting suggestions from people living in Lima who originally came from the community.

At present the following projects are under way: building of a road to link up with that from Lima to Yauyos; building of trenches on the *puna* for dipping sheep; improvement of the dam for the provision of water; building of premises for religious brotherhoods and institutions.

The prevailing system of individual ownership, together with the continual splitting up of landholdings by inheritance, is at the root of certain rivalries which are affecting the sense of community of interests, though the feeling is still seen to be strong at seed-time and the various festivals.

Tupe is a community in which craftsmanship is dying out. Not long ago the women's clothes were almost entirely made from materials woven by the peasants, but now manufactured products are gaining ground and the peasants are losing their old skill at the loom. The people are quick, alert and alive to developments, but conservative, as the survival of their language shows.

The extensive areas set aside for pasture could support large flocks and herds, which would enable the community to supply the coastal market. The sale of wool is already bringing in a large income, but the money is not very wisely used. The productive capacity of the narrow gorge where the peasants grow their crops on long-established terraces is steadily diminishing as a result of the use of unsatisfactory farm implements, unskilful repair of the terraces, and the shortage of water at certain times, although there are lakes on the mountain tops. The peasants all own small plots of land in various parts of the gorge and cultivate them by different methods. There are three separate forms of labour: *minga*, or work by a man or woman paid by the day; *turna* or voluntary help given in the hope of receiving similar help known as *returna* (this is the old system of *ayni*); and finally *jajina* or communal labour (the traditional *minka*).

The diet here, unlike that of the population of Taquile, is poor and inadequate although, generally speaking, the economic standard of the latter community is the lower. Trade is well established; the members of the community begin young and learn to trade by taking cattle or cheese down to the coast; some of them have opened small shops in the village, of which there are at present 15.

The influence of Catholicism is declining, although the religious institutions and brotherhoods dating from the seventeenth century are still powerful. From the economic standpoint, the latter act as small banks for their members. The loans they make by the year never exceed 200 soles (about £4) and the interest is constantly added to the capital. There are about thirty of these brotherhoods, and every peasant belongs to at least one of them. The idea that invested capital should produce interest is thus well established in this community.

The introduction of the products of modern technology, tools and utensils, ready-made clothing, books, magazines, powerful lamps, wireless sets, etc., is steadily proceeding. The members of the community are aware of what is needed in the way of machinery and organization to develop the area, and they try to give their children better opportunities by sending them to school in the towns. Tupe is a community in transition and, like many others, is waiting to become a part of a larger entity which will give it a new lease of life. For the time being, it is drifting along by itself, without problems of landownership, rivalries with its neighbours, or imminent dangers besetting it.

THE COMMUNITY OF MUQUIYAUYO[1]

This community enjoys a very definite prestige which, since 1921, has spread beyond the frontiers of Peru and accounts for the interest still taken by anthropologists in Muquiyauyo. It is a typical example of what a mestizo group in the central mountain area can achieve by its own unaided efforts and without guidance from any but its own members. Starting in 1921, the village, as a result of a combination of various circumstances, made a real advance which, however, could not be continued for a number of internal and external reasons. One reason was the fear to which any achievement by those regarded as 'natives' always gives rise. During the last 20 years they have, accordingly, been seriously hampered by a campaign of constant opposition, the result of which has been to some extent to break down their former sense of unity and common interest.

The factors which made the development of the community possible were the following:

1. Two thousand inhabitants, in possession of some eight square miles of fertile ground, producing such abundant crops as to permit the sale of the surplus, and who displayed a strong community spirit.
2. Until 1900 there was a clearly marked division into castes (mestizo and Indian), each of which had its own authorities. Since then the social organization has changed and the land has been divided up; collective ownership has given way to private ownership, but the pasture-grounds are still communal property, as are a few plots of cultivated ground allotted to the Church, the school and the community; these plots, incidentally, bring in a considerable income. Four divisions or quarters have been established, among which the population is divided; Indians and mestizos have thus been brought into the same system and their efforts united.
3. Through the school, an energetic education campaign benefited both Indians and mestizos and rapidly provided Muquiyauyo with qualified leaders whose influence was readily accepted. Education was the basis on which the teachers and organizers relied for the future development of the community.
4. The community found that its original capital, furnished by the contributions of its members, was considerably increased by the fines imposed for failure to take part in communal work and by the interest of 2 and 5 per cent charged on the loans granted, up to a maximum of 200 soles, to its members. The main reason for the economic success was the good agricultural yield and the existence of such markets in the vicinity as Jauja, the capital of the province, 6

1. Richard N. Adams, 'A Study of Labour Preference in Peru', in: *Human Organization*, Vol. 10, No. 3, Autumn 1951.

miles away; Huancayo, where the biggest market in Peru is held each Sunday, 30 miles away; and Lima, 167 miles away by rail and road. This economic prosperity is shared by all the communities in the valley of the Mantaro.

5. The steady development of neighbouring mining centres quickly began to attract workers. The influence was felt in Muquiyauyo as in the other communities, and gradually its young men went to work in the mines, the good wages paid them increasing the economic strength of the community. Those who were regarded as 'Indians' in the community saw that they could get good jobs there, and this gave rise to a spirit of real competition. (Within the group, the Indians and mestizos are still distinguished, although 'outsiders' class them all as Indians.)

The various circumstances created an atmosphere conducive to progress which, in 1918, led the members of the community to establish an electric power station. They formed a company, studied the relevant legislation, took the necessary steps and in 1921 opened the Febo Electricity Works, the establishment of which cost nearly 500,000 soles (£10,000). The station is equipped with two 75 h.p. Westinghouse units which have been working day and night since that date. The feed channel is 2 miles long and has a discharge of 3 cubic metres a second. Its maximum power is 150 kilowatts; it provides electric light for three settlements, including Jauja. The organization for running and maintaining it is still communally owned. The station has a staff of five and a manager. At present it is making a profit of 18,000 soles a month (£350), which is a high percentage on the initial investment, despite its bad administration.

Some of the money collected was invested in 1950 in a company, formed with a native of Muquiyauyo living at Huancayo, with the object of buying machinery for a spinning mill. The company, Textil Muquiyauyo, has a capital of 300,000 soles; it owns its premises, which have been handed over to it by the community. The machines have been installed but it has not so far been possible to get them going. This means that a considerable amount of capital is lying idle.

The other technical innovation is the Communal Mill which has been running since 1927. Each member of the company pays only 40 cents per *arroba* (25 lb) while others have to pay 80 cents. The mill is run by a 10 h.p. dynamo. The staff includes a miller, who is paid, on a percentage basis, by the month, and a voluntary manager.

Why did such a community, once embarked on the process of industrialization, fail to complete it, in spite of the equipment acquired?

The following are some of the factors that have helped to cause this stagnation:

1. The ratio of people to land has been completely changed. The population increased from 2,000 in 1918 to 5,100 in 1952. Of the eight square miles intended for the cultivation of food crops, half is now used for growing feeding-stuffs for the cattle and sheep. The ratio has thus been completely reversed. This is due to the very large production of milk—220 gallons a day for five months of the year and 70 for the remaining months, almost all of which is produced for sale outside Muquiyauyo and brings in a considerable income. Malnutrition is beginning to affect the community. There is clear evidence of it in the poor work done by the school-children. The problem is becoming serious and efforts are being made to solve it (mistakenly) by bringing into use part of the forest area, although there are still non-irrigated lands where the water problem, though difficult, is not insoluble.

2. The new generations have not fully replaced their predecessors, most of whom have now died or emigrated. The school has ceased to play the leading part

it did some thirty years ago; the old enthusiasm has abated. The best members of the population have left the district for the mining centres and there is no family which has not at least one of its members in the mines. This work pays well, especially as Muquiyauyo still has a good reputation and anyone coming from the community is well received. It is possible to earn from 25 to 30 soles a day, and workers who rise to be foremen may earn as much as 2,500 soles a month. Many of them die of silicosis and diseases of the lung. Any member of the community who is away pays 150 soles a month to the community for failing to take part in the communal work.

Another group, those who have continued their training for a trade or profession after leaving school, seek work in Lima or in the main towns of the departments, there being no opportunities for them in the community. Several members are given scholarships by the commune in order to complete their education, but the best of them are lost to the community (which was not so 30 or 40 years ago).

3. The hostility of the larger neighbouring villages and the indifference, and later the hostility, of the central government, have been a serious handicap, which many people consider to be at the root of the decline in initiative. The inevitable internal struggles for improvement called for considerable efforts. Stimulus, understanding and support from outside would have been invaluable in carrying out the plans. But the reverse occurred; the leaders, constantly accused for being political agitators of the extreme left or fomentors of sedition, were imprisoned, and controls thwarted all further advance.

4. The technical advances that the members of the community were trying to introduce confronted them with problems for which they were not mentally prepared. The management of the electric power station and the spinning mill was never efficient, and this was one of the fundamental reasons for failure. Four years ago, the people were cheated by a commercial firm from which they had purchased additional equipment to improve the power station for a sum of 300,000 soles; two transformers which could not be coupled to the existing machinery stood idle for two years although, in the end, one of them was adapted and is now in use. Several managers also embezzled large sums. No strict supervision was exercised over the installation of the street lamps in Jauja. If the receipts were well administered, the present income could be doubled.

Muquiyauyo is a mestizo community living in the western part of the lovely and fertile valley of the Mantaro; its fields lie on perfectly flat ground, which makes farming easier. Some of the people still speak Kechua at home. The village is built on the chequer-board plan of a Spanish town; it has 35 shops and an omnibus providing a daily service to Jauja and Huancayo; it has no drinking water or sanitary services.

In conclusion, we may draw attention to a few important aspects of the Peruvian Indian communities.

1. The Peruvian Indian communities take an inferior place in the cultural structure of present-day Peru. There are, however, shades of difference, and variations in the stage of development, to be seen among them, as in the cases of Taquile, Tupe and Muquiyauyo.

2. The common denominator is a consumption economy based on the combination of agriculture and stock-rearing (the latter on a small scale).

3. From the cultural point of view, they are ill equipped to cope with the changes

to which the introduction of modern technology for the purposes of industrial development may give rise.

4. They constitute ideal basic units for the development of a large region of Peru— the mountain district where more than half the population of the country lives. They can be made productive, supplying the nation with adequate quantities of foodstuffs, and can help in the development of modern industry, maintaining a proper balance between the number of people and the area of arable land available. They were able to produce a considerable quantity of crops between the twelfth and sixteenth centuries, under the Inca empire.

5. The cultural development of several of them (e.g., Muquiyauyo) shows that, in this respect, no advance is possible, even for an energetic and progressive community, unless an over-all plan, supported by the State, is brought into effect. Any such undertaking must be based on a firm determination to improve conditions in the communities. This means that a 'comprehensive' campaign is necessary.

6. Anthropological and statistical studies are absolutely necessary as a preliminary to any planning.

7. The process of acculturation is rapidly making Peru a predominantly mestizo nation and is bringing modern knowledge to the underdeveloped communities, but it is not working satisfactorily. Acculturation is proceeding haphazardly and there is no single body which can really be said to direct it. From this point of view, the setback in Muquiyauyo has much to teach us.

POSSIBLE CONSEQUENCES OF RECENT ECONOMIC AND SOCIAL DEVELOPMENTS AMONG THE ESKIMOS OF THULE

J. Malaurie

Until 1951 the polar Eskimos living in the region of Thule, on the north-west coast of Greenland, between latitudes 76° and 79° N., offered an interesting example of an archaic and comparatively isolated community—a surviving fragment of the past, as it were. The recent establishment of an American military base in the very heart of this tribe's territory has created a situation the results of which merit investigation, more especially as the future of the community is uncertain.

I spent over a year among the Thule Eskimos, making a survey from a purely geographical point of view, and by travelling a great deal in the region, collected much interesting information regarding means of subsistence, family incomes, the psychology of the Eskimo compared with that of the Greenlander, and vital statistics. But the conclusions to be drawn apply, of course, only to that particular area. Thule is undoubtedly an extreme case, in which physical factors are of decisive importance. Since the Eskimos live on the outskirts of the inhabited world, leading a necessarily precarious existence, their scope for adaptation is small and their creative capacity reduced to a minimum. I have no intention, therefore, of suggesting that these conclusions are universally valid; they apply only within the Arctic Circle, and to a certain part of that region.

It has long been realized that a problem arises when a primitive society is introduced to our forms of civilization. But the possible solutions of that problem have not always been very clearly described. In any case, a purely sociological approach to the question of contact and interaction between human communities differing in technological structure would lead us far astray if it were not preceded by a geographical study of the area concerned. An economic assessment of the situation and of ways in which it can be exploited has to be drawn up, and it may be thought desirable to attempt a geographical, or, one might say, oecological classification in preference to any other. Regional divisions are in the first place a matter of topology, and a civilization results in the first place from acclimatization in some particular spot. Since the 'real needs' of the Thule group are primarily material ones, and since their satisfaction is a prior condition of any social or cultural progress, this report does not deal with such social, religious or political phenomena as might be engendered by planned development. Such phenomena must, of course, be foreseen; and if given their rightful place in the general system they might lead to appreciable modification of the arguments here set forth

The small tribe of polar Eskimos (it has only 302 members), in the most northern of all human communities, is cut off from southern Greenland by Melville Bay, and from Baffin Island and Ellesmere Island by Lancaster Sound, Jones Sound and Smith Sound. In 1950 it was living in almost complete isolation from the rest of the world.

Range of movement is restricted, and sustained contact with neighbouring countries prevented, by variations in the condition of the ice due to the warming of the Arctic waters. This primitive civilization has seldom, in the course of its history, been able to enjoy the stimulating and enriching results of contact with peoples of differing culture. These Eskimos come, in all probability, from the south-west (Baffin Island). Recent studies devoted to them—and in particular to their music[1]—suggest that they are of American, not of Paleo-Asiatic origin, and that at some fairly remote period they were in touch with the Red Indians. In all likelihood, these northern nomads were settled on the coast of Smith Sound by the twelfth, or at latest the thirteenth century, if not before the year 1000. At a very early stage, the tribe—which was thus living on the route by which all Eskimos migrating from Canada travelled to the east and west coasts of Greenland—was cut off from the west coast (Upernivik, visited fairly regularly by Europeans). As is to be expected at this latitude, the climate is extremely harsh, with three months of darkness during the winter and only three months (June, July and August) with an average temperature above 0°C. The population is semi-nomadic, and has retained its traditional economic system, which was for a long period entirely self-sufficient. This is based on hunting, and is closely linked with local resources—walrus, seal, fox, an occasional bear, narwhal (these last are gradually disappearing). It might thus be supposed that their margin of existence is narrow, but this is not the case. They follow a system of semi-stocking and planned economy, and as they are few and their needs are small, the margin is quite adequate. Though it is difficult to estimate how many people could subsist on the available resources, it seems not unreasonable to estimate that if the standard of living remained low and hunting and fishing continued to be strictly regulated, the population could be doubled. Natural resources are varied and, in comparison with those on other parts of the Greenland coast, fairly considerable. A study of the incomes—in money and in kind—of the chief families in each village gives an approximate level which is much higher than that of the tribes in the southern regions of Upernivik and Umanak, who have a similar economic system. This is due to certain hydrographic and climatic conditions. Moreover, in such a thinly-populated area, hunting becomes really profitable. And thinly populated it certainly is—with 0.1 inhabitants per kilometre of coastline (1923), as against 0.51 per kilometre for the whole inhabited part of Greenland, and 0.89[2] for Julianehaab, the largest colony on the west coast.

Thanks to all these different factors, the colony of Thule is one of the most flourishing of Eskimo communities. This prosperity is reflected in its finances. During a single year (March 1950 to March 1951), the sale of skins and related products at the trading posts brought in 75,748 krone,[3] unequally divided between 70 to 75 families. Until recently, therefore, Thule was one of the few settlements of Eskimo hunters in Greenland, if not in the whole of the Arctic, whose budget showed a large credit balance.

Before entering upon a description of the way of life of the Thule Eskimos, it will perhaps be advisable to give a few dates. The tribe was discovered in

---

1. Ch. Leden, 'Ueber die Musik der Smith Sund Eskimos und ihre Verwandtschaft mit der Musik der Amerika-nischen Indianer', *Medd. Om Gronland* nr. 3, Copenhagen, 1952.
2. K. Birket-Smith, *Greenland*, Copenhagen, 1928.
3. One krone = one English shilling.

1818 by John Ross, but had no prolonged or formative relations with the outer world until visited by Robert E. Peary during the series of Polar expeditions which he carried out between 1892 and 1909. The first permanent trading station was established by Rasmussen in 1910, but it was not until 1937 that the Danish Government assumed official responsibility for the territory. The whole population is now Christian, the last member having been baptized in 1934.

This group of 302 persons provides a typical example of an isolated community: and while this is in itself a question of genetics, it has to be considered in connexion with an essentially demographic problem—that of the actual survival of so small a group.

'A study of vital statistics in small, isolated areas points to the conclusion that stability and continuity can be maintained only where are more than 500 inhabitants. Isolated groups of between 300 and 550 inhabitants are in an unbalanced state, from which they may either achieve stability or rapidly disappear.'[1]

A careful analysis[2] of the structure of the population in Thule indicates that these figures are too hard and fast, and should be modified. It is, however, true that the demographic situation of the tribe has always been precarious. It had 253 members in 1893, 207 in 1908, and 251 in 1923. The population is thus now slightly increasing, at the rate of 0.8 per cent per annum. Lengthy contact with whites has lowered resistance to disease. Tuberculosis has developed. Moreover, owing to considerable in-breeding, cases of deformity, though not numerous, are sufficiently frequent to have an economic effect (being a burden on the community).

The level of population is maintained only by a narrow margin. The birth rate is 173 per 1,000—a low figure for a community with a high marriage rate, and where birth control is unknown. This is to be explained by the unusual prevalence of sterility, due in part to in-breeding. Out of 51 women whose childbearing period was over, eight, or 16 per cent, had proved sterile. The introduction of Christianity may also have helped to lower the birth rate, since it has resulted in strict monogamy and the abolition of sexual promiscuity. In this connexion, the Thule group offers opportunities for investigating a number of problems affecting the structure of a very small population. It sets the problem of the isolated community in a clear light, and provides an interesting opportunity of testing the latest evolutionary theories regarding native peoples inhabiting a limited and sparsely-populated area. The investigation of these theories would certainly be facilitated by the provision of information concerning other isolated groups, especially in the arctic regions of Canada; but so far as I know, this is still very scarce.

One conclusion already emerges: if this tribe is to maintain its 1951 level, a certain amount of cross-breeding or, at best, immigration will be required. In any case, no reduction in the general cost of living (which is rising, because of improved living standards and the construction of public buildings, such as a school and a hospital) will be possible without an appreciable increase in population.

Are economic resources sufficient to allow of this? In other words, what is the optimum population? The impression is that 'the stability of such a population is ... ensured by its maintenance at a level somewhere between the biological

---

1. Livio Livi, *Population*. No. 3, 1951, p. 493.
2. J. Malaurie, L. Tabah, J. Sutter, 'L'Isolat Esquimau de Thulé', *Population*, Paris, 1952, No. 4, pp. 657-93.

minimum and the economic maximum. If it falls below the biological minimum, degeneracy sets in and the birth rate dwindles to vanishing point. If it rises above the economic maximum there is famine',[1] unless the protecting state intervenes.

The Eskimos have for centuries owed their existence to a well-established balance between local resources and their own minimum requirements. For some years past, in the arctic region, this balance has been disturbed—the needs of the population are increasing.

It is to the credit of the Danish Government that it has taken every possible opportunity of using the trading-post—that traditional lever of colonization—to awaken new interests among the inhabitants. The Eskimos have completely surrendered to European customs, and have become yearly more dependent upon fox-trapping from which they obtain their chief element of barter. The introduction of such an economic system in this part of the world was, both from the material and the psychological point of view, quite as revolutionary in its effect as the introduction of Christianity; but many people regarded it as necessary. While the experiment has succeeded in Thule—because the district is rich in game, hunters are few and the administrative authorities vigilant—it is inadvisable except in such conditions, and can in any case provide only a temporary solution. As a means of supplying food—'a small-scale system operating in surroundings where productivity is low'—its efficacy is limited, partly because of the natural increase in the population, and partly because of the rise in the standard of living.[2] For since they came into contact with Europeans, the Eskimos have introduced gradual changes in their diet (increased consumption of margarine, coffee, tea and tobacco) and in their other habits (textiles are replacing seal skins and reindeer hides, wood, fuel oils and coal are being used). Halfway along the road to civilization, they are becoming more exacting, and are no longer to be satisfied with their local resources alone. It is not improbable that, in these economic circumstances, the population will rise above the safe maximum within the fairly near future. If fresh local activities cannot be developed to supplement the traditional economy, the region will soon be over-populated in the Malthusian sense of the term. As the hunting-grounds cannot be indefinitely extended and it is impossible to introduce any activities based on further exploitation of animal life, such as whale fishing or cod fishing, it is already open to speculation whether the future of this handful of human beings does not depend in the last resort—as history has shown in the case of the inhabitants of other barren regions—upon migration to the more fertile sub-arctic borderlands.

The Danish Government is already faced with a similar problem on the west coast of Greenland. Owing to the rise in the temperature of the Baffin Sea, which has caused the seals to migrate, the authorities have encouraged the Greenlanders to transform their manner of life whenever the supply of game is judged to have fallen below an adequate level. Thus, without regard to the traditional social structure, the men have for the past twenty-five years been urged to give up hunting and turn to fishing or stock-breeding. So the half-breed Greenlanders of the next generation, assembled in four or five small towns, will, like their Icelandic neighbours, look to fishing or its associated industries to satisfy all their needs.

In the course of this process of development, Denmark is making every effort

---

1. P. George, *Introduction à l'Étude Géographique de la Population du Monde*, Institut National d'Études Démographiques, Paris, 1951, p. 77.
2. ibid.

to teach the natives to guide their own civilization in the right direction, preserving all those individual features which are still of value, such as their language and folk-lore. In other words, the government is striving to Europeanize the life of the Eskimos without impoverishing it. This aim cannot, perhaps, be attained in every case, but the urgency of the economic problems must be borne in mind.

Such are the main lines of the policy followed for nearly two and a half centuries on the west coast of this big island, between latitudes 70° and 60° N. In the light of the experience thus gained, it has become evident that any study of cultural and social motivations and incentives in an archaic community should always be preceded by an assessment of existing and potential resources, since these must, in the long run, determine what results can be achieved.[1]

The disintegration of Eskimo society calls for an assessment of resources—it is a social problem. Even a small fluctuation, caused, for instance, by an epidemic or a food shortage, can place this handful of people in an alarming situation, and, in 1950, I found that from the sociological point of view its structure was equally frail.

The structure of any Eskimo community is, of course, admittedly fragile. In a society which has never developed beyond the embryonic stage, the spread of Christianity and education, the visits—however brief and intermittent—of European expeditions, and the introduction of modern technical processes have set up a condition of latent traumatism. Under the continual impact of these new forces, the traditional methods of tribal government have gradually fallen into disuse; they survived until 1951 only because the Danish authorities, both private and governmental, had wisely refrained—in 1910 and again in 1938—from disturbing the segregated and isolated life of the tribe. To all appearances it still leads a balanced existence, but the real situation is not reassuring.

The traditional religious theories of the people strike them today as untenable. Their legends and beliefs, no longer backed by the authority of the medicine-man, are gradually being forgotten. Relationships within the tribe, having lost their religious implications, are changing. In former times they were based on respect for the most experienced hunter; now they are conditioned, among the young men, by their degree of Europeanization—diplomas, bank accounts, administrative responsibilities. Instead of hunting in parties for bear or walrus, they go out individually to set traps. The spririt of fellowship, which was maintained by common interests, is now declining and giving place to an individualistic and commercial spirit, which, because of the demands of trade, is directed towards the outer world.

In fact, if we follow Lévi-Strauss's suggestion[2] and consider those 'external characteristics which affect the structure of what we call a primitive society and distinguish it from the type of society we regard as modern or civilized', we are forced to admit that they are no longer to be found in Thule. It may seem surprising that in such circumstances development should not have been more marked—until we remember the exceptional isolation of the polar Eskimos, which it has been government policy to maintain. But no investigator can fail to perceive that, despite its present compact appearance and economic prosperity, the traditional structure of this community is now merely a brittle shell. At any sudden contact with a civilization which is technologically more

1. Similar observations have recently been made in regard to present trends among the Eskimos in Alaska, by Margaret Lantis ('Present Status of the Alaskan Eskimos', *Science in Alaska*. Alaskan Science Conference-Arctic Institute of North America, Washington, June 1952, pp. 38-51).
2. Claude Lévi-Strauss, 'La Notion d'Archaïsme', *Cahiers Internationaux de Sociologie*, Vol. XII, 1952, p. 7.

advanced, the shell may be expected to crack. Labour will then become available for fresh undertakings. And conditions are such as to attract it towards an expanding economic area—though if the attraction is to be sufficiently strong, that area must be in the neighbourhood of the region to which the Eskimos are attached by sentiment.

Such, in very brief outline, was the situation in July 1951, when an American military base—with 10,000 men in the first year, reduced to 5,000 in 1952—was established in Thule itself. Its site was, of course, chosen for strategic rather than economic reasons, and it was purely by chance that this gigantic airfield was created close to an Eskimo settlement. The future will show whether a base situated farther north, in a better position from the economic point of view, will not prove more suitable than Thule for civil aviation.

In any case, the construction of this airfield, by complicating the problem of the future of the Thule Eskimos, has hastened the need for investigation. It is hardly necessary to add that this sudden encounter between a small tribe which was still living in the seal age and a mechanized, military civilization has given cause for very serious thought to all concerned. In the course of a few weeks, this community has undergone a positive transformation. Will it be able to draw steady benefit from the change? This depends partly on the adaptability of the people themselves, which we know to be considerable, but partly, too, on the speed with which new native leaders succeed in modernizing the local way of life while preserving some of its essential features. The tribe was saved from disintegration in 1951 because the Danish authorities on the spot, in full agreement with the American commanders of the base, decided to maintain the Eskimos' isolation by putting the airfield, as it were, out of bounds. Moreover, the Eskimos themselves, seized by an instinctive fear—and also because there was no work for them at the base and because they could no longer carry on their ordinary occupations in the immediate neighbourhood of Thule (the water was polluted by petrol, the seals migrated and there was noise and dust)—decided of their own accord to move 200 kilometres farther north, to the old village of Kranak.

It must not, however, be supposed that this northward flight will settle the difficulty for very long. There have been some interesting examples of counter-acculturation, but these are bound to be ephemeral. Though the Thule of legend has changed its site, the problem remains to be solved, and time is not on the side of the Eskimos. Increasing needs, the desire for a higher standard of living, and the proximity of the military base will combine, in this reservation, which is not an entirely watertight compartment—no reservation ever is—to bring about the disappearance of this primitive group, regarded as a specific social unit.

If its members are to be integrated, it is highly advisable for their integration to take place before their former social structure has degenerated too far—and they themselves with it. The tests I carried out with school-age children (Rorschach, the Zazzo cross-out, the Prudhommeau copied drawing), the particulars supplied by the local authorities, and above all the technological history of this race, reveal the people's extraordinary adaptability (mechanical skill, talent for learning languages, evident willingness). The stage of development they have already reached, together with their natural qualities, suggest that at the present moment they run no risk of being overmodernized. Their integration must, of course, be carefully planned, and too abrupt contacts avoided. It should also be possible to make use of their particular aptitudes—fur-farming, training them as guides for work in the mountains or rescue teams for use in plane crashes—to instruct them and encourage them to specialize. Such a policy, if introduced without delay and carried out with moderation and caution, may perhaps lead to the formation of a new type of Eskimo society.

In view of the limited resources available to these people, and the danger that their tribal structure may collapse as a result of the establishment of the military base, one wonders (though this to some extent contradicts what I have written elsewhere[1]) whether the opening of the Arctic to air traffic may not turn out to be providential for the Eskimo people—not in every case, but wherever local resources are insufficient to enable them to eke out a living by adding sea-fishing to hunting: their attachment to their native soil makes them shrink from migrating to any considerable distance. Only in the requirements of the infrastructure can such groups find new and profitable activities through which to satisfy their recently-awakened material and cultural needs. It is sincerely to be hoped that these new developments will not end by creating a situation which it is their specific purpose to prevent[2]—a situation in which the native population becomes doubly proletarian, having lost its tribal structure without acquiring any vocational qualifications.

1. J. Malaurie, 'Problèmes Économiques et Humains au Groenland. Note sur Thulé,' *Annales de Géographie*, Paris 1952, Vol. 326, pp. 291-7.
2. G. Balandier, 'Contribution à une Sociologie de la Dépendance', *Cahiers Internationaux de Sociologie*, Paris, 1952, Vol. XII, pp. 47-9. See also p. 57.

WESTERN TECHNOLOGY AND THE AUSTRALIAN ABORIGINES

A. P. Elkin

The Australian aborigines are dark, chocolate-skinned people of varying but usually medium height, with black wavy to curly hair, deep-set eyes and, as a rule, narrow and retreating foreheads. Generally classified with the aboriginal hill tribes of southern India, they probably became differentiated in the islands north of Australia. Moving into that continent, their food-gathering, hunting and fishing economy was, and has been, the basic factor in their adaptation. This has involved living, foraging and hunting in small groups, often long distances apart. To be organized in large groups would quickly strip a locality of natural foods and either kill or frighten off the game, as the aborigines realize during ceremonial and social gatherings. Consequently, the process of occupying Australia was one of hiving-off from group to group, each one related by descent to those behind it, and maintaining contact by intermarriage and exchange of articles.

Obviously too, the density of population, that is the area required to sustain a food-gathering group of families, depended on the rainfall and on the natural-food supply throughout the annual cycle. Consequently, the tropical coastal regions and parts of other coasts with a regular rainfall or at least with constant rivers, carried the densest native population, and the arid central and western regions the sparsest.

Several contrasts appear in the life of the peoples of the different types of habitat. In the former, life is more settled. Permanent adjustment has been made to the environment. There is neither need nor desire to leave it. Groups can meet together more often and for some weeks or even longer, not having to disperse very far during the working hours, that is, if the season is favourable. Indeed, it is common to see quite large camps of from 60 to 150 and even more persons, belonging to different clans and even tribes, foraging in different directions, but not necessarily only on their own clan or tribal territories. In this type of good country, too, while there are names of many clans, tribal names and distinctions are hard to determine. In fact, these are not of great importance.

On the other hand, in the drier regions on the borders of the tropics or along the inland rivers, tribal areas are both large and distinct. Within these there are usually well-defined districts, over which certain clans or other sub-groups have the chief food-gathering rights, and to which they are bound by mythological and spiritual beliefs. These small groups spend most of their time in the food-quest apart from each other, only meeting in large bodies in good seasons. As a result, difference of dialect, and even of custom, arises within one tribe.

146

Finally, in the arid desert regions, the picture is of slow but continuous migration in a general south-easterly direction in search of oases and better country. The moving groups, stationary for a few generations or less, are linked by mythology not to regions, to tribal or other territories, but to ancestral roads along which the heroes of old, and their own forbears, ever moved forward, only occasionally and temporarily moving back north. In such a region, language, custom and belief vary little over vast areas, and because of the constant mobility and the struggle to live, the cultural heritage is meagre.

INTELLECTUAL AND TECHNOLOGICAL ADAPTATION

In each type and sub-type of habitat, the Australian food-gatherers have built up throughout the generations a detailed body of knowledge of the local environment and have developed skills in exploiting its food resources. The food-use of everything that lives, grows and moves has been learnt, and processes, some of them quite involved, have been developed for removing unpleasant or dangerous properties from certain fruits and roots. The times or seasons, the places and conditions for finding food and game, are known. So, too, are the signs or interrelationship of natural phenomena and species. The behaviour of forms of life, some of them of no direct value in themselves, have become, through association, indications of weather-changes or of the increase or appearance of animals or plants which are edibly important. It is this detailed and associative knowledge which explains the true saying that Europeans, never mind how clever, perish in the Australian bush in spite of the presence of sufficient food and water around them, but not recognized.

In addition, craftsmanship of no mean order is associated with the food quest. It is not merely a matter of collecting roots (yams); some creatures must be dug out, so a digging stick is made, and a wooden dish for carrying what is found. Tree-honey is obtained by cutting the bough open or off, stone tomahawks with handles being made and used for this and other purposes. The larger marsupials, emus and bustards, are not only tracked, wind direction being studied and camouflage used, but the spear is hurled truly and forcefully with the aid of a spear-thrower which extends the hunter's arm and adds to the leverage available. The spear itself, simple though it may seem, requires technical ability on the part of its maker, who works according to the tribal pattern. The shaft must be straight and well-balanced, and the point of wood or stone, whether barbed or not, firmly fixed. Heat is used for bending and straightening the shaft, and a stone chisel for smoothing it. Likewise, the making of stone spear-points by knapping or pressure-flaking, is a skilled process. Stone flakes with a sharp edge are used for cutting food, and nets, lines, hooks and special spears for fishing. The boomerang, especially the returning type, which is sometimes used for bringing down birds as they fly overhead in flocks, is a work of highly skilled craftsmanship. This weapon and the spear are also used in fighting, while shields and clubs are only made for that purpose.

SOCIAL AND RELIGIOUS ADAPTATION

The aborigines' adaptation to their environment is however not only ecological, intellectual and technological, it is also social and religious. Conformity is required to patterns of behaviour which have been proved satisfactory for mutual existence. It is sanctioned by mythology, and enforced by punishments which are ordered or allowed by the elders. This behaviour is based on the internal and external relations between members of the food-gathering groups. Its basis is reciprocity, correlated with kinship-groupings. This includes respect for each other's few possessions, mutual assistance under prescribed circumstances, and the duty of making gifts of food and implements, weapons and articles of adornment.

In spite, however, of knowledge, skill and social co-operation, the rain or flood sometimes fails and the normal food supply does not materialize. Such is the lesson of experience. It is a contingency which has occurred in the past more than once, with disastrous results. Tribal existence depends on forestalling, shortening or enduring it. The primary effort is to ensure that it does not occur. This is done by re-enacting in ritual the creative and formative period, that is, the acts which were associated, according to myth and doctrine, with the birth or first appearance in the region of the desired species and phenomena. These rites are often performed at sites directly connected with that formative epoch; or the places as well as the heroic deeds are represented in symbol, art, chant and act.

Such in brief outline was—and still is, in a few regions—the aborigines' integrated adaptation to the environment: ecological, intellectual, technological, social and religious.

PHASES OF CONTACT AND ITS EFFECTS

From 1788 onwards, European settlement began at selected coastal centres, on the bases of imports, of food production and of pasturage. It was rapid and comparatively dense. The food-gathering aborigines, unaccustomed to competition or invasion, and requiring all their country in order to live, were almost completely deprived of the means of existence before they could readjust themselves. Neither their body of knowledge, their skill and technical equipment, nor their social organization provided a means of meeting this ecological disturbance and this contingency. They became hangers-on on the outskirts of what had been their own hunting, social and ceremonial lands. Pauperism was their lot. The inadequate rations which they received from the white man did not make up for the loss of their natural foods, and this loss, together with alcohol, clothes and diseases, for none of which their experience or any mythological precedents had prepared them, brought about their extinction very rapidly. Some mixed-blood descendants remain, but very few full-bloods.

The spread of settlement into what became the rural regions was a slower process. Farms and pasturages gradually pushed out into tribal lands. The aborigines frequently gathered (stole) some of the settlers' crops and speared sheep and cattle, for their own best food-gathering and hunting areas were naturally the first to be occupied. The settlers, however, allowed by the government to take up the land, or at least not prevented from doing so, resented the aborigines' depredations, and clashes occurred. In some cases they received official sanction and help for their action; often they took the law into their own hands. With guns and force generally, the settlers established their position. Many aborigines in most rural areas were killed. The remnants became wanderers, roaming from one district to another in their own tribal territories, working occasionally, but homeless and aimless. In different parts of Australia from 1860 onwards, pity began to be felt and Protection Policies were drawn up; but these were only designed to protect them from further ill-treatment and injustice, and to dole out rations and blankets—in short, to smooth their dying pillow. Such was the comfortable rationalization of the era. Few full-bloods remain in these older settled regions, though most of the 30,000 mixed-blood aborigines belong there.

As the battle was won in the rural farming and denser pastoral regions of the continent, Europeans spread further with their flocks and herds, but into regions both tropical and arid, where to this day only sparse pastoral settlement prevails. The settlers, few in number and widely separated because of the need for large grazing areas, did not, to the outward eye, occupy the whole of the tribal territories into which they intruded. The aborigines could still go about their own affairs in much their old way over most of their country. It was only as the settler's cattle found or were driven to the permanent waters and best feeding grounds that clashes arose, for these were the natives' main camping and hunting grounds. They inevitably disturbed the cattle, and occasionally speared them. The settler's aim was to keep the aborigines away from such places. On the other hand, being almost completely dependent on the local natives for labour, he soon realized that if he antagonized them, he would be helpless. Neither driving them away, nor killing nor jailing them would get the stock mustered, branded and dispatched to market. The settler therefore encouraged some of the able-bodied men to work for him in return for rations, tobacco and some clothes. But this meant that older men and women and children soon camped near the settler's stockyards, and that what he paid to his workers went round the camp. He could do nothing about these dependants.

The aboriginal elders and leaders had learnt that hostility did not pay—that they could not get rid of the white intruder and his cattle. They also realized that the settlers, and later the pastoral company managers, depended on them for labour. Moreover they felt a growing desire for the white man's food and some of his goods. They therefore regarded the settler as part of the changed environment to which they had to adapt themselves. This they did by sitting down on the settler, and supplying workers who did just the minimum to keep his place going so that they would get their share of food and goods. Many a small settler has recognized that he was really working for the natives, but he had himself become so adapted to the situation that he would not be content elsewhere.

Thus a state of equilibrium was reached, broken only occasionally by loss of self-control. But it did not make for progress, either for the aborigines or for the country. The latter was not well worked, and the local native population decreased on almost all pastoral stations. The changed diet and manner of life, and the fundamental loss of purpose were factors involved. Women frequently objected to rearing children merely to be used by the white man.

This state of more or less adequate mutual adaptation (intelligent parasitism on the part of the aborigines) prevailed on the frontiers of settlement until the 1930s, and indeed still prevails in some parts. During the thirties, however, positive policies were evolved in the states and in the Northern Territory, which since the war have been increasingly put into operation. They are designed to ensure the aborigines' physical, educational and economic progress. The goal is assimilation into the general economic, social and political life of Australia. Efficient health services now operate in the north and centre of the continent, as well as in the settled regions. New employment regulations for aborigines have come into operation, particularly in the Northern Territory and adjacent regions, governing wages, housing, sanitation and the prices of goods sold in the settler's or pastoral station stores. In the same Territory in particular, a forward policy of education of full-blood children has been set in operation by the Commonwealth Office of Education, and—most significant—the Commonwealth Government's extension of child endowment to full-blood children living in institutions such as missions, State Homes or even on cattle stations under certain conditions, has proved, in some cases, that the aborigines can increase in numbers. This is the effect of providing adequate diet for, and care of, expectant and nursing mothers as well as supplementary foods and clinic services for infants and children.

Associated with these forward moves in policy is the growing realization by employers of aboriginal labour, often against their former custom and prejudices, that improved conditions of employment and of life generally for the aborigines will be to their own interest. In addition, particularly since the war, as a result of contact with, and work for, the fighting services, the aborigines in the north have shown an increasing appreciation of European culture, especially of its economic, recreational, medical and educational aspects. The white man no longer just symbolizes, or is a purveyor of, flour, beef, tea, sugar, tobacco, razors, knives, clothing and a few other articles. The younger aborigines are on the march to become part of, or to play an intelligent part in, the new way of life. This is the turning point for which some of us have been seeking. It is the tide in the affairs of man which must be taken at the flood.

PART-ABORIGINES

Every year in different parts of Australia a few persons of part-aboriginal descent pass quietly into the general community; they are either light-skinned, or have made good by steady work and independence. Some of these obtain certificates of exemption from acts and regulations governing aborigines. This enables them to apply for the state franchise if they do not already possess it, to purchase alcohol, or in the cases of persons of over 50 per cent aboriginal descent, to receive Commonwealth Social Service Benefits. For the purpose of these benefits and of the Commonwealth franchise, the Commonwealth regards half and lighter castes as full citizens. In New South Wales, Victoria and South Australia, all persons of whatever degree of aboriginal descent possess both the state and Commonwealth franchise.

About 40 per cent of acknowledged part-aborigines live in the poorer parts of cities and country towns or on the outskirts of the latter. The conditions are frequently unsatisfactory, but they regard themselves as independent and, when there is no economic depression, are able to obtain plenty of employment—the men mainly unskilled work in the towns, and farming and pastoral work of various kinds outside the towns. In cities they are mostly employed in semi-skilled tasks in factories, but some work as artisans and others as labourers. Females in the country do domestic work mainly, but some are now working in shops, and a few have become nurses and teachers. In the cities, many work in factories.

About 20 per cent of all part-aborigines live on government settlements under a prescribed degree of control. In some cases, as in Queensland and South Australia, these communities are industrialized, the men learning trades, and working for wages on the farm or cattle station, or in the sawmill, workshop or factory connected with the settlement. In New South Wales, these settlements are really only managed communities from which the employable men and women go out to daily or weekly work. Schools, hospitals, stores, churches and recreation facilities are provided.

Finally, in New South Wales in particular, there are many aboriginal reserves, on which a total of nearly 3,000 part-aborigines live, often in houses provided by the government, under the somewhat distant supervision of the police, or of a schoolteacher if a special school has been found necessary. The men go out to work. This scheme is a stage along the road to complete independence.

The problem of the part-aborigines is social and psychological. In country districts prejudice against them is marked, even to the extent of not wanting the children at the state schools. This causes an inferiority complex, with the result that many do not sustain the effort to make a success of the work they undertake. Thus a vicious circle is established. Further, with very few exceptions, they have not tried to establish themselves as independent farmers of tradesmen, although administrations are encouraging them to do this. In some states, too, the policy is to build standard houses in country towns, to be rented or sold to those part-aborigines who show that they are likely to live as self-respecting citizens.

In the larger cities, particularly in Sydney, there is little prejudice against these people. Their children attend the state schools, and no work of which they are capable is denied them. Some are living in good houses, even obtaining them in general housing schemes. Many, however, are congregated in congested areas so as to be together, and also because there is a housing shortage.

FULL-BLOOD ABORIGINES AND TECHNICAL CHANGE

There are about 50,000 full-blood aborigines in the sparsely populated regions of Australia. Given full implementation of present policies with regard to health, education and employment, depopulation should be arrested, particularly as they desire more and more to share in the material benefits of our economic system.

This desire, as already noted, is not new. The advantage of iron and steel over stone for implements and weapons was recognized in the early days of contact, whether with Macassans in Arnhem Land or with Europeans elsewhere. Ready-made axes and knives not only saved all the time previously required for making these articles from stone, but lessened the labour and time required for manufacturing all wooden implements, weapons and objects, from spear shafts to boomerangs, and from dishes to canoes. Stone chisels and engravers were still used, but gradually gave way to blades and points of iron and stout wire. In some regions too, iron and wire were used for spear-points, harpoons and fish-hooks. Skill and time, however, were still required in the processes of manufacture, and also in food-gathering and hunting. Ritual, too, was still believed to be necessary, with its severe call on time, thought and physical energy.

Thus, though iron made life somewhat easier from a technical point of view, it did not cause a revolution either in the way of life or in the standard of living. It was included in the system, and was sought, as in earlier days suitable stone was sought. Any pieces or type of iron which could be obtained from the white man or from his property were used. Sometimes hours of laborious work with stone tools were required to shape it, but the finished article had a lasting value which the stone tools did not possess. In other words, with the purpose and design in their minds, the aborigines showed themselves capable of patient industry and of some technical achievement.

The significant social change came when the aborigines saw that they could obtain meat without making spears and hunting, flour without gathering and grinding seeds, and sugar without running bees to their hives and chopping these down or out. The only requirements were to sit down on the settler or missionary and do what he wanted—to a limited extent. Other foods and tobacco were obtained. In addition, new wants were created by the white man's bias that some clothes should be worn, rugs used in the cold weather, and ground sheets by the stockmen. Matches, too, saved fire-making or carrying lighted fire-sticks; and leather straps, the necessity of making native rope. Finally mirrors, combs and other luxuries became desired.

Thus, instead of being parasitic on nature, with all the effort, skill and knowledge this required, the aborigines became parasitic, or at least dependent, on the white man. In this way they obtained enough to keep them alive with a minimum of effort. Instead of hunting, the young men rode after the cattle or sheep, and liked it. Instead of making implements and weapons, except occasionally, the men helped the white man erect buildings and fences, and—in later years—assisted him with his windmills, engines and even motor cars. The women, instead of foraging for roots, seeds and small animals, worked in and around the settler's or manager's house, cleaning, cooking, and carrying water in kerosene tins to the vegetable garden. The bigger the station, the more organized and varied the types of work.

Clearly this was a revolution in the aboriginal way of life, a revolution which has occurred on hundreds of pastoral properties in Australia; a revolution caused by the intrusion of a food-producing and highly technical economy—a revolution from which there could be no turning back. Aborigines whose tribal territory has been given over to pastoral pursuits for a couple of generations, have changed from semi-nomadic, separated groups of food-gatherers to a settled and more compact group associated directly and indirectly with that industry. Their corroborees (or public dances and songs) and sacred ceremonies are held near the main camp. Except for brief changes they have little desire to roam or 'go walkabout', as it is called. Mustering, branding and droving cattle have replaced the movement and excitement of the chase. Moreover, the country is no longer reliable for food-gathering and hunting, the cattle (or sheep) and horses having in dry times eaten it out, and the marsupials and reptiles having been starved out or frightened away. The aborigines' lot is henceforth cast with the white man and his means of livelihood, and this they have begun to recognize.

Opportunely so, because the white man's successful use and development of the usable inland parts of both tropical and arid Australia depends on the intelligent and willing labour of the aborigines—not on the static condition of equilibrium referred to above.

Therefore the present positive policies, their implementation and extension, must aim at ensuring the aborigines a just share in the pastoral industry or in any other industry which is developed in those regions where they have passed from a food-gathering economy to a settled way of life; mainly as an adjunct to the pastoral industry, though in some cases around missions and townships, where they provide labour. Moreover, they have not only passed from the use of stone to iron tools, but to familiarity with mechanical equipment of many kinds, windmills and road graders, engines and electric light, motor-cars and aeroplanes. When sick a flying-doctor comes; if arrested the policeman takes them in a motor vehicle; if they go somewhere along a road, they are unlucky if they are not given a lift in a passing lorry.

The mechanical side, however, is not only a matter of interest and use. Aborigines have shown that they make good technicians and mechanics. Given the training, based on good education and a growing understanding of responsibility, they will acquit themselves well. Further, experience on some stations and missions, and in Army Labour Corps, has shown that they quickly appreciate hygiene, housing, sleeping off the ground, eating at tables and caring for their clothes; especially when this is associated with just conditions of work, and with what they regard as adequate reward.

Finally, one other very big change is on the way as a result of the change of economy. Whereas authority in the past rested in the elders, through the secret life of which they were the masters, it is now passing to the head of the stock-camp, to the boss on the cattle station, and to the patrol officer of the Department of Native Affairs. The secret ceremonial life, which was integrated with the seasons and the food quest, and took a lot of time, tends to be modified and shortened, and to lose much of its significance. During the transition, some old men try to regain authority through a somewhat inverted use of rituals, or through magic. But it is a losing battle. The future is with the educated, money-earning aboriginal men and women within the general economic, political and legal system, which less than 100 years ago was unknown in the northern and inland regions of Australia.

The immediate problems are the relating of education to economic opportunity, region by region; the stepping up of the pastoral industry to contribute to the world's meat supply, as well as to increase opportunities for what should be an increasing aboriginal population; and the development of other industries or subordinate industries and types of employment and livelihood; and all this in regions where, for geographical reasons, white settlers have not increased and, generally speaking, have not been successful. The problem is partly one of social anthropology; it is also one of scientific research within the region, and of intensive economic study.

FACING THE PROBLEM

The Council for Scientific and Industrial Research Organization is engaged in research into problems of soil, water, crops and animal husbandry in the northern and inland regions. The use of heavy machinery, to which the war gave an impetus, on roads and stations, and the increasing use of motor lorry and aeroplane for transporting necessities and luxuries to townships and stations, and cattle and sheep (in some circumstances) and other products to the ports or railheads, are giving an impetus to a more efficient development of the country. Directors of pastoral firms and government officials are, not for the first time, concentrating on the economic aspects of the problem of transport and markets. Lastly, research in social anthropology[1] has for the past 20 years been concerned not only with the indigenous culture of the aborigines, but also with the changes in their culture, in their social organization, economy, and way of life generally, and with the effect of such changes on their numbers and distribution. On the basis of this research representations have been made, and advice and help given, to the administrative departments concerned and to the missions. At the same time public opinion has been kept informed, and to some extent has been influenced by disseminating knowledge of the aborigines and of the problems involved.

---

1. This has been organized almost solely by the Department of Anthropology, University of Sydney, in conjunction with the Australian National Research Council.

The anthropological emphasis is important; whatever foundations be laid for increased development of the centre and north of the continent by scientific research and economic planning, and by the provision of advanced technical equipment, willing and acclimatized labour will be essential. According to past experience, this will not be provided adequately by the white man. He and his womenfolk are not acclimatized, and unless he has a definite vocation, he prefers to live in more populous and more comfortable regions. On the other hand the aborigines are acclimatized; they are interested, realizing, as already stated, that their livelihood is associated with the white man and his enterprises; and they have the ability to undertake the work required. But they must be educated, trained technically, employed justly and rationally, and given the opportunity to be self-dependent within new communities of their own centred on a modern economy. The present Commonwealth education policy should therefore be wholeheartedly pursued and expanded, the themes emphasized being literacy, technical training, and social responsibility in the new age.[1]

---

1. The background and principles of the policies at present in operation are analysed in A. P. Elkin, *Citizenship for the Aborigines*, 1944.

NOTES AND
DOCUMENTARY STUDIES

PROBLEMS OF INDUSTRIALIZATION
OF UNDERDEVELOPED COUNTRIES

H. W. Singer

AGRICULTURAL IMPROVEMENT AND INDUSTRIALIZATION

The title of this paper implies that industrialization is necessary to economic development, and that underdeveloped countries are also 'underindustrialized'. But are underdeveloped countries necessarily underindustrialized; are developed countries always industrialized?

There is no controversy over two negative propositions: underdeveloped countries are not industrialized; industrialized countries are not underdeveloped. This however ignores a group of wealthy countries like Australia or Denmark, exporters of agricultural commodities, but not industrialized if judged by their foreign trade.

If we consider their internal employment structure, countries like Australia are, surprisingly, industrialized. Their agricultural productivity is so great that quite a small proportion of their workers can produce enough primary produce to give high-level supplies at home, and ample exports too. In their internal employment structures, these countries resemble developed manufacturing countries rather than underdeveloped primary producers. Thus, if one regards 'developed' and 'industrialized' countries as synonymous, one should understand that the term 'industrialized' describes only the employment structure. In that sense, all are industrialized.

Poor, underdeveloped countries have 60 to 80 per cent of their population in agriculture; national income is very low, as are *per capita* incomes and productivity in agriculture. This would be true even if agriculture in underdeveloped countries were as productive as other sectors. In fact, average productivity in agriculture tends to be even lower than in industry. *Per capita* income in agriculture is often about two-thirds of the national average. Both productivity and *per capita* incomes in the few non-agricultural industries are appreciably higher, if exceedingly low compared with even agricultural incomes in wealthy countries. Discrepancies between agricultural and non-agricultural incomes are much less in developed countries, even if productivity in agriculture bears the same ratio to national productivity, simply because a smaller proportion of workers are in agriculture.

There are two main roads to economic development: one can accept the internal structure of the country and concentrate on raising the low productivity, particularly in agriculture, within the existing structure. Alternatively, one can concentrate on the great difference between agricultural and non-agricultural productivity, increasing *per capita* national income by shifts away from agriculture. In the first case, the existing, predominantly agricultural, structure is improved. In the second, structural change is attempted.

The choice between improving the existing structure or making structural changes must be an economic one, decided by which of the two approaches is cheaper. There is no ready-made solution. There are cheap and expensive ways of improving agriculture. There are cheap and expensive ways of changing from agriculture to industry. Moreover, the two are alternatives only in the limited sense of which is to come first.

In the last resort, both types of change are bound together, in complex yet important ways. We are here concerned only with what is to be changed first, which is a matter of economic choice. A great deal of agricultural improvement can be carried out cheaply, for example by changing institutions like land tenure or practices such as rotation and by better seed selection, or the use of fertilizers. But there are also expensive ways of agricultural improvement, for example, where great irrigation works are necessary.

Similarly, in non-agricultural sectors of underdeveloped countries, existing industries can sometimes be improved by better management, better care of machines, etc. But improvement of existing industries may also mean extensive and costly re-equipment or relocation. Nor is a change to industrialization necessarily either 'cheap' or 'expensive.'

In general, the cost of industrialization can be lowered in three ways:

1. By avoiding urbanization with its heavy overheads like transport or water. This means bringing industry to the existing population rather than encouraging a general drift to the towns.
2. By concentrating on industries requiring little capital, and skimping on public utilities. Ultimately, however, the reduction in cost is more than offset by falling output.
3. By applying a technology which uses much labour and little capital. This is important in overpopulated countries, where capital and natural resources cannot maintain full employment and there is underemployment on the farms. A shortage of capital relatively to labour afflicts underdeveloped countries generally, but at present the possibilities of developing labour-intensive technologies are limited because such a development itself marks economic advance.

There are thus cheap and expensive ways of development, whether one improves the existing structure or attempts structural change. Relative cheapness in any specific instance depends on various factors. First, on the relationship of population to natural resources. Where there is overpopulation, agricultural development will be more expensive than industrialization. By definition, there is no land for ready extension of agriculture; agricultural improvement without any reduction of the agricultural population, if possible at all, requires costly investment.

Yet industrialization can be relatively cheap. There is a pool of unemployed or underemployed manpower, mainly in the countryside; the need for urbanization can be reduced by constructing public services and capital facilities there. Where population is sparse, development of primary production is likely to be relatively cheap compared with industrialization.

The test of expense means that the choice will rarely be of agricultural improvement or industrialization. Some agricultural improvements will be cheaper than industrialization and vice versa. At some point, the yield from further structural changes will be less than from improvements within the structure, and vice versa. Further, beyond the first step, improvement is bound to lead to structural changes, and structural change to bring improvement. For a continued rise in agricultural productivity will increase both real incomes and the demand for non-agricultural, particularly manufactured, goods. There will also be a derived demand for capital goods.

The operation of Engels' Law means that improvement leads to structural change. As incomes increase, a smaller proportion of any increase is spent on food. In a closed economy, it is impossible to increase agricultural productivity without causing structural change, if demand is reasonably free. One could maintain the position by exporting proportionally more of the increasing agricultural output, and importing correspondingly more manufactured goods. This would postpone structural changes in the developing country, but only by inducing them elsewhere.

Similarly, structural change implies improvement. Structural change in underdeveloped countries shifts people from the agricultural to the non-agricultural sector, and whether such a transfer means an absolute or only a relative fall in the agricultural population, it implies an increase in average productivity in agriculture. Otherwise the supply of food and other raw materials would fall, particularly for the non-agricultural population. This situation is incompatible with rising real incomes, for when real incomes increase, people consume more agricultural products. Engels' Law does not say that they want less, only that demand increases less than in proportion to incomes.

Hence, industrialization implies agricultural development designed to increase yields of primary produce, though this change, again, can be shifted to other countries through foreign trade. But the improvements in productivity must occur somewhere within the existing structure. For the whole world the relationship between structural changes and improvements persists. The choice between improvement in agriculture and industrialization is mainly one of time sequence.

TECHNOLOGY AND INDUSTRIALIZATION OF UNDERDEVELOPED COUNTRIES[1]

Underdeveloped countries today use derived technologies. This distinguishes their industrialization from that in the nineteenth century, when the very process of industrialization depended on constant technical innovation. In attempting to industrialize, modern underdeveloped countries have to introduce a technology evolved over many years in much more highly developed countries. This is most dramatically evident in present-day technical assistance programmes. The more developed countries have a practical monopoly of industrial and scientific research and experience. Modern technology depends both deliberately and instinctively on requirements and factor endowments in industrialized countries. This has several results. First, it causes the rapid evolution of new, superior, technologies, and the correspondingly rapid scrapping of slightly obsolete capital goods. Second, the modern technology has concentrated on inventing labour-saving devices. Third, it requires certain levels of scientific training and of education, widely reached only in industrial societies.

Even in industrialized countries, these particular features of technological development create problems, particularly in times of unemployment and de-

---

[1] The writer has here drawn extensively on his article, 'Obstacles to Economic Development in a Non-Schumpeterian World', *Social Research*, 1953.

pression, when the underlying assumption of relative labour shortage is less true. By and large, however, technological advances suit the conditions in developed countries.

This is not true of underdeveloped countries. For them, a different and in many ways older or 'inferior' technology would be more appropriate. Capital is acutely short and labour relatively, even acutely, abundant. The technology of 1850 might well make economic development easier. But this technology has been scrapped, and rightly. The only existing technology is that of the industrialized countries.

An old industrial country like Britain could begin with a technology requiring few, simple, capital goods and develop that technology in step with changing factor endowments. Countries whose economic development occurred rather later perhaps had the best of both worlds. They avoided some of the inevitable blind alleys and experimental costs; yet technology had not advanced sufficiently to be out of line with their 'pre-industrial' factor endowments. This is particularly true of the United States where, in the early stages of development, labour was relatively scarce.

The underdeveloped countries today are in a worse position. Modern technology is not compatible with their endowments and their natural requirements. They cannot develop a technology harmoniously unless it is their own technology— and absence of an original technology is characteristic. At some stages it may have been an advantage to be a late-comer in economic development. By now, it is a serious disadvantage.

The modern capital-intensive technology affects underdeveloped economies in several ways:

1. The initial expense of investment is very high and makes the scanty resources of underdeveloped countries insufficient for balanced development.
2. Modern technology requires elaborate and expensive capital goods which have to be imported. This causes balance of payments problems and increases costs of installation.
3. Labour-saving devices are largely wasted since alternative jobs are lacking, prevented by the very lack of investment.
4. The effective life of expensive equipment is often shorter. Operators are less careful, standards of maintenance are lower, etc.

The absence of a technology which is both modern and in harmony with existing factor endowments is a major problem of underdeveloped areas. By adopting the technology of industrialized countries, they put themselves at an immediate disadvantage.

POPULATION PROBLEMS IN RELATION TO INDUSTRIALIZATION

It is a widespread belief that the first 'requirement for industrialization' is a reduction of population pressure. I shall deal here only with two problems, first that of population density, second the more dynamic one of population increase.

The first proposition to be considered is population in underdeveloped countries. This is so dense that agricultural returns are diminished and national incomes reduced; poverty is the inevitable result of population pressure, and one cannot 'promote economic development' otherwise than through population factors.

There is much to be said for this view, but not for the conclusion derived from it. It is not an argument against economic development. Dense population does indeed cause great poverty. Since underdeveloped countries are predominantly primary producers, dense populations on limited areas of land create a Malthusian deterioration through the law of diminishing returns.

But population pressure can be adjusted and yet not cause impoverishment. The internal employment structure can be changed so as to move excess population from the agricultural sector, thus raising *per capita* agricultural incomes, and to transfer it to occupations not subject to diminishing returns. Agreed, the automatic increase in *per capita* production in agriculture is not sufficient, since absolute output will fall even when excess population is removed. Hence, there is a need for some agricultural improvement beyond the automatic increase in productivity arising from the removal of excess population. Agricultural development, in the sense of increasing total production with smaller numbers, is an essential concomitant of transferring population from the agricultural sector.

Thus, the solution to this first problem is a move away from agriculture, which aligns the employment structure of the country with the dictates of population pressure. Excess population may be a valid explanation for poverty, taking existing structures as given. But it is also a most urgent argument for simultaneously adjusting structures and improving agricultural productivity. Since these two things constitute economic development, overpopulation is an argument for, not against, economic development, especially for industrialization.

At worst, population pressure works in both directions: by reducing average incomes, it reduces the margin of resources available for development. It also increases prospects of development beyond what would normally correspond to the low income level.

With development policies adjusted to population factors, excess population carries its own 'built-in stabilizer'. If it causes poverty, it also indicates a way of curing it.

We now consider the more dynamic proposition that 'population in underdeveloped countries increases so rapidly that provision for the increasing population swallows up their meagre savings'. In many underdeveloped countries with low incomes, voluntary gross saving is no higher than 10 per cent of income, and may be less, and much of this gross saving may assume the form of hoarded gold, cattle, palatial public buildings, or bank accounts abroad.

Even if gross savings are wasted in this manner, about half of them will be needed to make good depreciation. There is little capital in underdeveloped countries, but the burden of maintaining it intact is as great, in relation to national income, as in developed countries. Indeed, for two reasons it may be higher. First, the capital-income ratio tends to be high in early stages of economic development. Second, existing capital tends to wear out more rapidly than in developed countries because of less efficient repair and maintenance, and the failure to adapt capital equipment to specific conditions and requirements. To assume that maintaining existing capital will take 5 per cent of the national income is to be conservative.

This leaves 5 per cent net savings. But before economic development can proceed, provision must be made for the increasing population. As in *Alice in Wonderland*, a developing country with an increasing population has to run in order to keep in the same place. Development requires an increase in *per capita* income.

How much of the 5 per cent net savings will remain for such development after provision for the increased population has been made? Probably nothing.

If the rate of increase of population is $1\frac{1}{4}$ per cent and the capital-income ratio 4 : 1, it takes 5 per cent of the national income merely to maintain *per capita* capital.

This looks gloomy, but some qualifications are possible. First, it is assumed that increased population, while requiring capital for its productivity, will not in itself contribute to production, and capital formation. Yet, even in the developed countries, where capital-intensive techniques are important, additional labour, even without additional capital, can give significant, though not proportionate, increases in output.[1]

Second, increased output may not require correspondingly increased capital. Technical progress can, over a period of time, increase output, without such an increase in capital. One could even imagine population pressure stimulating technological improvements.

Third, not all capital would have to be increased. The existing roads might be sufficient for the greater population and might even be better utilized. Population increase may create external economies in the form of better use of existing capital. Population pressure itself may form an inducement to better utilization of existing capital.

Fourth, even if domestic savings disappeared in providing for the population increase, it would still be possible to use foreign capital to increase production and income *per capita*, and once generated such development might create a sufficient margin over consumption to maintain the impetus of development from domestic sources alone.

Thus, there is no inevitable necessity for increase in population to prevent economic development, except in very extreme circumstances. Again, contrary to a widespread impression, the rate of population increase in underdeveloped countries as a whole does not appear to be significantly greater than in developed countries, though the figures are not complete nor easy to interpret. It is true, however, that in underdeveloped countries, the way in which population increases is particularly wasteful. It results from high birth and death rates. It is the wastefulness of the method rather than the rate of population increase which is the real obstacle to economic development.

The age distribution in underdeveloped countries is also unfavourable to a high production and high capital formation. The combination of high birth and death rates results in large numbers of children, too few of whom survive to repay by sustained production throughout their working lives the 'investment' made in them in their youth. Paradoxically, one trouble of underdeveloped countries is that there is too much unproductive investment devoted to feeding and bringing up a new generation for productive work. If this is included as investment, it may well be that investment in underdeveloped countries takes more of the national income than in more developed countries, perhaps even on a *per capita* basis.

If the preceding argument is true, important policy conclusions follow: lower death rates will increase the rate of population growth and may make the provision of capital for the increase of population more burdensome. But it will also increase the proportion of children who survive and thus raise the productivity of investment in their upbringing. Hence, the net effects of a fall in death rates are doubtful, except that the more immediate effect is more likely to be harmful than the long-run effect. A simultaneous fall in birth and death rates, however,

---

1. Cf. Tinbergen and Polak, *Dynamics of Business Cycles*, p. 128.

is likely to be economically beneficial, simultaneously diminishing the investment in the upbringing of children and increasing the productivity of the smaller investment actually made.

It is noteworthy that such an 'unfavourable age distribution' is common to underdeveloped countries generally, whether normally considered as 'over-populated' or 'underpopulated'.

TECHNICAL KNOWLEDGE AND MANAGERIAL CAPACITY AS LIMITING FACTORS ON INDUSTRIAL EXPANSION IN UNDERDEVELOPED COUNTRIES

C. N. Vakil and P. R. Brahmanand

The rate of a country's economic development depends on many complementary factors; deficiencies in any of these may slow down or even inhibit economic growth. Underdevelopment is often attributed to a low rate of capital accumulation; certainly, shortage of capital compels changes in technique and organization so that existing resources can be used to best advantage. Technical knowledge and managerial capacity are both necessary and complementary. Mere technological knowledge is of little avail; managerial efficiency in an underdeveloped economy in large part determines whether full advantage is taken of new techniques. The more efficient management is, the greater the demand for technical knowledge.

The essence of technical progress is to reduce the volume of resources needed to produce a given output. The relative efficiency of different technical developments thus depends upon how scarce the resources saved are. An economy where a particular factor is scarce, or which urgently needs new techniques, calls technical knowledge to its aid. But new methods will not necessarily be found. Otherwise existing international differences in development would be less. Technical knowledge has not developed autonomously in underdeveloped countries, because certain essential conditions are not satisfied.

Technological advance can occur at various levels. It can come from experienced workers, from research departments of large firms, or from independent specialized laboratories and research institutions. How far the individual worker can himself modify known methods or invent new ones depends upon the extent of specialization. In underdeveloped economies there is too little specialization; nor does the high labour turnover allow long-period concentration. Again, whether industrial or State resources can be devoted to technical research depends on general economic development. Poor countries have no surplus resources for such long-term investment. Most firms are small and lack research departments; nor do specialized research agencies develop autonomously. The State's responsibility in developing technological knowledge is widely recognized; but since the State is poor, underdeveloped countries inevitably depend in part on accumulated technical knowledge in advanced countries.

Technical knowledge can be broadly classified as:

1. Knowledge with economic possibilities and which can be utilized in the socioeconomic environment, but which is not available because developed countries will not impart it, or only on conditions. This occurs particularly with international combines which have pioneered industrial expansion in undeveloped

164

countries, and whose technical knowledge is closely guarded. Again, a country might industrialize without its own citizens knowing how to construct or operate particular industries. This would raise serious problems if friction caused foreigners to leave, which partly explains the attitude of underdeveloped countries to foreign capital.

2. Knowledge available on reasonable terms, but which is useless without changes in industrial organization or social policy.
3. Knowledge which is available, but which requires easy access to capital. Here, known technology is of little value, unless it develops more suitable methods.
4. Knowledge which could be used only if the country has sufficient capital.

First, one must establish training institutions. But in underdeveloped economies existing institutions often cannot be used because of high training costs, uncertainty in employment, and caste or class rigidities. Expenditure on technical training is a long-term investment, which few families can afford. A literary education is preferred; those who can afford technical education usually seek it abroad. Local employers tend to prefer persons trained abroad, with unfortunate effects on home development of technical training institutions. Again, some industrialists in underdeveloped countries depend on technicians trained in their own firms rather than at universities. Apprenticeship is not common, and technical colleges do not own factories. Qualified men tend to be under-used and accept jobs where their hard-won specialized knowledge is of little avail.

The desire for higher technical education, implying great specialization, depends on both size and certainty of demand. Unless many industries are expanding, highly specialized individuals risk unemployment.

Some underdeveloped economies have powerful obstacles to labour mobility. Communities are divided into watertight compartments, perhaps by caste systems. Such obstacles persist, despite changing social opinion, largely through vested interests. Those who are better off consolidate their relatively high standard of living by preventing the flow of talent, though democracy is slowly eliminating this. It therefore takes some time for wage and salary differentials to adjust labour supplies. Pecuniary rewards cannot break the rigidities of tradition.

Even if technical schools and research organizations are successfully established, superior methods of production may not be used. It is difficult to introduce changes in countries with an intrinsic dislike of new methods. Old methods persist, despite their inadequacy; routine and inertia create an atmosphere unreceptive to new methods. Unless the need for improvement is keenly felt, superior methods are not used. This new attitude requires the individual to feel that conscious effort can substantially improve his living standards. The difficulties come from sheer conservatism; from opposition by groups whose importance is threatened by new methods; or from opposition to the economic and social consequences of such methods.

Obviously the application of technical knowledge must lead to economies in using labour. In most undeveloped countries labour is abundant. Thus, new methods do reduce costs, but often cause unwelcome unemployment or underemployment. Admittedly the savings may enable individual firms to expand output and employment, but only much later. Initially, new methods tend to create unemployment which, if population pressure is heavy, causes serious social frictions. In fast-developing countries technological unemployment, though sometimes important, does not persist, because increased activity absorbs displaced labour. Industrial development can remedy these difficulties, but only if rapid and certain.

Again, new production methods may displace particular types of workers; for example, those in cottage industry. Admittedly, individual entrepreneurs can use superior methods, despite the dislocation and distress they cause. But, in a democracy, changes which seriously disturb the existing fabric are frowned upon. The new conception of the Welfare State sometimes prevents countries from taking full advantage of technical knowledge.

Other drawbacks of Western technology are: rapid urbanization and consequent overcrowding and slums; undue concentration of industry in particular areas; glaring discrepancies in living standards between different groups; and numerous consequent social problems. These difficulties can be overcome by expenditure on social policies; but a poor community can afford little such spending.

The socio-political environment thus tends to be unreceptive to modern techniques. There are also doubts about the practical application of improved technology. The economic unit must be large enough for the techniques to be reasonably applied. Capital must be available, also effective organization— big 'ifs' in underdeveloped economies. The unit of activity often hardly warrants applying improved methods. Co-operative farms would help; but how can they be organized? Unless industries are monopolistic, technological knowledge is unlikely to be used autonomously. New techniques need new capital.

But can present technical knowledge itself help to produce more rapid industrial expansion? Past industrial development in advanced countries suggests that technical and organizational changes were linked; and that continuously expanding markets enabled industry to absorb new knowledge, and gave it freedom, despite the economic and social disturbances involved. When public opinion had crystallized in favour of a social policy to temper adverse effects, these countries were already highly developed. In most underdeveloped countries, modern technical knowledge has to be superimposed upon a retrograde system, and the social conscience will hardly give technology a free field. To desire industrialization in these countries, without wishing to pay its heavy price in supplying capital and dealing with social upheavals, is to ignore very grave difficulties.

Again, underdeveloped countries lack the appropriate technological knowledge. Each country has to work out its own salvation, and, particularly, to find out which production methods are feasible for it. In this sense technological knowledge is a limiting factor.

The following techniques seem best for underdeveloped countries: (a) ones which can be quickly learned; (b) requiring little initial investment and no increase in the size of firms; (c) reducing the 'gestation' period; (d) requiring less investment in specialized and skilled workers and being appropriate to current educational standards; (e) saving scarce resources other than labour; (f) expanding production horizons, and increasing supplies such as minerals or electricity. The limited resources available for acquiring technical knowledge necessitate careful choice of fields in which to become proficient. Natural aptitudes, expected requirements in various fields, and activities in which specilization is desired, show the fields of knowledge appropriate for concentrated development. Without careful planning, resources may be dispersed. The choice between pure and applied research is also important. Scarcity of resources makes it desirable to seek knowledge with immediate practical application.

Again, what type of specialist technical training is most useful? Should it be based on a wide general training, or should specialization start early? In backward countries, specialization might be preferable. The pace of industrial expansion in backward countries depends on modifying Western techniques and creating a suitable organizational framework. Here managerial capacity has a significant role.

Managerial capacity must be distinguished from innovation or entrepreneurship. Managers direct existing enterprises; innovators cause radical, discontinuous, changes in the economic environment. The manager's function is to adapt production as efficiently as possible to changes in external conditions, including changed production methods, forms of organization, markets and legal systems. The 'optimum' organization is continuously changing with the economic environment. Co-ordination is essentially dynamic; its efficiency determines the reserves which firms can create. Thus it limits future expansion. Further, the speed with which firms adapt themselves determines the rapidity of social change.

Deficiencies in management limit expansion in two main ways:

1. Management becomes more difficult as firms expand; entrepreneurs prefer limited development. With more adequate managerial talent, individual firms might grow faster. Such limits on expansion occur at two extremes. First, firms denied specialized managers suffer from a deficiency in managerial capacity. Since management has to be performed anyhow the choice lies between a specialized manager, able to adopt highly scientific management methods, and the native, untrained ability of owners or their nominees. Such firms could attain greater efficiency if assisted by specialized management. Second, firms may grow so large that even the best managerial talent cannot cope with them. In underdeveloped countries the former limitation is more important.

2. Fewer new firms may be established because entrepreneurs are lacking. How is management related to enterprise? In most underdeveloped countries entrepreneurs are scarce enough; the position only worsens when they become entangled in actual management. This happens when enterprise and management are not sufficiently diversified. If proprietors prefer to manage their own firms, then, from the community's point of view, the more they perform actual management the less their time for starting or expanding enterprises. Modern management is highly complicated, and specialization on management or entrepreneurship is essential. Development in backward countries depends too much on a small group of leaders; they should not fritter away their resources. Why do not entrepreneurs realize this? It is a vicious circle. Efficient managers are scarce. Entrepreneurs therefore cling to responsible functions. Yet unless there is a sustained demand from entrepreneurs, the best men do not specialize in management. Until proprietors trust in managers, such a specialized cadre will not develop.

There are, broadly, three stages in developing the management function. First, the entrepreneur himself is the manager. Second, as responsibilities increase, he may delegate them; but not if he is old-fashioned, or disapproves of decentralizing responsibility, or cannot find or afford specialized managers. In any case, a firm's progress may be hampered by insufficient personal interest or organizational ability. As a result, the owner's energy may be dispersed between several concerns, all run inefficiently. Gradually, as the concerns grow, the owner will probably have to delegate his functions. Thus, third, the management function becomes subdivided, and the manager allows greater functional specialization.

The attitude of industry generally, the rate at which firms expand, and the conscious need for functional specialization, all largely determine the demand for managers. If most firms are small and moderately poor, the demand for specialized managers is limited. 'Average' managerial capacity is abundant, but specialized management can only be used after the business has become fairly large. Somewhat later, diminishing returns set in and co-ordination exceeds the individual's capacity. Since management is an admixture of diverse talents, the supply of efficient managers is limited. The indivisible nature of managerial capacity and the predominance of small firms explain why the general level of managerial efficiency is relatively low in underdeveloped countries. Yet if large corporations developed, the demand for specialized managers might fall. The demand for managers depends on the number of individual firms and on their rate of growth.

As firms grow, they may find it desirable to delegate management to an external agency looking after several concerns and with a financial interest in them. This system makes specialized managers unnecessary in individual firms—and large-scale management is more economical. But the system can lead to abuse. An agency interested in several competing firms may use its funds so that their respective interests are set at naught. Again, when some industrial development has occurred, such agencies hinder growth by preventing the separation of ownership from control, and prevent specialized business leaders and managers emerging. Hence the managing agency system in India has become outmoded.

To make good deficiencies in managerial capacity, one first needs to teach entrepreneurs how to employ specialized talent and to encourage its development. If reliance on family relationships cannot be reduced, adequate training should be given to managers. Even in advanced countries, entrepreneurs often look down on scientific training. They are doubtful of qualified persons' ability to adapt themselves. Industrialists in advanced countries are beginning to realize that scientific management pays; but not yet in underdeveloped countries.

Again, the scale of rewards must attract the right kind of managers. In underdeveloped countries government service takes the best talent, partly because of better conditions and higher income, more because of the high social status of government service. To attract good men, private business must offer unduly high rewards, great security and possibilities of advancement.

In developed economies, changes in ownership or control do not cause large management changes. In underdeveloped countries, the tendency to appoint relations to key positions does frequently cause changes in top management. New men come from outside the firm, giving little opportunity for advancement to those inside. The consequent uncertainty and lack of incentive helps to perpetuate inefficiency.

Managerial talent also develops slowly because of the general 'unenlightened' attitude of entrepreneurs. Industrial development depends on capital, and hence on the pattern of wealth distribution. Since there are few investment institutions, industrial advance largely depends on the attitude of wealth-owning groups. If they prefer short-term gains, even the best manager has limited scope. Indeed, interests of owners and managers may diverge. The latter stress the continuity of the concern and its efficient organization. The rewards of this are reaped only after much time, and often lead only to intangible returns like increased prestige. Managers would like to create reserves for expansion; proprietors only judge managers by their ability to earn immediate profits. Unless owners are enlightened, management has little scope and good managers will continue to be scarce.

Private enterprise in an underdeveloped economy can hardly offer the same opportunities as government service. Firms can only give security within their own organization. Unless industry generally is highly developed, and promotion chances are reasonable, too little talent will enter industry, and the best of it will go to the larger, well-established firms, which, by definition, need it less. Average industrial efficiency will not increase. Small wonder, then, that in many underdeveloped economies foreign-owned industry attracts the best talent. Again, social prestige in business may not tempt able men. If standards of education of businessmen—and morale and standards in private business—are low, social status in industry will suffer.

The remedy is to separate management from ownership and enterprise; to make management a profession; to improve conditions of work; to increase rewards, and to raise morale. This would help to attract the right type of manager. Managers should have the latest information about business conditions and methods, if necessary from specialized agencies. Established houses may thus gain little. They may even stand to lose because less-established firms will develop; but the reserves of developed firms can enter other fields. The considerable outlay on specialized management leaves the majority of small firms, unable, at present, to use modern organization methods. Specialized agencies able to perform various management functions should be developed, and their services made available widely and cheaply, until firms grow big enough to employ specialized talent. Yet no outside agency can alter the internal problems of firms, which must themselves see that their employees are trained in scientific management.

THE RECRUITMENT OF
WHITE-COLLAR WORKERS IN
UNDERDEVELOPED COUNTRIES

B. F. Hoselitz

In the discussion of the human problems arising in underdeveloped countries undergoing a process of technological change, the question of the formation and training of an industrial labour force stands in the foreground. It is, indeed, a most important problem, especially if a process of relatively rapid industrialization is envisaged, and if not merely the acquisition of new manual and technical skills, but the entire alteration of the way of life of large masses of the population takes place. Most of the past discussions of the development of an industrial labour force have concentrated on two groups within the new industries: the industrial labourers at the bottom of the scale, and the technical élite, the engineers. Some attention has also been given to the problem of how managers concerned with the organizational and 'business' problems of the new industries can be trained and, in some underdeveloped countries, what steps could be taken to induce the development of a class of private entrepreneurs in industry.

The problems which arise in all these areas are complex and differ from one another considerably. The transformation of 'peasants and primitives' into industrial labourers is a task involving masses of people, and which affects not merely the place and manner of their daily activity, but their entire social existence.[1] The training of engineers and top managers involves fewer individuals, but because of the strategic positions which these obtain in an industrializing economy, their selection and their most appropriate employment also involve, from the viewpoint of the economy as a whole, various difficult problems.[2]

With all the attention which has been given to the incentives and motivations which may exist for industrial workers on the one hand and managers, entrepreneurs, technical leaders, and engineers on the other, one group has received little attention, though, in the last resort, their successful recruitment and effective co-operation is indispensable for a process of industrialization. This group is that of the white-collar workers. In the subsequent paragraphs I propose to suggest a few thoughts on the role which this group may play in a process of industrialization and on some problems which arise.

Before entering into a discussion of the problem itself I wish to express two caveats:

---

1. On this problem, see Wilbert E. Moore. *Industrialization and Labor*, New York, 1951.
2. See on some aspects of this point my article 'Entrepreneurship and Economic Growth', *The American Journal of Economics and Sociology*, Vol. XII, No. 1, October 1952.

1. The countries which are commonly designated as 'underdeveloped' exhibit great differences in culture, relative level of economic advancement, political structure, and internal social relations. Since my remarks will be couched in general terms, some of them may be inapplicable to individual countries. In fact, it would be impossible to present significant propositions on this (as on almost any other) topic, if one were to make sure that they were really applicable to *all* underdeveloped countries. Some assertions made in this paper must, therefore, be interpreted as describing tendencies in some countries, a real situation in others, and to be of subordinate or no importance for certain others.

2. For reasons of space, some of the situations described will be schematized to a certain extent. I readily admit that such a procedure constitutes a simplification of the real situations, but I hope that over-simplifications can be avoided, and that in spite of some schematization the analysis of at least the core problems will not lose its validity.

When we speak of white-collar workers we deal with a group of people who, in terms of economic position and social ranking, exhibit great heterogeneity. In most of the theoretical treatments, white-collar workers, as a group, are counted among the middle class, and I will follow this practice by making use of the classification of the middle class presented by Professor F. Marbach.[1] Marbach distinguishes between the 'old' and the 'new' middle class, and further between the 'self-employed' and the 'non-self-employed' members of the middle class. Although, on the whole, there is some overlapping between the 'old' and the 'self-employed', on the one hand, and the 'new' and the 'non-self-employed', on the other, the two principles of classification yield four easily distinguishable categories. In this paper we are concerned only with white-collar workers, i.e., with members of the non-self-employed sector of the middle class. And here, we may distinguish two groups again, one of which corresponds, on the whole, with Marbach's old, and the other with his new middle class.

The new non-self-employed middle class is made up of white-collar workers who perform relatively unskilled labour. Although they do not work with their hands, their real income, in the advanced countries, is normally not above, and frequently even below that of semi-skilled and skilled manual workers. In this group belong the typists, bookkeepers, shipping clerks, filing clerks, and other persons engaged in commercial and industrial establishments and in public service. This group will be designated in this paper as 'employees'.

The old non-self-supporting middle class is made up almost entirely of public officials, normally in the higher ranks of the public service. To this group should be added persons engaged in occupations of similar complexity in the service of private firms or individuals. We will designate this group hereinafter as 'officials'.

The 'employees' are distinguished from the manual labourers in that they work in an office rather than a workshop or a factory, and that their work requires, in general, a higher degree of literacy than most manual jobs. A typist must know how to spell, and a bookkeeper must have, on the whole, a greater ability for arithmetic than most manual workers. The 'employees' are distinguished on the other hand from the 'officials' in that their jobs usually do not involve, nor permit them to make, decisions of any significance. The work of employees is mostly routine work, it requires, apart from certain relatively non-complex skills, chiefly the ability to be attentive, patient, and careful. Moreover, as a rule, the incomes

1. Fritz Marbach, *Theorie des Mittelstandes*, Berne, 1942, esp. p. 188ff.

and also the social position of officials is considerably higher than that of employees, as also of skilled manual workers.

The most characteristic aspect of the economic role of officials is their intermediary position in a bureaucratic hierarchy.[1] This means that they are normally in a position in which they receive general directives from the persons in *élite* positions within their bureaucratic hierarchy, and it is their task to translate these general directives for their subordinates. In addition they are usually called upon to make decisions within a rigorously prescribed field, to iron out differences between their subordinates, and to maintain channels of communication with co-ordinated portions of their bureaucratic hierarchy. The most significant difference between officials and the members of the *élite* is that only the latter make policy decisions, and occupy, in governmental hierarchies or in business organizations, the positions of ultimate responsibility. As a rule, there is also some difference in the level of income and general social ranking between members of the *élite* and even the highest-placed officials.

From the distinctions made, it is clear that there exist important differences in the incentives and motivations of employees, on the one hand, and officials, on the other. I shall first briefly consider the former group.

The employees are, in the advanced countries, the 'proletarianized' portion of the middle class. Their income often remains below that of manual workers, and this appears to be a correct reflection of the over-all social value of their economic contribution. The particular jobs which they perform require few specialized skills, apart from those acquired by almost all children in school. Whatever skills are needed in addition can usually be learned by a very short training or by some process of on-the-job training. Moreover, since many of the jobs performed by employees are on a low level of technical complexity, the human factor can be replaced relatively easily by machines. In other words, machines plus high-grade engineers can often be substituted for employees—the various types of office equipment from the simple typewriter to the most complex Hollerith machine are examples of this. Whether or not, and under what conditions such substitutions will take place is a question of relative prices. But the ease with which such substitution can be accomplished is another factor pressing the incomes of employees to a low level.

Compared with this situation in the advanced countries, a different situation is likely to persist in many underdeveloped countries, at least during the early period of the industrialization process. The differences are due mainly to two factors: the much greater illiteracy rates in underdeveloped countries and the very low prestige that in many of these societies is attributed to manual work which 'dirties one's hands'. (This last factor plays a certain role too in advanced countries.) Some employees endure their economically unenviable position, because being a white-collar worker gives the illusion to the outside world—and sometimes even to oneself—that one is above the ordinary crowd of common labourers. This has the consequence, as Marbach has shown, that employees in advanced countries are recruited, on the whole, from a higher social layer than manual labourers, even though the amount and quality of education required for the two types of position are not very different.

In many underdeveloped countries the relative social prestige which attaches to white-collar jobs is even greater, and that is in close correlation with the relatively

---

1. I shall not distinguish in what follows always between public, i.e., governmental, and private, i.e., business bureaucracies. Although I shall be concerned mostly with public bureaucracies, most of what applies to them also applies, *mutatis mutandis*, to business bureaucracies.

greater scarcity of literate persons. For this reason white-collar jobs which require few or no advanced skills are in great demand, often by people who do not even possess these skills—although they only know how to read and write. This makes the problem of selection difficult and here another characteristic of many developing countries comes in: the partial absence of impersonal market relations and the much greater weight of family and other primary group relationships in these countries.

In practice these factors have the following consequence: lower-rank employee positions become available to persons with a minimum degree of literacy. In view of the social prestige of white-collar positions as compared with manual labour, and because of the relatively greater scarcity of individuals even with a minimum degree of literacy, such positions will normally pay higher wages than those of manual workers and most occupations in agriculture. Hence, with an increase of the rudiments of literacy there will be a race for these jobs and selection for them will depend, to a large extent, on personal connexions and friendships between applicants and persons in the higher echelons of an administrative organization. It is no secret that, in many underdeveloped countries, the staffs of certain government offices are composed of relatives or co-villagers and other personal friends of one or several heads of a department or division. It is not necessary to point out that this method of recruitment of even the lowest ranks of a public bureaucracy has many undesirable aspects. It tends to keep out many qualified persons; it places professional relationships within the bureaucratic hierarchy on a non-rational basis; it produces vested, almost clannish, interests within the public service; and it endangers the principle of promotion within the bureaucracy from the ranks, since not effective performance but personal friendship is the decisive criterion. At the same time, this system bears the seeds of producing corrupt administrations, since every applicant for a position will find it desirable to 'become a friend' of persons with the power of appointment—if necessary by means of gifts or bribes.

It is, of course, not suggested that this must be the rule in all public administrations in underdeveloped countries. But we must consider that even its sporadic occurrence may have serious adverse consequences, and we must moreover bear in mind that with progressive industrialization, the expansion of public and semi-public bureaucracies of various kinds is inevitable. Industrialization leads to great population shifts. New cities arise, villages become towns. New administrative functions become necessary, called forth by the increased need for speedy and accurate communication and transportation and by the new functions which national, provincial, and local governments are forced to adopt.

Moreover, the drafting into industry of peasants and other persons without urban background requires the increase of various welfare, educational, and other administrative agencies which normally only central or local governments can provide. All these trends make necessary a large increase of bureaucracy and thus pose a problem in the recruitment of employees, as well as officials. In view of the pressures which are likely to arise, it is most desirable to found effective 'community-oriented' administrations, and the ambiguity in the social and economic position of lower-rank employees may operate against this objective.

An alternative would be the attempt to substitute, wherever possible, machines for employees. But this would lead to the contradictory result that in countries in which labour is cheap, labour-saving machinery would be employed in occupations where a number of new career opportunities could be created which, in the long run, would have an important beneficial effect on the economic growth potential of the country. It would have the other unfavourable result that the scarce foreign exchange would have to be used for the purchase of expensive equipment and that the middle and upper ranks of the bureaucracy would be even more heavily overburdened with work and responsibility. And these persons, who are in crucial positions, are already in short supply. Whatever dangers and inadequacies may lie in the recruitment of employees, the chief bottleneck in the building up of administrative bureaucracies in underdeveloped countries is in fact in the lack of trained officials.

Many of the problems which we observe in the recruitment of employees are also encountered in the building up of a staff of officials, and vice versa. Some of the points which will be discussed below apply also to the expansion of the lower ranks of an administrative organization. The constitution of a bureaucracy is fraught, on all levels, with analogous problems. But the important difference between inducting employees and officials is that because of the differences in the nature of their respective roles different factors are of chief importance in the case of each of the two groups.

As has been pointed out, the peculiarity of the role of officials consists in that they make decisions. They cannot, therefore, be replaced by machines. But in a well-functioning bureaucracy their decisions are not arbitrary, however independently they may be made. I do not refer to the fact that the decisions made by any official are limited by the competence of his department, division, or section, but rather that however free he may be, and may need to be, in some respects, he is merely an instrument implementing policies which were not designed by him, but imposed upon him. To fill the position of an official properly, it is, therefore, necessary that the holder of such an office be ready to place himself fully at the service of the bureaucratic hierarchy he serves and that he ask himself at every juncture whether his activity is in pursuit of the general policy directives under which he functions. In addition he is charged with doing his work in the most efficient manner possible. Efficiency in this context means something very similar to what economists have in mind when they speak of 'economizing': the attainment of a given goal with a minimum of means.

These limitations ideally impose upon an official a perfectly 'rational' method of action. There is a close analogy between an ideal-typical official and an ideal-typical entrepreneur. The latter 'economizes' means in order to maximize profit, the former in order to maximize the implementation of whatever policy he is charged to execute. It is no wonder, therefore, that really efficient bureaucracies exist only in a social framework in which rationality (in Max Weber's sense) has become a widely generalized principle of social action. Weber sums up thus his penetrating discussion of the bureaucracy.

'Bureaucratic structure is everywhere a late product of development. The farther we go back in historical development, the more typical become forms of government which lack a bureaucracy and officialdom altogether. Bureaucracy has a "rational" character: it is dominated by rules, purposiveness, means, "objective" impersonality. Its origin and growth has had everywhere a "revolutionary" effect, in a special sense; an effect which the advance of rationalism usually produces wherever it occurs. In this process structural forms of government became annihilated which did not have a rational character, in this special sense.'[1]

The specific conditions which are associated with this kind of rational action, and without which it cannot function properly as a generalized principle of social

1. Max Weber, *Wirtschaft und Gesellschaft*, Tuebingen, 1947, Vol. II, pp. 677-8.

action, include at least the following: tasks in a society must be distributed on the basis of achievement, rather than on the basis of a person's status. That is, in order to implement his job effectively, an official must select those persons and other means which, on the basis of known scientific and technological relations, are most efficient. This demands, moreover, that the exercise of the functions of an official must be 'democratic', in that he disregards, in a formal sense, special claims of individuals which are not based on objective criteria of achievement or on clearly established legal claims. Moreover, this rationality of an official's actions will normally lead to his making use of whatever specialized skills exist, in order to achieve an end. Hence rational bureaucratic activity tends to support and sometimes even to initiate division of labour and specialization. Finally, the impersonal quality of the official's purpose requires that he be 'community-oriented', i.e., that he regards his office as a trust which he administers in the interest of the community as a whole, rather than as a benefice which leads to his own enrichment or the accumulation of power.[1]

Many of these principles of social action are foreign to the value systems dominant in some underdeveloped countries. Moreover, in some countries the social structure and its maintenance work against the introduction of these principles. Hence the development of effective bureaucracies encounters great obstacles. Indeed, really efficient administrative organizations have been created only in economically advanced countries; the governmental and administrative apparatuses of most underdeveloped countries were, until recently, either manned in their higher positions by non-natives, or experienced periodic breakdowns.[2] In other words, the administrations of native governments or enterprises in many countries of, say Latin America or the Middle East, exhibited a degree of inefficiency and instability which was one of the factors accountable for the relative economic backwardness of these countries. The administrations of colonies and foreign-owned enterprises in underdeveloped countries were manned, at least in their higher positions, by citizens of the metropolitan country who transplanted their own organizational and administrative procedures. With the attainment of independence by many former colonies, and the increasing trend to place foreign investments in all underdeveloped countries under the supervison of the national government, the growth and extension of native bureaucracies is necessary. These must take over the functions exercised until recently by non-natives. In other instances they must modernize themselves and replace their often inefficient and non-rational methods of operation by the introduction of the principle of rational action on an impersonal, formally egalitarian, basis. This process of innovation makes great demands on a new type of manpower, and it is not surprising that the recruitment of officials equal to the tasks demanded of them forms a serious bottleneck in the economic development of underdeveloped countries.

In the subsequent paragraphs I shall try to analyse some of the factors which exert an influence on the number and types of persons who become officials

---

1. A more extensive discussion of these interrelations can be found in my essay, 'Social Structure and Economic. Growth', *Economia Internazionale*, Vol. VI, No. 3, August 1953. See also Marion J. Levy, Jr., 'Some Sources of the Vulnerability of the Structures of Relatively Non-Industrialized Societies to those of Highly Industrialized Societies' in B. F. Hoselitz, ed., *The Progress of Underdeveloped Areas*, Chicago, 1952.

2. On some of the bureaucracies in antiquity and the middle ages and their differences with the modern type of governmental and business bureaucracies, see Weber, op. cit., p. 655ff. One of the outstanding examples of a bureaucracy in a country which did not belong to the group of economically advanced areas was imperial China. But whatever may be said about the merits of the Chinese imperial bureaucracy, one of its main features was its instability which made it incapable of functioning in a period of social and economic transition imposing increased stresses. See on this point, Marion J. Levy, Jr., 'Contrasting Factors in the Modernization of China and Japan', *Economic Development and Cultural Change*, Vol. II, No. 3, October 1953, esp. p. 165ff.

in the bureaucracies of underdeveloped countries. This may explain why the shortages exist and how they might be overcome. One important factor is the absence, in most underdeveloped countries, of well-ordered administrative procedures. Existing bureaucratic procedures are outdated and often derived from the practice of some more advanced country with entirely different conditions. The previous colonial status of some countries and the fact that others, though politically independent, were culturally dependent on an advanced country have caused the adoption of certain European systems of administration which sometimes were altered a little to suit local conditions better, but which in general need considerable overhauling. These very procedures often make public, as well as business, bureaucracies in underdeveloped countries topheavy, cumbersome and ill-adapted to the needs of the country. Examples of this can be found in the tax and fiscal administrations of many underdeveloped countries, but they exist also in other fields.[1] The most appropriate method to deal with this situation is the substitution of existing administrative procedures by more suitable ones, a task in which the United Nations and its Specialized Agencies may provide considerable assistance.

In addition to the external cumbersomeness of administrative structures which could be relatively easily removed, if it were not for a multitude of vested interests of office holders or other beneficiaries of the system, there are factors in the social structure of some countries which make the formation of rationally operating bureaucracies difficult. I refer to the excessive inequalities in social position and, resulting from it, the quasi-feudal character of some underdeveloped societies. At the top of the social pyramid is a small group which has a virtual monopoly of wealth, political power, and education—the three main status-conferring variables. The officials who are appointed under such a system usually stand in a relation to the political power holders which resembles that of the mediæval *ministeriales* to their clerical or secular overlords. In other words, the officials do not serve the community as a whole, but the special interests of a politically powerful group. This has the consequence that not only excessive emphasis is placed on the preservation of the *status quo*, at least as far as the distribution of political power and social prestige is concerned, but it also tends to keep out of the administration persons who have undoubted objective qualifications, but who do not stand in a quasi-retainer position to the members of the community's *élite*. Quite apart from the fact that such bureaucracies are in any case unsatisfactory because recruitment is based not on the principle of achievement, but on that of personal status, a class of discontented intellectuals is created, who often turn to various radical movements in order to attain positions in which their capacity for political leadership can find some expression. But in the shadow of the division of the world into two great camps, the formation of political opposition groups often leads to a repetition of the world conflict between communism and democracy within the underdeveloped country. Although the radical groups are sometimes illegal and may exist only underground, they are present nevertheless and impose serious difficulties on the smooth economic progress of the country. Furthermore, this very situation makes the introduction of more rational community-oriented bureaucracies even more difficult. For, as Weber has pointed out, this process of rationalization is 'revolutionary' in a certain sense. It has the

---

1. On this point, see Henry S. Bloch, 'Economic Development and Public Finance', in B. F. Hoselitz, op. cit. I was able to observe personally the extreme clumsiness of the customs administration of a Latin American country in which I served on a United Nations Technical Assistance Mission.

tendency of reshaping social relations and introducing a principle of formal egalitarianism which the political *élite* may regard as dangerous to its interests and whose introduction it will therefore attempt to resist. In such countries— and some of the Middle Eastern and Latin American nations belong to this group —the introduction of modern bureaucracies may encounter great difficulties. This will, at the same time, affect the speed and ease with which an over-all process of economic development can be accomplished.

Fortunately, the majority of the larger and more important underdeveloped countries do not have quite such rigid social structures. Some rigidities exist there also, and they impede the extension of rational, impersonally operating administrations. For example, Daniel Thorner recently surveyed the prospects of reshaping the village administrations in India through the establishment of village *panchayats*. He found that in most parts of India the *panchayats* have no power whatever and are not likely to obtain it, and that in those parts where they are effective they have been built into old-established power and social structures reinforcing the caste system where it still exists, and a class system based on differential landownership and wealth, where the caste system is weaker. Thorner sums up his observations with the remark 'that to rebuild village life would require far greater vision, authority and popular support than is commanded by the *panchayats* anywhere in India. To approach the goal of rural economic development through the agency of the existing village *panchayats* would appear to be an exercise in frustration'.[1]

But although such impediments to the formation of modern rational bureaucracies exist probably in all underdeveloped countries, they have become relatively subordinated in some, especially in the formation of governmental bureaucracies in the larger administrative units and, above all, also in the business bureaucracies. Yet even there some obstacles still exist, which are due partly to the lack of adequate training facilities for officials, and partly to the absence of traditions of officialdom which prescribe a strong ethic for the profession and produce the sentiment of responsibility and loyalty to one's task so characteristic of bureaucracies in advanced countries.

Although the systems of professional and higher education are being re-examined in almost all underdeveloped countries, there is still too great an emphasis on literary-historical and narrowly legal training. This is also the case with requirements for positions in the higher ranks of the bureaucracy. The notion that an official is often, even predominantly, not a 'generalist', but a specialist in a particular field of knowledge has not yet fully penetrated the public administrations of advanced countries and lags badly behind in underdeveloped countries. One consequence of this fact is that in advanced countries, as well as in underdeveloped countries, private bureaucracies are often staffed with better qualified and sometimes better educated men than public bureaucracies. In underdeveloped countries where specialized technical and professional skills are relatively scarce, the loss of many qualified individuals who might have performed valuable public service to private enterprises is a serious blow to government administration. Again, many officials who go abroad on government fellowships in order to acquire special skills soon after their return drift into better paid or more honorific positions in private business administration.

A sufficiently large supply of adequately trained persons for higher positions

---

1. Daniel Thorner, 'The Village *Panchayat* as a Vehicle of Change', *Economic Development and Cultural Change*, Vol. II, No. 3, October 1953, p. 215.

in public bureaucracies will only be forthcoming when educational facilities are increased and improved. But here, as in so many other instances, the intermediate schools are in the greatest need of improvement. In some underdeveloped countries there exist excellent universities, and a small number of persons may even receive a university education abroad. The extension and improvement of elementary education is also given high priority in all development plans, and this is quite appropriate in view of the still high illiteracy rates. But it is of almost equal importance to modernize and improve secondary education and technical training. Here is a great field of development in which Unesco can be of inestimable service.

Even the provision of more adequate educational facilities on the secondary level and in special technical fields will have only limited results if traditions of loyalty in service and responsibility are not developed. There are many factors which operate against the rapid and easy introduction of these values. As already stated, in some underdeveloped countries, public officials—and within a somewhat different context officials in business enterprises—often occupy positions similar to those of personal retainers of their superiors. Although this may be acceptable in business bureaucracies, in the long run, it defeats the effective operation of a public administration. But the replacement of this personal tie of service to one's superior by the integration of an official into an impersonal hierarchy is a most difficult process, requiring a total readaptation in thinking and values. It is clear that in order to achieve such a transformation powerful incentives must be present. I can think of only two developments in the societies of underdeveloped countries which may support it. One is the elevation of the prestige and power of officials and the other is the persistence of nationalist sentiments. Neither of these alternatives appears attractive to a person educated in and adhering to the values of Western society. The first tendency seems to increase greatly the danger of creating a managerial class, possibly with totalitarian predilections, and the second to contribute to a growth of ethnocentrism and rejection of cultural and other influences from abroad which may ultimately endanger the peaceful development of international relations.

But the dilemma may appear greater than it really is. The growth of managerial tendencies in public administrations may be tempered with an enhanced emphasis on popular democratic processes, and nationalism may perform a positive function in destroying primary loyalties to a family, tribe, or local village group, and replacing them by loyalties to the nation as a whole. We should not forget that also in Europe nationalism passed through this positive constructive phase, and is responsible, in part, for the consolidation of the great nations of contemporary Europe. If the underdeveloped countries can achieve the creation of smoothly functioning bureaucracies without giving way to the excesses of managerialism or nationalism—both of which contain the seeds of political and social totalitarianism—they will have made a contribution to socio-political practice in this matter equivalent to any achievement of the already advanced countries.

THE UNSETTLED ATTITUDE OF NEGRO
WORKERS IN THE BELGIAN CONGO

A. DOUCY

PROBLEMS OF VALUES

It is now becoming increasingly evident that the main problem which governments have to face in Africa south of the Sahara is that of Negro manpower. In the Belgian Congo the colonial authorities, anxious to meet the requirements of the present economic development, and realizing the extent of the problems it involves, are doing their best to find a solution. No solution can be satisfactory, however, unless it is adapted to the mentality of the local population. For the Negro mentality is different from ours; it results from a combination of historical circumstances affecting successive generations, and upon which—as Professor Glansdorff points out—are grafted certain particular tendencies which can in most cases be traced to external sources and are of a psychological character.

In the sphere with which we are here concerned, the mentality of the Negroes in the Belgian Congo explains why their idea of work is in complete contradiction to our theories of 'work as a duty' and 'work as a source of prosperity'. So the colonial authorities, faced—as elsewere in Africa—with the need to employ local labour, have tried to introduce a number of new conditions, aimed at modifying the traditional mentality of the workers and bringing it somewhat nearer to our own.

Since the Negroes in the Belgian Congo are—to quote Professor Glansdorff again—'strongly influenced by the habit of seeing, owning or using any particular object', these new mental tendencies should have the effect of awakening in them needs which they had not hitherto felt, and which could be satisfied only by undertaking some European form of work. But the new mentality cannot be created unless the new social and psychological conditions introduced by the colonial authorities make full allowance for the old one.

And it cannot, I think, be confidently asserted that this has been done anywhere in Negro Africa. That is probably why our Western ideas have made so little impression on the Negro mind. As regards the workers' needs, however, there has been a great change in the situation. Those needs are more numerous and extensive than they were fifty years ago; and they are also more numerous and extensive than those of Negroes who have remained in their traditional surroundings. But the things the Negro wants, and the order and quantity in which he wants them, are bewildering to a Western mind.

The Negro mentality has not been fundamentally transformed, so that for him the value of an object is determined, in many cases, not so much by its usefulness or rarity as by the actual conditions under which it can be bartered. This is in fact quite logical, at any rate from the superficial point of view, for the process of bartering goods with the 'whites' was what first brought African and Europeans into contact. So the Negroes have gradually come to consider that an intrinsic value attaches to objects thus exchanged, and barter has left its mark on their mentality.

After studying the question and making certain experiments, I have come to the conclusion that it would be possible, on this basis, to foster the development of other mental tendencies, favourable to our conception of work. This fundamental difference of conception is woven like a filigree through the considerations advanced in the following pages.

CHARACTERISTICS OF THE AFRICAN WORKER

The African worker, it must be emphasized, is nearly always a migrant. Wilfrid Benson, discussing the extent of migration in Africa[1] in an article published in *International Labour Review* in 1939,[2] states that the whole continent is still an area of migration, and that workers are sometimes found to have travelled from one end of it to the other: 'Even where the local demand and supply are equal, it is not unusual to find local labour emigrating to distant employment, and local employments being filled by immigrants. Migration may be enforced by economic conditions. It may be encouraged by economic opportunities. It is also based on African traditions.'[3] And the author stresses the fact that these migrations are no merely temporary phenomenon. Most of the workers concerned return home after an absence rarely exceeding two years. The volume of migration is increased by the comparative brevity of the period away from home, and sometimes reaches alarming proportions—as, for instance, in Nyasaland, where economic and social development is impossible because, every year, 140,000 persons, out of a population of slightly more than 400,000, go off to Southern Rhodesia and South Africa.

Another characteristic of the African worker is that he is unskilled. His principal handicap is his complete ignorance of any technique. He cannot do his work efficiently until he has been given some training. Technical training increases his self-respect and also the respect in which he is held by others, and this is very important.[4] Lack of training gives rise to many problems, which are all the more difficult to solve because, in the territory we are now considering, the demand for labour is constantly increasing. Reading the reports of the missions sent out by the governments of various countries to study the economic situation in certain parts of Africa, one soon notes that the chief concern of their authors is the shortage of manpower, particularly skilled workers.

One mission, reporting to the governments of British East Africa in 1942, pointed out that these territories were confronted by two problems. In the first place they had to overcome a general shortage of skilled workers, which was not

---

1. With the exception of countries where Arab influence predominates.
2. W. Benson, 'Some International Features of African Labour Problems', *International Labour Review*, Vol. XXXIX, No. 1, January 1939.
3. W. Benson, op. cit. p. 34.
4. Statement made by the ILO delegation to the African Labour Conference, Elizabethville, 1950.

only impeding normal economic activity, but constituted a serious threat to the government's extensive schemes for developing the mines and for the cultivation of ground-nuts.[1]

In the second place they had to ensure that children, on leaving school, would regularly enter industry or commerce. The report went on to say that the school system should normally provide a general education, to be followed by apprenticeship or by some other form of vocational training organized within the industry or trade concerned, adding that in all the territories under consideration there was a shortage of highly skilled, reliable workers capable of working without close and constant supervision.

Similar considerations are put forward in the reports issued in 1947 and 1948 respectively by the Government of Nyasaland[2] and the Government of Northern Rhodesia.[3]

This lack of trained and qualified Negro workers in Africa south of the Sahara is due to a complex series of sociological factors for which the authorities are obliged to make allowance, and which render the problems relating to the employment of local labour much more difficult to solve.

When a man leaves his familiar surroundings in order to work for a European concern, he does not entirely shake off the influence of those surroundings. His sociological background remains unaffected, so it is not surprising if he disappoints us by failing to understand the principles of our industrial civilization.

This does not mean that the authorities—those in control—are not entitled to plan the social economy of Africa on European lines. It simply means that no institution can be established or social progress achieved in the territories we are here considering, without reference to the permanent sociological factors which govern Negro life. We may therefore anticipate that in connexion with employment, circumstances may arise which have no apparent relation to social policy, but which governments will have to take into account.

These circumstances arise, for instance, when the attempt is made:
1. To obtain the necessary manpower for European industrial and commercial undertakings.
2. To avoid disturbing the demographic balance of the tribes, and consequently the agricultural economy of the territory (having regard to the preceding paragraph).
3. To protect the workers, when necessary, in their relations with employers.
4. To ensure them against injury and other risks involved in industrial employment.

I shall now attempt to determine the influence exerted by each of the different circumstances which, in my opinion, affect stability of employment among Africans who work in industry or on plantations in the Belgian Congo.

The information on which this survey is based was obtained partly by Mr. Pierre Feldheim, Director of Research at the Solvay Institute of Sociology, and partly by myself, during two study trips which I made to the Belgian Congo, in 1951 and 1953, on behalf of the University of Brussels and the Institute for Scientific Research in Central Africa.

---

1. Kenya, Tanganyika, Uganda and Zanzibar, *Technical Education and Vocational Training in East Africa*, London, 1948. See also United Nations, *Non-Self-Governing Territories: summaries and analyses of information transmitted to the Secretary-General during 1949.*
2. Nyasaland, *Annual Report of the Public Works Department*, Zomba, 1947.
3. Northern Rhodesia, *Labour Department Report for the Year 1947*, Lusaka, 1948.

As I have already mentioned, the authorities in the Belgian Congo were faced with the problem of native labour in an even more acute form than it assumes elsewhere. In 1948 the authors of the 10-year plan declared that if conditions in the labour market underwent no change, African workers would number about 1.1 million by 1959. At that time the total number of workers was 755,000. A survey made by the General Government in 1950 revealed that even during its initial period the plan would require from 97,000 to 160,000 additional workers. In 1953 the same department stated that there would be no exaggeration in claiming that at that time and in the prevailing circumstances, between 1.1 million and 1.2 million African workers were needed. These figures are taken from an official memorandum prepared by the Department of Native Affairs and Manpower of the General Government of the Belgian Congo, which was discussed by the Léopoldville Provincial Council in 1952.

This shows that already, before a third of the 10-year period has elapsed, the need for workers is in excess of the figure of 1.1 million which the authors of the plan had set as the target to be reached at its conclusion. 'The situation is thus extremely serious'—I quote from the department's report—'for it cannot be denied that at the present stage of development of the peoples of the Congo, it would be very dangerous to recruit more than a million workers'. All the more dangerous since, if all the able-bodied men who are theoretically available in their own homes were employed in European undertakings, the wage-earners would represent nearly 39 per cent of the total number of able-bodied men in the population. The entire population would suffer from such a disturbance of the economic balance in this vast territory where industry, in the widest sense of the word, is still confined to a few isolated areas. Other solutions must therefore be sought. I myself have a preference for those which are based on the assumption that any policy aimed at increasing productivity will have results of the first importance in the underdeveloped areas.

As soon as one begins to examine the problem of the output of Negro workers in Africa, one is reminded that the dominating feature of the market is its instability. As I have indicated earlier, the Belgian colonial authorities, realizing the fundamental importance of this phenomenon, have expressed their determination to introduce more stable conditions, as one of the goals of the 10-year plan.[1] Since the absorption capacity of the home market depends chiefly on the level and stability of Negro incomes, the temptation is to try to prevent fluctuations in the labour market by raising wages. The question is whether this is a practical policy and, if so, how it can best be applied.

Before attempting to answer this question, however, we should investigate the causes of the instability of the labour market and try to assess their importance and practical effect, and their bearing on the problem as a whole. For if there is to be any attempt to make organized use of African manpower or to raise output to a satisfactory level, the labour market must first be stabilized. Only then will it become possible to contemplate a gradual, general reduction in production costs, accompanied by a considerable improvement in the living standards of the population. Having thus indicated the order of procedure, I will now attempt to analyse the factors which, in my opinion, have a decisive influence on the stability of the Negro labour market in the Belgian Congo.

---

1. *Plan Décennal du Congo Belge*, Vol. I, p. 17.

The problem of fluctuations in the labour market might be summed up in the word 'absenteeism', were it not that allowance must also be made for the sometimes decisive influence of the employers' behaviour and of varying circumstances. I mention this last point only by way of reminder.

Absenteeism, which is endemic among Negro workers in some parts of the Belgian Congo, is the most frequent cause of fluctuations in the labour market. In industry, it is among manual labourers that it occurs most frequently. In the plantations it is most often found among workers employed on weeding, fruit picking and general maintenance. I shall return later to this point.

Without claiming to give a complete list of the causes of absenteeism, I will indicate those which have come to my personal knowledge.

The influence of tradition

The influence of tradition is still very strong in the Belgian Congo, and makes demands upon the workers to which even those who seem most Europeanized usually submit.

It cannot, however, be denied that many Negroes go to work in European undertakings simply because they are anxious to escape from the burden of these traditions. But though tribal pressure may then be reduced, it continues to be exerted, if only through the influence of the women who, being much less affected than the men by European education and training, and having much less understanding of our Western ideas, remain warmly attached to their own kith and kin. In such a case, a husband and wife will disagree in their attitude towards their respective families. As I have already explained, tribal pressure is still exerted even over a man who has left his village in order to escape from the demands of tradition: this pressure is immediately brought to bear if a worker wishes to get married! He is forced to accept the dowry system and the other rules observed in his community, and thus falls back into the clutches of tradition.

Some people may be tempted to suppose that since dowries are often very high, they must represent a very useful means of encouraging the Negro to work. There is some truth in this. But the fact remains that the man is positively plundered by his wife's family; and if he belongs to a matrilinear community the chances are that its regulations will prevent him from taking his wife with him to his place of work. In many cases he will refuse to accept a fixed-term contract, and it is by no means unusual for him to give up his job and go home to his village. Industrial concerns in the colonies, being aware of the prominent part played by the Negro wives, usually provide a number of facilities to enable their employees to pay dowries and get married. Some companies have gone so far as to adopt a policy of family stabilization which has often given excellent results (the Union Minière du Haut Katanga has been particularly successful in this respect). I have also come across many instances proving that the Negro woman—a habitual cause of absenteeism and therefore of instability—could also have a valuable stabilizing influence.

Another effect of tradition on the workers is their casual attitude towards their employment. A man who leaves his job or is dismissed knows that he will always find support and help in his own village, especially as there is no individual ownership of land, so that any member of the group is entitled to cultivate the soil and reap the resultant harvest. He can thus be off-hand at no risk to himself, and fall back on the village at any time. This tug of war between the clan and the colonial economic system is becoming more and more strenuous.

In the large towns, such as Léopoldville and Elizabethville, there are signs that economic pressure is becoming stronger than home influences. This was apparent, for instance, towards the end of 1953, when the danger of unemployment which arose in certain branches of activity seemed to have brought about an appreciable change in the attitude of workers towards their jobs. But in working for a European concern, the Negro is still embarking upon an unnatural kind of life; and giving up such work still means, for him, a return to a natural life. Thus, as he can find a livelihood in his village, he is very seldom placed in the position of a work-shy labourer in Europe.

The type of work

Another prominent cause of absenteeism is to be found in the type of work. To begin with, it should be mentioned that workers settle down better in industrial undertakings than on the plantations—probably because in the factories they feel they have drawn closer to the European employees, that they have surmounted yet another of the barriers separating them from the whites: whereas on the plantations they feel—as they told me quite frankly—that they are doing 'nigger work'. The proportion of absenteeism varies, however, from one factory or plantation to another and, other things being equal, the work itself appears to be the deciding factor.

It has now become a truism to say that in factories the extent to which a worker settles down depends on his degree of skill. In factories, too, night work is particularly unpopular, and absenteeism is rife among employees on night shift. On the plantations, the unskilled work, such as weeding, or keeping the plants in straight rows, does much to unsettle the employees. There are two reasons for this: in the villages, such work has always been left to women; and on the plantations, employers have always given it to the weakest and least skilled men— thus bringing the work itself into disrepute, a fact of which the men are keenly aware. On the other hand, the teams employed to cut down trees and clear the ground for the enlargement of the plantations show a most satisfactory enthusiasm for their work, although it is much the hardest, most dangerous and most exhausting of all types of agricultural labour. This popularity is due to the fact that work of this kind has always been done by men; moreover, many Europeans regard forest clearance as one of their finest tasks, and this certainly affects their attitude towards the workers they employ. It is equally certain that it creates a desirable psychological atmosphere for the work.

There is another factor which should perhaps not be underestimated. Like most plantation work, forest clearance is made up of clearly-defined tasks. The African is always anxious to know exactly how much work is expected of him in a particular job, and how long it is to take: and this cannot always be predicted in other types of agricultural work.

Proximity of Negro villages

This is a factor which usually has an unfavourable effect upon workers employed on the plantations. In the equatorial province, for instance, absenteeism is encouraged, for various reasons, by the proximity of the villages from which the employees come.

The first reason is that their wives often leave the camp and return to the village—because they are summoned back, because they are cultivating a plot of land there, or because they have some other reason for staying at home. In such cases, the worker often leaves his job—either because he wants to see how his wife's crop is coming along, or because he feels he ought to keep an eye on her personally! In the Mayumbe district (province of Léopoldville) the proximity of the Negro villages produces this effect chiefly towards the middle of the dry season, when the workers go home to repair their huts before the rains begin. On several plantations in the Eastern Province (Stanleyville) the workers go off as soon as they are paid, to hand over their money to their families at home.

Several agricultural concerns have realized the extreme importance of this question of proximity and have tried, usually with success, to reconstruct the entire Negro village on their own concession. In thus replacing the camp, which workers rarely like, by the village, they get rid of one cause of absenteeism.

The problem is more serious in the palm plantations than in the rubber plan-tations, for workers who go away for any of the above reasons can usually be sure of making up the wages they forfeit by their absence. When they get back to the village they need only cut the fruits from the palm trees and take them to the nearest purchasing station. Even if this belongs to the concern by which they are employed, they can rely on selling their produce.

The proximity of the home gives rise to precisely the type of absenteeism which employers find most difficult to prevent—frequent, temporary absen-teeism, which disorganizes the work to an even greater extent than desertion or long absence. And geographical considerations, combined with the effect of the regulations governing the recruitment of labour, usually lead employers to hire their workers locally.

Proximity of large towns

Here the problem is one of abandonment of jobs and general instability of the labour market, rather than of absenteeism properly so-called. Undertakings (especially plantations) situated in the neighbourhood of Europeanized towns, or of African settlements attached to such towns, find that their chief handicap in this respect is the workers' tendency to move to such places. I will not enter into the various reasons why they do this, but merely point out that the attraction exists.

Other causes of absenteeism

Under this heading I have listed a number of causes which came to my notice, but which are less far reaching in their effect than those already mentioned.

Gambling. In about ten of the plantations I visited, gambling was a positive scourge. The workers stake their pay, lose it, and are disheartened—especially as they find that absentees, both those who have dropped their work altogether and those who are simply slacking, spend their entire time practising the games concerned, then fleece the workers and live very largely at their expense!

Food supplies. In some districts, despite the efforts made by the employers and the measures introduced by the authorities, food supplies are unsatisfactory. If the workers are given, in kind, the legal rations which form part of their pay, the situation is considerably improved. But for some years they have been demanding money instead of rations, and in most cases the authorities and the employers have been obliged to give way. If local food supplies are scarce, the men go hunting and fishing, to obtain 'extras' which they greatly appreciate. The employer very often does much to help them, but the urge to improve their diet frequently results, nevertheless, in their dropping their work for two or three days, to go hunting in the bush. This cause of absenteeism is too important to be ignored.

Policy regarding breaches of contract. At present, penalties are incurred by Negroes who commit a breach of their work contract.[1]

During the last few years, under the influence of the liberal principles advocated by the International Labour Organisation, the idea has been gaining ground in Belgium that these penalties should be abolished. The colonial authorities have not so far taken any steps to rescind them, but the law courts in the Belgian Congo are adopting an increasingly lenient policy in this respect. The result is—most unfortunately—that the workers are beginning to consider that their contracts cease to be binding from the moment they feel inclined to stop work. This feeling helps to account for the increase of absenteeism in the Belgian Congo—especially as the public prosecutor often refuses to apply the existing regulations, anticipating that they will soon be altered.

So far I have dealt with absenteeism as a prominent factor in the instability of the labour market in the Belgian Congo, illustrating its extent by a number of examples, some of which contribute not only to absenteeism but to permanent withdrawal from employment.

In addition to this factor, which in itself would repay further investigation, there are others, among which I would include *inflated wages, lack of vocational training among Negro workers,* and *the behaviour of white overseers.*

INFLATED WAGES

During the post-war boom in the building trade, particularly in the larger towns of the colony, contractors began to offer workmen wages and remuneration in kind on a scale which attracted them in large numbers, thus disorganizing the labour market. This also led to an extraordinary waste of manpower, for as labour was comparatively cheap, these contractors hired their workers *en masse,* even if they were completely unskilled. This same policy of inflated wages has been adopted, to a varying extent, in other branches of activity.

LACK OF VOCATIONAL TRAINING

This also helps to unsettle the workers. So far there has been no effective organization of vocational training in the Belgian Congo, and school trained workers

---

1. Three decrees making this a punishable offence are in force in the Belgian Congo and in Ruanda-Urundi: decree of 16 March 1922, relating to work contracts, Articles 46-53, Chapter IX, dealing with repressive measures; decree of 11 January 1926, relating to indentures, Article 29, Chapter VIII; decree of 1 April 1933, relating to work contracts for boatmen, Articles 28-35, Section III. This decree stipulates that the penalties mentioned in the decree of 16 March 1922 shall be applicable to Negroes employed on the waterways.

were soon heavily outnumbered by Negroes from the villages, who had to be recruited and employed after the war because of the rapid economic expansion.

Many of these men were workers only in name. Apprenticeship and vocational training courses were organized for them in several enterprises. But the sociological and psychological factors whose persistence I have already described came into play and were responsible for an immense amount of disturbance in the labour market.

THE BEHAVIOUR OF WHITE WORKERS

Colonial authorities and private employers in the Belgian Congo recruit as few European overseers as possible, because of the high salaries they are obliged to pay them. It is generally agreed, however, that the overseers have a decisive influence on the attitude of the African workers. Lack of supervision and inadequate technical guidance result in low output and this in its turn unsettles the workers. Matters are often made worse by the employment of insufficiently trained European workers in the lower grades, since their behaviour frequently causes the Negroes to give up their jobs.

THE PROBLEMS OF THE AFRICAN WORKER
IN THE GABOON AND THE CONGO

G. BALANDIER

The region of the Gaboon and the Middle Congo, where, between 1948 and 1951, I carried out a survey and took steps to encourage certain practical reforms, is one whose economic and social development presents great difficulties. Not that the peoples living in this region are exceptionally backward from the cultural standpoint: in certain respects, owing to their long-established direct and indirect relations with the West, they seem better prepared than the larger national groups of West Africa to embark upon the 'modern' tasks which now confront them. The difficulty is due rather to geographical and historical causes. This area has an extremely sparse population (hardly more than a million inhabitants); distances are considerable and communications, right up to recent years, poor, while improvements—such as the Congo-Océan railway—have been very costly. The physical hardships and material difficulties inseparable from life in the equatorial zone have also to be reckoned with. There are only two areas with a comparatively 'dense' population—the Ba-Kongo country in the neighbourhood of Brazzaville (with 12-15 inhabitants per square kilometre) and the Wole-Ntem, bordering on the Cameroons, where Fang peasants have recently established cocoa plantations (over 5 inhabitants per square kilometre).

Moreover, the peoples occupying this territory suffered heavily in former times from the slave trade, which reduced the population and led to many tribal wars. They have also felt the repercussions of the trading methods of more modern times, which gave rise, until quite recently, to a considerable flow of population towards the trading posts and to fierce competition for monopolies. Instability still characterizes most communities in the Gaboon-Congo region. It has been intensified by colonization, which, through its need to recruit labour, was responsible for a rush to the towns which it made no attempt to stem—with the result that in the Middle Congo, one out of every five inhabitants is now living either temporarily or permanently in a town.

Economic development is retarded by what may be called 'indigenous' obstacles. These, as already explained, include—in addition to the serious difficulties so liberally provided by nature itself in the equatorial zone—underpopulation, the impermanent character of the local communities, and an economic system which has been based since remote times, at least so far as the male population is concerned, more on barter and the acquisition of commodities for bartering than on agriculture. But the difficulties inherent in the economic activities of colonists must also be taken into account. Until recently, barter—conducted through the medium of the 'Sociétés' and of a number of middlemen—was the chief occupation in the region. Not until after 1920 was the timber (*okumé*) industry developed on an extensive scale; mining did not begin until after 1930, when the first important lines of communication were being opened up (one mining company was formed at an earlier date, but it soon lapsed into inactivity). It is in the public works enterprises, in the logging and mining camps, that the villagers—in large numbers and without passing through a transitional stage—gain their first experience of wage-earning. These types of work employ a large quantity of labour, but provide a minimum of training. This has an inevitable effect on the behaviour of the African worker who 'emerges' from such activities. Any survey of his problems, such as is required before practical action can be taken, must be based on an understanding of this situation.

In an underpopulated country, where there is a local shortage of manpower (in the neighbourhood of a given industry) coupled with a comparatively high demand, there are only three possible methods of supplying requirements—by compulsion (the policy of 'drafting' labour), by calling in help from outside, or by introducing technical improvements, which has been the tendency for the past ten years. Taking our examples from the Gaboon, we will now consider how manpower problems have affected village communities by disturbing their demographic structure, contributed towards the growth of a proletariat, and given rise to a policy of direct or indirect compulsion which has been maintained over a long period.

Until the present day, when the whole process is being mechanized, the timber industry required from 20,000 to 30,000 workers, known as 'hired hands'. This demand was made upon a country with only 420,000 inhabitants, where manpower was needed for other purposes as well. A rough estimate, based on the age-groups generally recruited—men between the ages of 20 and 40—will show that this number of workers represents the total number of males in that age-group in a population of 150,000 to 180,000. Over 40 per cent of the population of the Gaboon was thus affected by the demands of the lumber camps; this figure gives some idea of the contribution provided by communities outside the area of the industry.

The local authorities were quick to realize the demographic and social consequences of this policy, which adversely affected the inhabitants of the Gaboon without satisfying the requirements of the contractors. The annual report for 1928 states that 'much remains to be done in order to compensate for the decrease in the native population which has resulted from the large-scale recruitment of labour'. It refers to the 'grave consequences' of this 'emigration', saying that 'family life is completely disorganized when the grown men leave their villages, to work in industries on the coast'. In addition to all this, there were growing up alongside these industries so-called *villages de vagabonds* (shanty towns), the spread of which was contributing to the growth of a very unstable proletariat.

Furthermore, the voracious demands of the timber industry are directed almost entirely towards unskilled labour; the villagers are uprooted, without being permanently settled in a new sphere of activity, and without receiving any training. As recently as 1950, according to figures published by the Inspectorate of Labour, more than 80 per cent of the labour force in the Gaboon were unskilled manual workers and only 13 per cent so-called skilled workers—these percentages cover all types of activity, some of which are less 'primary' than the timber industry.

A further example may be drawn from one particular district—that of the administrative area of Ngounia (Gaboon), which is both a 'reserve of manpower' and an industrial zone. In 1950, the total number of wage-earners employed in the mines and lumber camps of this area amounted to 23 per cent of the adult male population over 15 years of age, while during the previous ten years nearly 18,000 men had left the district to work elsewhere. This illustrates the high proportion of wage-earners in the region, and the cost in terms of male population to regions which abide by the traditional ways of life. The study of economic motivations and incentives can be undertaken only in conjunction with a thorough investigation of the circumstances in which a peasant becomes a wage-earning worker, and the opportunities available to him in this sphere. According to my own observations in the southern part of French Equatorial Africa—which were confirmed by my colleague, G. Sautter, the geographer—there is every reason to suppose that 'jungle' enterprises find great difficulty in keeping their workers—especially since the introduction of the new laws of 1946, which, by recognizing the principle of freedom of employment, have diminished the possibility of recourse to coercion. It should be added that the 'social welfare' measures adopted by certain agricultural and mining undertakings in the Middle Congo have done little to reduce this tendency to drift. Once 'uprooted', the peasant makes his way by gradual stages, through one industrial job after another, towards one of the big urban centres. It is to these, therefore, that a considerable part of this survey will be devoted: they undoubtedly attract like a magnet. For this purpose I shall draw upon the results of my survey of the 'Black Brazzavilles',[1] by which I mean the African towns of Poto-Poto, Wenzé and Bacongo, bordering on the white town.

Let us consider the situation of the wage-earner in these towns.

The two main criticisms suggested by a perusal of the Inspectorate of Labour's reports are that the labour market is in a state of continual flux—the comparative stability referred to above characterizes the urban population, but is not reflected in urban business enterprises—and that skilled workers are very rare. There is, incidentally, an inescapable connexion between these two facts.

The state of flux is due to the very nature of salaried employment in Africa, and to the particular types of economy which exist in this region. The Negro is forced into wage-earning by an ever-growing need of money, by the rapid disappearance of traditional methods of subsistence, and by he necessity of paying his taxes; the wage he receives is very low, whereas his financial requirements are becoming more and more numerous. In the towns, the worker's chief incentive is the desire to obtain the best paid work available; and to this end the more ambitious go to the Belgian Congo to get some type of special training in demand at Brazzaville. In most cases, wages and purchasing power are not high enough to attract the workers. This is shown by the efforts they make to obtain the better paid jobs, as mechanics, chauffeurs, etc., and by the comparative stability in this class of employment. Many prefer not to take permanent jobs; they hope to get back to their villages, for varying periods, or to establish themselves in some form of commercial activity which is not only profitable, but satisfies their need of freedom. This is another cause of mobility, originating in the system of barter which was for a long time the dominant feature of the local economy. It emphasizes the fundamental weakness of a labour market which is in itself precarious and subject to fluctuation because it is governed by purely external circumstances.

The reaction of workers to the reforms introduced since 1945 is significant.

1. A survey carried out during my visit to the Congo and the Gaboon, from 1948 to 1951.

The report drawn up in 1947 by the General Inspectorate of Labour stresses the following factors: insufficient attraction of salaried work, 'because the advantages it offers are regarded as inadequate, compared with the effort involved and the profits which accrue'; refusal to subscribe to long-term engagements, which are governed by arbitrary contracts. Here the report explains that: 'In urban centres, the tendency to accept employment only for brief periods developed at a much earlier date. It is due to the fact that in such places workers were, and still are, drawn from a large floating population, difficult to supervise and, on the whole, reluctant to accept regular, long-term work. Employers thus became accustomed to hiring manual labourers on a day-to-day basis. . . . Skilled workers, though tending to remain longer in their jobs, have always objected to signing long-term contracts, which offered them no appreciable advantages in exchange for their independence.'[1] This document calls attention to the role of urban centres as reserves of manpower, and the failure of the workers to adapt themselves to town life and steady employment—a failure resulting from the conditions of that employment.

Surveys conducted among workers at Brazzaville show that about 50 per cent of them would like to change their jobs—with the exception of the shop-keepers and fishermen, who are satisfied with their comparatively high profits. This desire springs from the hope of finding employment which will enable them to 'live better', or which will confer a certain prestige, or by the wish to have several strings to their bow and thus stand a better chance in periods of depression. During the survey I carried out in co-operation with various technical departments, it was found that manual labour was regarded by almost all workers as 'the worst', because it meant hard work for the lowest wage, and earned no esteem for the worker. This sheds an interesting light on the problem of the influence of local conditions on the choice of employment. The most 'attractive' professions are those involving the new techniques introduced by Europeans—civil service and teaching (clerk, schoolmaster), health (nurse, doctor, laboratory assistant), mechanization (chauffeur, tractor driver, mechanic, etc.). And these, being the fields in which the whites have proved themselves to be superior, and in which they predominate, are all the more alluring, since they seem to be reserved for a privileged minority. This fact is mentioned in the official reports: 'Experience has shown that Negroes find a unique attraction in machines—to such an extent that they lose interest in other activities of outstanding importance, such as building or carpentry.'[2] Moreover, the first observations, made in various parts of Africa, go to show that Negro workers are very efficient in dealing with machines.[3] For a long time it was maintained that 'progressive' Africans were interested only in 'white-collar' jobs. This was true only when office work was the sole alternative to domestic service or manual labour—in which circumstances it was natural that they should prefer it.

These inclinations are hard to satisfy under the present economic and social system: in the course of the survey already mentioned, many of those questioned admitted that they 'had not been able to get other work', or 'learn any other job', or 'go to school'. An analysis of wage-earning in the Middle Congo, where the towns of Brazzaville and Pointe-Noire provide the majority of the statistics,

1. Inspection Générale du Travail, *Rapport Annuel 1947*, chapter on Labour Laws.
2. Inspection Générale du Travail, *Rapport Annuel 1949*, Annexes.
3. Unpublished report on possibilities of industrialization in Africa, drawn up by the International African Institute, London.

serves to illustrate this point:[1] domestic servants, 4.5 per cent; clerical workers, 7.5 per cent; technicians and skilled labourers, 25.5 per cent; unskilled labourers, 62.5 per cent.

To these particulars should be added the fact that salaried employees in the 'management and supervision' category make up less than 1 per cent of the total of African workers, and that, like many of the clerical workers, they are often foreigners.

All this points to what is described, in official parlance, as 'an excessive proportion of unskilled workers', and raises the question of vocational training. What demand is there for trained personnel, and what attempts have been made to satisfy them? The answer to this question is supplied in part by the information given above, concerning the economic situation in this part of Central Africa: owing to the lack of industrial equipment and the prevalence, until recent years, of the system of barter, such a demand hardly existed until 1945, when the so-called 10-year plan was put into operation. As for the training of skilled personnel, the reports drawn up during the emergency period which followed that date refer with some bitterness to 'the negligence shown by many employers, during the past few years, in training and supervising their workmen'.[2] In connexion with this remark, it should be remembered that technical training, whether government-organized or in private hands, was of very poor quality, no attempt to place it on a sound footing having been made until 1937, when the vocational training school at Brazzaville was reorganized. This establishment is still the only real school of its kind; and except for the apprenticeship centre at Pointe Noire—which had 266 pupils in 1950-51—it is the largest. In 1950-51 there were 190 pupils divided among the three sections (industrial, technical and commercial) of which the school has consisted since 1946. The future prospects of these pupils vary considerably, according to whether they enter government or private employment. Figures issued by the Inspectorate of Labour show that in the former case they receive much higher salaries (7,000 as against 3,000 francs, in 1949-50), together with special allowances, and have good prospects. The contrast, says the report, gives rise to 'grave dissatisfaction, which may result in aversion for manual work'.[3] This remark is illuminating: the existing enterprises have as yet no need for highly skilled workers. Only the building trade and the public works undertakings have a great need of 'specialists' at the moment, to meet the demands of the plan. This accounts for the eight-month 'intensive vocational training courses' offered by the four industrial 'sections' (masonry and bricklaying, reinforced concrete, timber work, carpentry) which were set up as an emergency measure. These are the consequences of an economic system which was for long in a state of stagnation, and which owes its new lease of life entirely to the exceptional circumstances of the present post-war period.

Further proof that vocational training has been neglected is furnished by the numerous cases of 'casual' apprenticeship, where boys go to some older worker, who may be only semi-skilled, to receive a smattering of instruction for which a high payment is often asked. This practice exists among carpenters, bricklayers, cobblers, tailors, chauffeurs, and even typists. But it is the chauffeurs who find it the most profitable, because of the attraction exerted by their work—which entails handling a machine and dealing with travellers and goods, and offers the possibility of taking on many apprentices.

---

1. Inspection du Travail du Moyen Congo, *Rapport Annuel 1949*.
2. Inspection Générale du Travail, *Rapport Annuel 1947*.
3. Inspection Générale du Travail, *Rapport Annuel 1949*.

In such circumstances it is naturally difficult to assess the workers' output or the quality of their work. The Inspectorate of Labour describes the situation as 'characterized by lack of diligence, great changeability, and an average output which is usually much below that of a European worker in the same type of employment'.[1] The report at once goes on to say, however, that this cannot be due only to physiological causes. It admits that the workers are insufficiently prepared for their tasks, makes a brief reference to the effect upon them of having left their familiar surroundings, which in the majority of cases is a very recent event, and states that 'the African worker is unfamiliar with the technical methods and the tools used by his European colleagues, and he is not accustomed, by tradition, to work to a time-table'. This latter observation, like all statements concerning the output of Negro workers, points to the need for certain specific investigations—an example of which was provided by Dr. Ombredane in the Belgian Congo, when he called for a comparison between incentives in familiar surroundings and surroundings where white influence predominates. His report draws attention to fundamental points of contrast: 'Contrary to the practice in familiar surroundings, the wage we offer the Negro depends on his output in a job which tends to be continuous for fixed intervals, which is organized, imposed upon him and supervised by others and is often so fragmentary and ant-like that its ultimate value is hardly apparent to those who do it.'[2]

Dr. Ombredane also emphasizes that the African worker remains alien to the task imposed upon him and to the undertaking which makes use of his services; he 'is seldom a permanent part of the undertaking for which he works; in most cases he remains an alien and unstable element'. This absence of interest accounts for the lack of diligence of which employers complain, and which is even more marked among manual labourers than among skilled workers. At Brazzaville, according to a very rough estimate, absenteeism varies 'from 8 to 12 per cent'—a very high percentage.

In view of all these unfavourable circumstances, some of which must be attributed to unfamiliar surroundings and the rest to a backward economic system, the question of the incentive provided by wages becomes important. The Inspectorate of Labour's reports indicate that 'in the great majority of cases, increased output has little effect on wages'; and that, furthermore, workers usually have but slight interest in receiving better pay, 'as they can seldom buy what they want in the market to which they have access'. This raises the question of the relation between wages and the prices in the market where the Negroes have to buy. Broad statements of this kind must, however, be qualified: one experiment carried out at Brazzaville showed that an appreciable rise in salary may lead to a proportionately higher increase in output. One undertaking which hires casual labour has two work sites, on one of which it pays the legal wage rate, while on the other it offers from 20 to 25 per cent above the legal rates. Output is notably higher in the latter case, and the difference exceeds 25 per cent. No appreciable improvement in output can be expected without greater security for the worker; and present insecurity is due not only to the state of flux in the labour market, but also to the low purchasing power of money and the lack of an adequate welfare service.

Added to all this, it should be observed that the bonds created by team-work

---

1. Inspection Générale du Travail, *Rapport Annuel 1949*, Annexes.
2. Dr. A. Ombredane, 'Principes pour Une Étude Psychologique des Noirs du Congo Belge', in *L'Année Psychologique*, 50th year, 1951.

are still very fragile, and are often broken by long-standing antagonisms based on ethnical factors. This instability is due in great part to the preference for short-term employment, the recent origin and doubtful duration of many undertakings, and the high proportion of 'new' citizens in the towns. From the topographical point of view it is reflected in the fact that the population shows no tendency to sort itself into occupational groups—no such groups are being formed, even in the newest parts of the towns. Except in the case of the railway workers, who live together in a special camp—which, incidentally, has helped them to develop a certain interest in their work as such, and has led to a comparatively successful trade union movement among them—the chief impression is that the wage-earners, as a body, are widely dispersed and exert very little influence. The difficulties encountered by the trade union movement (suspect, at first, as being a type of organization introduced by the colonizing power, and later divided against itself by individualistic tendencies) are significant.

It is not enough to consider only those difficulties which arise from the peculiar features of the wage system and the modernized sector of economy in an underdeveloped country. Cultural conditions must also be taken into account—and anthropologists have been active in investigating them. Economic progress among African Negroes may be seriously impeded by the persistence of certain types of behaviour, or of methods of organization which are not really adequate.

The Fang tribe, in the Gaboon, shows a 'maladjustment' which is due to the survival of a traditional attitude towards wealth. The social structure of this people is fairly flexible, individual eminence being more regarded than constituted authority; for instance a rich man (*nkuma-kuma*) enjoys so much respect that strangers are apt to take him for the local chief. But wealth here consists chiefly of wives (a local proverb says 'Our wives are our real wealth') and of goods locked up in chests, which may in a sense be considered as 'potential wives', since they help to make up the dowry. A good deal of the tribal income undoubtedly comes into circulation in the first place in the form of dowries, and these are governed by local fluctuations in prices. Now that money is being earned by an increasing number of individuals, competition for wives is intensified, and the dowry figure is constantly rising, while involuntary bachelors are becoming more and more numerous. Once the system under which wealth and women were kept in circulation has been thus disturbed, it causes more discontent and strife than satisfaction. However, it still remains, as one young Fang writer puts it, 'the starting point and the goal of Fang economy'. This tips the scales in a way which discourages the economic activity of the young men, who are the first to suffer from the situation. The resultant lack of balance is typical of a society where the production of human beings (the size of the social group which one person controls either directly or by 'alliance') has remained more important than the production of property and the amount of controlled wealth. This is not an isolated case.

A second type of maladjustment occurs because traditional forms of authority (a maternal uncle's authority over his nephew, the authority of an older over a younger brother, etc.) are often exerted in such a way as to bring about the economic exploitation of the dominated person. The same applies to traditional rights over women which, where they are maintained, give scope for 'blackmailing' the husband with perpetual requests for 'presents'. Families (in the widest sense of the word) and 'associates' invoke tradition to justify their claim to a considerable proportion of an individual's income. Economic activity is, of course, discouraged rather than stimulated by this 'commercialization' of social relationships.

These are only two typical examples of unfavourable factors. But it should be remembered that favourable factors exist as well. Reference to traditional customs may bring to light methods of organization which can be adapted without great difficulty to the new economic conditions. This has been the case with the *Ki-temo* evolved by the Ba-kongo, the practical value of which has been proved by the many services it has rendered. I should like, therefore, to give a somewhat detailed description of this type of economic organization, which is known chiefly as a savings association.

The *mwan' a temo*[1] members of such an association vary in number from the 3 to 4 needed to form a 'little *temo*' to the 10 to 20 of a 'big *temo*'; they all pay in an equal sum, the amount of which, and the frequency of the payments (fortnightly or monthly), are fixed in the light of their financial position and their aims. Workers earning an average wage usually organize '500-franc' or '1,000-franc' *temos*, to be paid in at the end of each month; while tradesmen and certain government employees manage to make deposits amounting to several thousand francs. Strict discipline is maintained; fines are imposed for delay, and if any member cannot pay his contribution, he must either find someone to take his place, or borrow the necessary sum.

The chief purpose of such an association is to build up a sum giving a higher purchasing power than that of the individual members; to oblige the members to save, by means of strict discipline; and to protect them from extortionate money-lenders by a system of mutual assistance. But the *mwan' a temo* often gets into debt in order to keep up his contributions and has to use his share, when he receives it, to pay his debts. The preliminary condition for the establishment of such an association is that the prospective members all need to build up a capital sum within a relatively short period—to put the finishing touches to a dowry, pay for a fence, build or repair a hut, etc. Members must all be of the same tribe (the association is confined to natives of the Ba-kongo) and there must be a certain affinity between them, so that they trust one another. According to tradition, the member who receives all the contributions must provide the palm-wine which is drunk by the entire company, in token of the sacred nature of the pledges given and of the alliance into which they have entered. This attempt to adapt tradition to the new economic circumstances helps to strengthen the bonds of fellowship the importance of which has already been indicated. Mr. H. Labouret emphasizes the fact that 'urban sedentary workers have (thus) brought with them to the towns those sentiments of fellowship and interdependence which are highly developed in most local communities'.

It is interesting to note the changes resulting from this transference to town conditions: the *temo* ceremonial has been simplified, losing its solemn and formal aspect and becoming a commonplace instead of an exceptional event. The average number of members has decreased, and the links between them have lost much of their significance. These were originally intended to mark the establishment of friendly business relations between former enemies. Later, they developed into a kind of mutual assistance among planters, to raise sums for capital expenditure. This type of *temo* is widespread in a number of Ba-kongo and Ba-soundi villages, and in some cases is not unlike a commercial partnership. Some of the younger Ba-kongo men are now considering the possibility of transforming the *ki-temo* into a co-operative society. All this shows that the system is highly diversified, but its permanent characteristics are the pooling of wealth on a basis of complete solidarity, with interchange of assurances, and—still more important—the provi-

---

1. *Mwan'a temo*, child of the *temo*.

sion of a traditional framework which inspires confidence and involves the 'partners' in commitments which they clearly understand.

It is not possible to consider the problem of economic motivations and incentives as an isolated one, merely in the light of its psychological and cultural implications (inasmuch as culture tends to be defined, to an ever-increasing extent, in terms of behaviour). It needs a thorough investigation, which can only be undertaken with an exact knowledge of the economic conditions resulting from European interference and after a precise assessment of the present state of the society to which the African worker belongs. No full description of the impediments and adaptations which are affecting the economic activity of the Negroes can be provided without a comprehensive survey of that society; and the anthropological method is of great value here, since it deals with the question in all its aspects. The need for such an approach is evident—in African Negro communities everything may be said to hinge on economics and religion.

Moreover, the need for a comprehensive investigation, covering all the subjects concerned, is increased by the fact that indissoluble bonds exist between the 'traditional' and 'modernist' environments, each of which reacts on the other. This gives rise to a further problem, which cannot be considered here: how is the transition to be made from this comprehensive study—dealing with subjects not all equally susceptible of generalization—to the advancing of any really significant theory?

THE ARAB DEVELOPMENT SOCIETY'S
PROJECT IN JERICHO, JORDAN

C. HOURANI

Perhaps the most interesting agricultural, social and educational experiment being conducted in the Middle East today is the project of the Arab Development Society near the town of Jericho on the west bank of the Jordan. This project is at one and the same time an experiment in the utilization of underground sources of water (the existence of which was not suspected until the Society, under the guidance and inspiration of its President, Musa Alami, dug its first well in 1949); an experiment in housing, which has established certain facts about costs and standards involved in providing homes for refugees now living in tents and caves; an experiment in educating the 'lost generation' of Arab youth from the refugee camps to become useful members of society; an experiment in agricultural and irrigation techniques which will have to be developed if and when the Jordan Valley is cultivated on a large scale; and above all an experiment in self-help conducted exclusively by Palestinian Arabs seeking by their own efforts to redeem themselves and to restore a self-confidence badly shattered by the events of 1948.

The importance of the project has received international recognition in learned publications such as the *Middle East Journal*,[1] recent articles appearing in *Time* magazine[2] and in the *New York Times*,[3] the interest displayed by visiting foreign diplomats, experts and technicians, and by a recent grant from the Ford Foundation to expand the educational side of the project.

HISTORY OF THE PROJECT

The project of the Arab Development Society in its actual state today is the outcome of years of experiment and reflection. The fluid political, social and economic conditions of Palestine and Jordan in recent times have not provided the stable climate in which long-term planning could be carried out, and it was the ability of the Society to adapt itself to changing conditions, and its President's brilliant flair for improvisation which enabled it to survive and make a success of its efforts.

---

1. See *Middle East Journal*, Washington, D.C., Vol. 5, No. 4, Autumn 1951.
2. See *Time*, 20 July 1953 (Atlantic edition).
3. The *New York Times* on two successive days, 6 and 7 July 1953, published front-page and leading articles about the project, which it called 'Mr Alami's Oasis'.

The origin of the project is to be found in the attempts made by Musa Alami[1] in 1944 and 1945 to interest the Arab League in a programme of village welfare in Palestine designed to check the progressive alienation of land from Arab to Jewish hands which was a consequence of the poverty, ignorance, lack of credit facilities and general backwardness of the Arab fellahin.[2] In order to administer this programme Musa Alami formed a group in Jerusalem, composed of prominent Palestinian Arab personalities, under the name of the Arab Development Society.[3] The members of the group adopted Musa Alami's proposals, and the Government of Iraq generously subscribed the sum of 250,000 Iraq dinars (equivalent to £250,000 sterling); this has been the main fund from which the Society has financed its work.

With the intention of founding a model village which would set standards for village housing, the Society purchased a large tract of land in the Jenin area and a smaller piece in the upper Jordan Valley. The former tract, however, fell into Israeli hands in 1949 and the capital expenditure and effort made there and in other districts by the Society were wiped out.[4] With the destruction of the former Palestine, the establishment of Israel, and the annexation of what remained in Arab hands to Transjordan, the problem of raising the standards of village life in a settled community was transcended by a new and vastly more difficult one—what could be done to save the uprooted Palestinian Arab community from complete disintegration and dispersion? Almost the whole of that community was now uprooted; moreover the greater part of the refugees were from rural areas, and with the loss of their lands and the possibility of carrying on a way of life which had been pursued for centuries, they were threatened with speedy destruction as a community if left to rot in camps, with their demoralizing life of inactivity.

Faced by this vast problem, and at the same time now having only very limited financial assets,[5] the Society had to re-think its programme and purpose. What remained of their funds could be spent on relief, but it would not go very far, and then the Society would have to close down. The money left was not sufficient to rehabilitate or resettle any significant number of refugees, even had resettlement been then a practical policy. There remained the possibility of using their funds for an experiment which would demonstrate certain basic facts simultaneously to the refugees themselves, to the Arab Government, and to the international organizations concerned with the problem either on the political or humanitarian level. It was this last course which Musa Alami decided to take.

For the purpose which he had in mind Musa Alami chose as the site of his experiment the southern end of the Jordan Valley, just north of the Dead Sea, which is the lowest place on the surface of the globe. In June 1949 the Society obtained permission from the Government of Jordan to take possession of an area of land to the extent of some 5,000 acres and to develop it. This area was officially registered as 'dead and waste'; except after the scanty rains (an average of three inches per year) no vegetation grew on it, and to all intents and purposes it was a desert, as hot and desolate as any in Arabia.

---

1. For biographical details, see *Middle East Journal*, October 1949.
2. For details of this programme, see *Middle East Journal*, Autumn 1951, pp. 497-8.
3. For the constitution and programme of the Arab Development Society, see pamphlet published by the Society in July 1953 at Jerusalem.
4. Pending of course the possibility of compensation.
5. 200,000 Jordan dinars.

The first basic fact which Musa Alami wished to make clear, particularly to the United Nations organization in charge of relief and works projects, was that before dismissing an area of land as unsuitable for development because of lack of water or for any other reason, it was necessary to explore its possibilities to the full. UNRWA was of the opinion that the Jordan Valley offered no attractive possibilities for refugee rehabilitation, and favoured the transfer of the bulk of the refugees to Syria, Iraq and Libya. This opinion was based on the premise that there was not enough water to make the Jordan Valley, and in particular its southern end, cultivable.

Accordingly the Arab Development Society proceeded to dig a well, with a primitive rig of their own construction. The result was immediately encouraging. Water was found at less than a hundred feet: it was sweet, with an extremely low salinity, and it was plentiful. Since the first well was dug, 24 more wells have been dug, all of them showing similar results.[1] The average flow from each well now in operation[2] is 100 cubic metres per hour. No diminution in the flow has been observed after three years of continuous pumping.

With this underground supply of water, the Society could begin to cultivate the land at its disposal. To date 2,500 dunams (625 acres) have been desalted and made cultivable. On this area 16,000 forest trees, 10,000 banana trees, 5,000 citrus trees, and 8,000 vines have been planted and are flourishing, in addition to highly successful crops of vegetables, cereals and cotton. The great fertility of the soil, the plentiful supply of water and the intense heat combine to produce extraordinary results, and the face of nature has already been changed by the green oasis which the Society has created in just over three years.

Accordingly, the first objective which Musa Alami and the Society set themselves has been achieved. The existence of hitherto unsuspected underground sources of water has been proved, and what was previously regarded as uncultivable land has become the most fertile and productive land in the region. One of the immediate results has been to stimulate private enterprise to look for water in the vicinity of the Society's land, and 15 wells have been successfully dug and gardens and orchards planted. The price of land in the neighbourhood has risen from practically nothing to 30 Jordan dinars.

Another result of the Society's success in finding new water supplies has been to compel UNRWA and the governments which are its main supporters to turn their attention back to the Jordan Valley as the one area which in the near future could enable any considerable number of refugees to be rehabilitated. The utilization of the water of the Yarmuk and Jordan rivers, of such surface water as can be trapped and stored, and of underground water, would permit a considerable portion of the 600,000 dunams (150,000 acres) of the valley to be cultivated, giving employment and land to perhaps 250,000 refugees.

The second basic fact which Musa Alami wished to demonstrate both to the refugees themselves and to the Arab governments was that there was an alternative line of action to allowing the refugees to remain in the camps until they could return to their homes. The choice was not one between settlement or repatriation, but between the demoralizing life of the camps or a life which would restore to the refugees their usefulness as productive members of society and their dignity and self-respect as human beings. Whatever their future destiny

---

1. In 1953 the Society received a well-boring machine as a joint gift from Tapline and Aramco; till then it had had, at great expense, to hire a rig.
2. The Society does not have money to buy pumps and motors for the others.

might be, the important thing was to rescue them from inactivity and to point out to them a way by which they could work out their own salvation. To the local governments, moreover, Musa Alami wished to demonstrate that the refugees were not a burden on the economy of the country, but could assist in the process of developing hitherto undeveloped areas; and that the problem of raising living standards through increased productivity was a problem common to all the inhabitants, refugee or other.

A third objective which Musa Alami and the Arab Development Society set themselves was to discover the costs of refugee rehabilitation not by sitting in offices behind adding machines, but by process of actual experiment; and thereby to reach certain conclusions about the living standards which could be achieved with a given amount of money. It was the belief of Musa Alami that any attempt to provide homes other than tents for the refugees should aim at providing living standards higher than those from which they had come, and so act as a lever whereby the living standards of the non-refugee population could be raised. What this would cost could only be determined by trial and error. The Society's project therefore included the building of a model village with all community facilities. The village consists of 65 houses, a school, clinic, storehouses, pump-houses and public oven. The houses are of two sizes: the larger consists of two living rooms, kitchen, lavatory, shower, and a small verandah, covering 82 square metres of floor space; the smaller have the same facilities but only one living room. The building material is mud, baked in the sun to make hard bricks which provide excellent insulation against the heat. In spite of the fact that cement, timber and plumbing material all had to be purchased at high prices,[1] the average cost of each house worked out at 340 Jordan dinars ($952).

Taking into account all the expenses involved in the discovery of water, land reclamation, the purchase of machinery and agricultural equipment, the construction of buildings and the provision of social services, the Society reached for the average cost of rehabilitating one refugee family a figure much lower than the figure of $3,000 per family which the Director of UNRWA, Mr. John Blandford, estimated as the cost where considerable irrigation and desalting of the land is necessary (this figure including the estimated cost of 45 Jordan dinars ($126) for a mud hut).[2]

DEVELOPMENT OF THE PROJECT

It was the original intention of the Society that the village constructed on the site of the project should be a co-operative village, and that on the completion of work on land reclamation the refugee settlers would constitute a self-governing community. Certain factors, however, intervened to modify the Society's policy. In the first place, although enthusiastic about the discovery of water, the refugees showed no willingness to leave the camps and settle on the project. They were reluctant to risk losing their rations by finding employment which in their minds might not last and, above all, they feared that by settling on the project they might somehow lose their rights to the homes now under Israeli control which remain the object of all their thoughts and hopes, or to compensation. In the dim twilight

1. Jordan having practically no raw materials needed for construction.
2. See New York Times, 16 July 1951.

of the camps it is what has been lost that still beckons, not what can be done to take its place.[1]

In the second place, a new problem was arising among the refugees owing to the existence of a large number of boys and girls for whom there were either the most meagre educational facilities or none at all, and who were growing up in a world which offered them no country, no future, no hope. Unless something was done to rescue this 'lost generation' of Arab youth, there was a serious danger that they would constitute a disruptive force throughout the Arab countries, nihilistic because the world offered them nothing, destructive because they had known nothing but destruction. In the third place, there was an increasing possibility, created by the discovery of underground water and the growing attention of international experts and engineers to the Yarmuk River Project, that the Jordan Valley would become the site of large-scale development; this would create the demand for farmers with the special skills which irrigated cultivation in the Jordan Valley demands, and for the technicians and artisans who would be needed to build a new community.

All these three factors combined to convince Musa Alami and the Arab Development Society to change the emphasis of their project from being primarily an agricultural to becoming chiefly an educational one. In March 1952, a Vocational Training Centre was opened which is being built up to a strength of 120 boys.[2]

The students of the Vocational Training Centre are chosen mainly from the large class of orphans which the war in Palestine created. Since they have no homes, the Society must assume complete responsibility for them all year round, and assume the functions of parents. Boys are accepted between the ages of 11 and 15, and will remain until they are 19. In addition to elementary education they are taught practical agriculture and crafts. They live in the houses constructed on the project, and when they have finished their training they will be given the chance of settling on the land. As far as possible they run their own affairs; it is part of the training to instil into them the spirit of co-operation and self-reliance.

If funds can be found, it is the intention of the Society to expand the boys' centre so that it can take 250 students, and to found a centre for girls, also to the number of 250. The vocational training which it is hoped will eventually be offered will include: (a) agriculture, comprising tree growing, cultivation of cereals, vegetables, cotton, sugar cane and beet, horticulture, apiculture, poultry farming, dairy farming including pasteurization and cheese and butter manufacture, and certain industries connected with agriculture such as canning of vegetables and fruits and a flour mill; (b) crafts, comprising carpentry, mechanical and electrical training, plumbing, tailoring and sewing, shoe-making, embroidery; (c) industries, including weaving, tile and brick manufacture, and a printing and binding press.

The boys and girls trained in the centre will, it is hoped, constitute an important element in the building of a new community in the Jordan Valley which will follow on the development of the water resources of the region. Not only will they provide a farming class skilled in the special techniques of cultivation required by the climatic and soil conditions of the valley; they will also provide some of the skilled labour force which will be necessary for the construction,

---

1. The mentality of refugees everywhere is similar; it can only be fought by changing the conditions in which they live, not by argument and reason.
2. A grant of $149,000 from the Ford Foundation in July 1953 will enable the Society to increase the buildings and services of the centre, and thus help to raise the standard of agricultural training.

repair and servicing of the new communities. If the vision of a Jordan Valley Authority should become real, the Vocational Training Centre will play an important role as experimental station and training ground. 'Even if it did not exist, it would be necessary to invent it.'

The future development of the Arab Development Society's project will depend largely on the financial resources available. With present resources, and the existing stage of utilization of the land, the Society expects by 1955 to receive an income from its crops sufficient to support the Vocational Training Centre. The full utilization of the land and other resources of the Society would enable it to expand the centre by the addition of the industrial branch and the enlargement of the agricultural and crafts sections, and to take care of 500 boys and girls, 100 of whom would graduate yearly. It would also enable the Society to give employment to between 500 and 1,000 refugee families on the work of the project. On the basis of the experience gained in the development of the project to date, the total cost of this complete utilization of resources is estimated at 500,000 Jordan dinars.

Whether or not this further expansion takes place, the progress so far achieved justifies the description of the project as a most significant experiment in developing unused land and water resources, it has pointed the way to the development of a vast area of territory in the Jordan Valley and is doing pioneer work in the great task of reconstituting the dispersed Palestinian Arab community.

BIBLIOGRAPHY

The literature dealing with the consequences of technical progress in the so-called underdeveloped countries is considerable and is often difficult to distinguish from that even richer describing the phenomena of acculturation or confronting social development to economic development. The present bibliography does not therefore pretend to be exhaustive. It lists the main works which have been published on the subject during the last ten years—books which themselves often include a bibliography—and mentions a few articles which illustrate vividly the various themes connected with the influence of technical progress in countries undergoing development. When a book or periodical has been simultaneously published in several languages the bibliography lists only the original language in which this work has been written.

ADAM, A. 'L'influence de l'industrialisation sur la vie sociale au Maroc', *Way Forum* 32, July 1959, p. 18-21.
AKADEMIJA NAUK SSSR. *Social'no-ekonomiceskie problemy tehniceskogo progressa* (Social and economic problems of technical progress). Moskva, Izdatel'stvo Akademii Nauk SSSR, 1961. 480 p.
ALLEN, R., *et al. Technology and social change.* New York, Appleton-Century-Crofts, 1957. 529 p.
ALTHABE, G. *Le chômage à Brazzaville (étude psychologique).* Paris, Office de la Recherche scientifique et technique outre-mer, 1959, 163 p.
ANKARA UNIVERSITY. Faculty of Political Science. *Economic and social aspects of farm mechanization in Turkey.* Ankara, 1953, 105 p.
'Social aspects of industrialization in Africa South of the Sahara in rural areas', *International social science bulletin* 9 (3) 1957, p. 397-412.
Aspetti sociali dello sviluppo economico (Gli) (Social aspects of economic development). Milano, Vita e Pensiero, 1961. 155 p.
BALANDIER, G. 'Conséquences sociales du progrès technique dans les pays sous-développés. Revue des recherches significatives / Social implications of technical advance in underdeveloped countries. A trend report and bibliography', *Sociologie contemporaine / Current Sociology* 3(1), 1954-1955, p. 1-75.
——. 'Déséquilibres socio-culturels et modernisation des pays sous-développés', *Cahiers internationaux de sociologie* 3(20), 1956, p. 30-44.
——. 'Le développement industriel et la prolétarisation en Afrique noire', *Afrique et Asie* 20, 4th quarter 1952, p. 45-53.
——. 'Les implications sociales du développement économique: introduction', in: CONSEIL INTERNATIONAL DES SCIENCES SOCIALES. *Les implications sociales du développement économique*, p. 5-27. Paris, Presses universitaires de France, 1962.
——. (ed.) *Les implications sociales du progrès technique.* Paris, Presses universitaires de France, 1959. IX + 355 p.

BALANDIER, G. 'Problèmes de désorganisation sociale liés à l'industrialisation et à l'urbanisation dans les pays en cours de développement économique rapide', *Information (ISSC/CISS)* 6, Oct. 1955, p. 1-15.
——. *Sociologie actuelle de l'Afrique noire. Dynamique des changements sociaux en Afrique centrale.* Paris, Presses universitaires de France, 1955. XII + 511 p.
——. *Sociologie des Brazzavilles noires.* Paris, A. Colin, 1955, 274 p. (Cahiers de la Fondation nationale des sciences politiques, no. 67.)
——. 'Structures sociales traditionnelles et changements économiques', *Revue de l'institut de sociologie* 1, 1959, p. 27-40; *Cahiers d'études africaines* 1, Jan. 1960, p. 1-14.
——. (ed.), *Le tiers-monde. Sous-développement et développement.* Paris, Presses universitaires de France, 1956. New revised edition, by A. Sauvy, 1961, XXI + 404 p.
——; BERNARD, S; DAVIS, K., et al. *Changements techniques, économiques et sociaux.* Paris, Conseil international des sciences sociales, 1959. IX + 355 p.
BANKS, J. A. 'Social implications of technological change', in: CONSEIL INTERNATIONAL DES SCIENCES SOCIALES. *Lex implications sociales du développement économique,* p. 61-106. Paris, Presses universitaires de France, 1962.
BANTON, M. P. 'Les implications sociales de l'industrialisation en Afrique au sud du Sahara', *Information (ISSC/CISS)* 25, July 1960, p. 1-6.
——; DOSSER, D. G. M. 'The balance between social and economic development in Africa South of the Sahara', *Information (ISSC/CISS)* 27, June 1961, p. 5-20.
BARANSON, J. 'New technologies for emerging economies', *Harvard Business Review* 39(4), July-Aug. 1961, p. 144-152.
BARBER, W. J. *The economy of British Central Africa: a case study of economic development in a dualistic society.* Stanford, Calif., Stanford University Press, 1961. XII + 271 p.
BASCOM, W. R.; HERSKOVITS, M. J. (eds.), *Continuity and change in African cultures.* Chicago, University of Chicago Press, 1959. VII + 309 p.
BEAGLEHOLE, E. 'Evaluation techniques for enduced technological change', *International social science bulletin* 7 (3), 1955, p. 376-386.
BEHRENDT, R. F. W. *Die wirtschaftliche und soziale Revolution in den unentwickelten Ländern* (The economic and social revolution in the underdeveloped countries). Bern, H. Lang, 1959. 53 p.
BELSHAW, C. S. *Changing Melanesia: social economics of culture contact.* Melbourne, Oxford University Press, 1954. X + 197 p.
BENDIX, R. 'Industrialization, ideologies and social structure', *American sociological Review* 24(5), Oct. 1959, p. 613-622.
BENEDETTI, A. 'Sviluppo tecnologico e formazione sociale (Technical progress and social development), *Politico* 26(1), March 1961, p. 83-92.
BERGER, G., et al. *Le progrès scientifique et technique, et la condition de l'homme.* Paris, Presses universitaires de France, 1960. 136 p.
BERNA, J. J. 'Industrialization in underdeveloped countries', *Social Order* 7(1), Jan. 1957, p. 14-28.
BERNARD, S. *Les conséquences sociales du progrès technique.* Brussels (Institut de sociologie Solvay), les Éditions du Parthénon, 1956. 217 p.
BIGET, J. 'Industrialisation et sociétés africaines', *Revue de l'Action populaire* 144, Jan. 1961, p. 49-63.
BONAZZI, G. 'Alcune ipotesi sul rapporto tra reclutamento di manodopera industriale e processo di acculturazione in communità arretrate (Some hypotheses on the relation between the industrial manpower supply and the process of accumulation in backward areas), *Quaderni di Sociologia* II (40), Spring 1961, p. 160-170.
BROZEN, Y. 'Technological change, ideology and productivity', *Political science quarterly* 70(4), Dec. 1955, p. 522-542.
BUSIA, K. A. 'Africa in transition: technical civilization', *Practical anthropology* 6(5), Sept.-Oct. 1959, p. 223-230.
——. 'The impact of industrialism on African communities', in: *Annual Conference: Sociology section. Ibadan,* March 1953, p. 31-37. Ibadan, West African Institute of Social and Economic Research, 1953.

Busino, G. 'Aspetti sociali dell' industrializzazione in Asia' (Social aspects of industrialization in Asia), *Tempi moderni* 3(3), Oct.-Dec. 1960, p. 125-141.

Cabrita, H. 'Aspectos humanos e sociais de industrialização na Africa portuguesa' (Human and social aspects of industrialization in Portuguese Africa), *Belotim geral do Ultramar* 29(340), Oct. 1953, p. 55-80.

Capelle, M. 'The industrial employment of women in the Belgian Congo', *African women* 3(3), Dec. 1959, p. 59-61.

Cardoso, F. E.; Ianni, O. 'Condiciones y efectos de la industrialización de São Paulo' (Conditions and effects of industrialization of São Paulo), *Ciencias políticas y sociales italiana*. Milano, A. Giuffrè, 1961. 842 p.

Carlton, F. T. 'Human relations in an era of rapid technical change', *American journal of economics and sociology* 15(2), Jan. 1956, p. 183-188.

Centro nazionale di prevenzione e difesa sociale. *Il progresso tecnologico e la società italiana* (Technical progress and the Italian people). Milano, A. Giuffrè, 1961. 842 p.

Cola Alberich, J. 'Derivaciones sociológicas de la industrialización de Africa' (Sociological consequences of industrialization of Africa), *Cuadernos de estudios africanos* 27(3), 1954, p. 41-50.

Comhaire, J. 'Some aspects of urbanization in the Belgian Congo', *American journal of sociology* 62(1), July 1956, p. 8-13.

Conseil international des sciences sociales. Bureau international de recherche sur les implications sociales du progrès technique. *Conséquences sociales de l'industrialisation et problèmes urbains en Afrique*. Paris, 1954, 77 p.

'Conséquences sociales de l'industrialisation rapide des pays insuffisamment développés (Les)', *Progrès social* 56, July 1958, p. 3-48.

Costa Pinta, L. A. 'Economic development in Brazil. A general view of its sociological implications', in: Conseil international des sciences sociales. *Les implications sociales du développement économique*, p. 131-142. Paris, Presses universitaires de France, 1962.

——; Bazzanella, W. 'Economic development, social change and population problems in Brazil', *Annals of the American Academy of Political and Social Science* 316, March 1958, p. 121-126.

Courthéoux, J.-P. 'Sur la "socialisation" du progrès technique', *Revue économique (Paris)* 12(6), Nov. 1961, p. 905-917.

Curle, A. 'Tradition, development and planning', *Sociological Review* 8(2), Dec. 1960, p. 223-238. [Pakistan.]

Datta, B. *Economics of industrialization: a study of the basic problems of underdeveloped economy*. Calcutta, World Press, 1957. x + 332 p.

Davydov, B. I.; Ščedrenok, V. P. 'K voprosu o korennoj protivopoložnosti social'noe-konomičeskih posledstvij tehničeskogo progressa pri socializme i kapitalizme' (The basic opposition of social and economic consequences of technical development under socialism and capitalism), *Trudy (Leningradskij inženerno-ekônomičeskij Institut)* 35, 1961, p. 3-23.

Devauges, R. *Le chômage à Brazzaville en 1957 (étude sociologique)*. Paris, Office de la recherche scientifique et technique outre-mer, 1958. XII + 258 p.

Edokpayi, S. I. 'Industrialisation in West Africa', *African Affairs* 56(225), Oct. 1957, p. 317-324.

'Effet de l'industrialisation sur l'Inde (Les)', *Chronique sociale de France* 66(7), 15 Dec. 1958, p. 525-539.

Ellis, H. S.; Wallich, H. C. (eds.), *Economic development for Latin America*. Proceedings of a conference held by the International Economic Association. New York, St. Martin's Press, 1961. x + 478 p. [Some papers refer to the implications of technology].

El-Saaty, H. 'Some aspects of the social implications of technological change in Egypt, U. A. R.', in: Conseil international des sciences sociales. *Les implications sociales du développement économique*, p. 153-166. Paris, Presses universitaires de France, 1962.

FABREGAT, C. E. *Industrialización e integración social* (Industrialization and social integration). Madrid, Camara Oficial de Comercio, 1960. 36 p.

FAIRBANK, J. K. 'The influence of modern Western science and technology on Japan and China', in: *X Congresso internazionale di Scienze storiche, Roma*, 4-11 settembre 1955. *Relazioni*, vol. 5, p. 241-270. Florence, G. C. Sansoni, 1955.

FALIX, D. 'Industrialization and stabilization dilemmas in Latin America', *Journal of economic history* 19(4), Dec. 1959, p. 584-599. [With a discussion by W. N. Parker, p. 619-620.]

FELDMAN, A. S. 'The interpenetration of firm and society', in: CONSEIL INTERNATIONAL DES SCIENCES SOCIALES. *Les implications sociales du développement économique*, p. 179-198. Paris, Presses universitaires de France, 1962.

FIRTH, R.; FISHER, F. J.; McRAE, D. G. 'Social implications of technological change as regards patterns and models', in: G. BALANDIER (ed.), *Les implications sociales du progrès technique*, p. 261-293. Paris, Presses universitaires de France, 1959.

FITZGIBBON, R. H. 'Columbia as a laboratory for change', *Civilisations* 11(2), 1961, p. 130-142.

FORD, E. 'Impact of industry on African peoples', *African World*, July 1955, p. 13-14.

FORDE, D. (ed.) *Social implications of industrialization and urbanization in Africa South of the Sahara*, prepared by the International African Institute. Paris, Unesco, 1956, 743 p. [See also the International social science bulletin 7(1), 1955.]

FORTHOMME, G. *Mariage et industrialisation; évolution de la mentalité indigène dans une cité de travailleurs d'Élisabethville*. Liège, Institut de sociologie de l'université, 1957. VII + 104 p.

FRANKEL, S. H. *The economic impact on underdeveloped societies: essays on international investment and social change*. Cambridge, Mass., Harvard University Press, 1953. VII + 179 p.

FRIEDMAN, G. 'The social consequences of technical progress', International social science bulletin 4 (2), 1952, p. 243-260.

FRIEDMANN, F. G. 'The impact of technically advanced civilizations on underdeveloped areas', *Confluence* 4(4), Jan. 1956, p. 391-406.

FROELICH, W. (ed.), *Land tenure, industrialization, and social stability: experience and prospects in Asia*. Milwaukee, Marquette University Press, 1961. xv + 301 p.

GALIBERT, G. 'Problèmes humains et économiques de mise en valeur industrielle au Sahara occidental', *Cahiers d'outre-mer* 11(42), April-June 1958, p. 142-172.

GERMANI, G. 'Algunos aspectos de la familia en transición en Argentina' (Some aspects of the evolution of family in Argentina), in: CONSEIL INTERNATIONAL DES SCIENCES SOCIALES, p. 29-44. *Les implications sociales du développement économique*. Paris, Presses universitaires de France, 1962.

GINI, C. 'Efectos sociológicos de la aviación' (Sociological effects of aviation); *Revista internacional de sociología* 14(54), April-June 1956, p. 181-203.

GOLDSMITH, R. W. *The comparative study of economic growth and culture*. New York, National Bureau of Economic Research, 1959. 201 p.

GOULD, H. A. 'Some preliminary observations concerning the anthropology of industrialization', *Eastern anthropologist* 14(1), Jan.-Apr. 1961, p. 30-47. [India.]

GREEN, T. 'Technology and education in South-East Asia', *Oversea education* 26(2), July 1954, p. 70-74.

GRUBER, R. (ed.), *Science and the new nations*. Proceedings of the International Conference on Science in the Advancement of New States, held at Rehovot (Israel), 1960. New York, Basic Books, 1961. xv + 314 p.

GUNDAPPA, D. V. 'Industrial technology and Indian society', *Pacific Spectator* 9(2), 1955, p. 199-209.

HALPERIN, M. 'La América latina en transición' (Latin America in transition), *Ciencias políticas y sociales* 1(2), Oct.-Dec. 1955, p. 77-89. [Social and political consequences of industrialization.]

HAUSER, P. M. *Le phénomène de l'urbanisation en Asie et en Extrême-Orient*. Calcutta, Unesco Research Centre, 1959. 321 p.

HOLAS, B. 'Le paysannat africain devant le problème des cultures industrielles. L'exemple des Oubi (Côte-d'Ivoire)', *Revue de l'Institut de sociologie* (2), 1957, p. 219-233.

Holness, J. 'The crisis of colonial industrial technique', *Présence africaine* 14-15, June-Sept. 1957, p. 84-106.

Hoselitz, B. F. 'Population pressure, industrialization and social mobility', *Population studies* 11(2), Nov. 1957, p. 123-135.

Hoselitz, B. F. 'Problems of adapting and communicating modern techniques to less-developed areas', *Economic development and cultural change* 2(4), Mar. 1954, p. 249-269.

—— (ed.), *The progress of underdeveloped areas*. Chicago, University of Chicago Press, 1952. x + 296 p.

——. *Sociological aspects of economic growth*. Glencoe, Ill., Free Press, 1960. 205 p.

——. 'Some potentialities and limitations of research on social implications of technical change', *Civilisations* 6(2), Apr.-June 1956, p. 157-178.

Houghton, D. H. (ed.), *Economic development in a plural society: studies in the border region of the Cape Province*. Cape Town and London, Oxford University Press, 1960. xv + 401 p.

Ianni, O. 'Factores humanos de la industrialización en Brazil' (Human factors of industrialization in Brazil), *Cienc. polit. soc.* 6(20), April-June 1960, p. 325-338.

Inman, S. G. 'The impact of the modern world on Latin America: a politico-economic and technological approach', *Civilisations* 5(4), 1955, p. 549-568.

Itel'son, L. B. 'Sovremennaja tehnika i psihologičeskie vozmožnosti čeloveka' (Modern technology and the psychological potential of man), *Voprosy Filosofii* 15(4), 1961, p. 60-70.

Iwai, H. 'Kindai Gijitsu no Kazoku Seikatsu ni ataeru Kinpaku' (The impact of modern technique on the Japanese family), *Jimbun-Gakuhô* 21, 1959, p. 135-202.

Jalink, W. P. 'Sociale implicaties van technische veranderingen' (Social implication of technical development), *Mens en Onderneming* 13(2), 1959, p. 7.

Kahl, J. A. 'Some social concomitants of industrialization and urbanization', *Human organization* 18(2), Summer 1959, p. 53-74.

Karpat, K. H. 'Social effects of farm mechanization in Turkish villages', *Social research* 27(1), Spr. 1960, p. 83-103.

Karve, D. G. 'Some sociological implications of planned development', *Eastern Anthropologist* 13(3), Mar.-May 1960, p. 64-74.

King, R. W. 'Technology and social progress', *Political science quarterly* 76(1), Mar. 1961, p. 3-10.

Klineberg, O. 'A psychologist's approach to technological change', *Mens en Maatschappij* 35(5), Sept.-Oct. 1960, p. 373-377.

Koyama, E. 'Social implications of technological change in Japan', in: Conseil international des sciences sociales. *Les implications sociales du développement économique*. Paris, Presses universitaires de France, 1962, p. 107-116.

Kuhne, O. 'El progreso técnico y el progreso social' (Technical and social progress), *Revista mexicana de sociología* 22(3), Sept.-Dec. 1960, p. 823-846.

Kuželev, N. S. 'Ekonomičeskoe i social'noe značenie tehničeskogo progressa' (The economic and social significance of technical progress), *Sbornik Statej po ekonomičeskim Voprosam (Leningradskaja vysšaja partijnaja Škola)* 1, 1960, p. 20-35.

Labisa, A. S. 'Alguns problemas da produção e mão-de-obra indigenas em Angola' (Some problems relating to production and local manpower in Angola), *Estudos ultramarinos* 4, 1959, p. 75-116.

Lebret, L. J. *Dynamique concrète du développement*. Paris, Économie et humanisme, les Éditions ouvrières, 1961. 551 p.

Lefrançois, P. 'Les problèmes de l'industrialisation de la Communauté française outre-mer', *Tropiques* 57(413), Jan. 1959, p. 33-36.

Lerner, D. *The passing of traditional society: modernizing the Middle East*. Glencoe, Ill., Free Press, 1958, xiii + 466 p.

Lewis, O. 'The effects of technical progress on mental health in rural populations', *América indígena* 12(4), Oct. 1952, p. 299-307.

Mallart, J. 'Un exemple des implications sociales du progrès technique', *Travail humain* 20(3-4), July-Dec. 1957, p. 305-312. [The Coming of Modern Technique to the Haciana Valley in Spain.]

MANNDORF, H. 'Auswirkungen der Industrialisierung und Verstädterung auf die indische Kasten-Gesellschaft' (The impact of industrialization and urbanization on the Indian caste system), *Sociologus* 8(1), 1958, p. 40-57.

——. 'Soziale Umwandlungprozesse als Folgeerscheinung der Industrialisierung in Südasien (The process of social transformation as a consequence of industrialization in South Asia), *Sociologus* 7(2), 1957, p. 181-183.

——. 'Die sozialen und kulturellen Auswirkungen den Industrialisierung auf die indische Kasten-Gesellschaft (The social and cultural effects of industrialization on the Indian caste system), *Mitteilungen der anthropologischen Gesellschaft in Wien* 87, 1957, p. 103-105.

MEAD, M. (ed.), *Cultural patterns and technical change.* New York, The New American Library, 1955. 352 p.

——, *et al. Society, tradition and technology.* Paris, Unesco, 1953. 397 p.

MITCHELL, J. C. 'Social change and the new towns of Bantu Africa', in: CONSEIL INTERNATIONAL DES SCIENCES SOCIALES. *Les implications sociales du développement économique,* p. 117-130. Paris, Presses universitaires de France, 1962.

MOORE, J. F. 'Some aspects of industrialization and co-operative development in underdeveloped areas', *Indian economic review* 1(4), Aug. 1953, p. 1-21.

MOORE, W. E. *Industrialization and labor; social aspects of economic development.* Ithaca, N. Y., Cornell University Press, 1951. XX + 410 p.

——. 'Social consequences of technical change from the sociological standpoint', *International social science bulletin* 4(2), Summer 1952, p. 280-288.

——. 'Technological change and industrial organization', in: CONSEIL INTERNATIONAL DES SCIENCES SOCIALES. *Les implications sociales du développement économique,* p. 199-209. Paris, Presses universitaires de France, 1962.

——; FELMAN, A. S. *Labour commitment and social change in developing areas.* New York Social Science Research Council, 1960. VI + 378 p.

MORAES FILHO, E. DE. 'Algunas consecuencias de la industrialización sobre la dinámica de la empresa' (Some effects of industrialization on the dynamics of undertakings), *Revista mexicana de Sociología* 22(1), Jan.-April 1960, p. 67-75. [En Amérique latine.] p. 67-75. [En Amérique latine.]

MORGAUT, M.-E. *L'Afrique et l'industrie.* Paris, Fayard, 1959. 206 p.

——. 'Évolution africaine et civilisation industrielle', *Communautés et Continents* 52(5), Jan.-Mar. 1960, p. 27-41.

MOULY, J. 'Quelques aspects économiques et sociaux de la planification dans les pays sous-développés', *Économie appliquée* 12(3), July-Sept. 1959, p. 307-335.

NAJDENOV, V. S. 'Social'no-ekonomičeskie posledstvija tehničeskogo progressa pri social</zme (The social and economic consequences of technical progress towards socialism), *Voprosy Filosofii* 14(8), August 1960, p. 14-24.

NAKAMURA, T. 'Gipitsu Henka to Sonraku Shakai' (Dynamic of technical change in a village community), *Jinruigaku Zasshi* 66(3), Mar. 1958, p. 37-43. [Japon.]

NARAGHI, E. 'Conséquences sociales de développement économique et technique en Iran', *Information (ISSC/CISS)* 20, April 1959, p. 1-13.

NASH, M. *Machine age Maya; the industrialization of a Guatemalan community.* Glencoe, Ill., Free Press; Chicago, Research Center in Economic Development and Cultural Change, University of Chicago, 1958. VI+ 118 p.

——. 'The multiple society in economic development: Mexico and Guatemala', *American anthropologist* 59(5), Oct. 1957, p. 825-833.

——. 'Some cultural and social aspects of economic development', *Economic development and cultural change* 7(2), Jan. 1959, p. 137-150.

NASH, M. 'Some notes on village industrialization in South and East Asia', *Economic development and cultural change* 3(3), April 1955, p. 271-277.

UNITED NATIONS LIBRARY. '*Bibliography on industrialization in underdeveloped countries.* New York, United Nations. 1956. XI + 216 p. [Bibliographical series, no. 6.]

NIEHOFF, A. 'Caste and industrial organization in North India', *Administrative science quarterly* 3(4), Mar. 1959, p. 494-508.

NOLTE, R. H. *Social change and industrialization in Egypt*. New York, American Universities Field Staff, 1955. 31 p.

OGBURN, W. F. 'Social implications of technical advance. A trend report and bibliography / Conséquences sociales du progrès technique. Tendances actuelles et bibliographie', *Current sociology / Sociologie contemporaine* 1(4), 1953, p. 187-266.

——; NIMKOFF, M. F. *Technology and the changing family*. Boston, Houghton Mifflin, 1955. v + 329 p.

OPLER, M. E. 'Technological change and social organization in a village of North India', *Anthropological quarterly* 32(3), July 1959, p. 127-133.

ORANS, M. 'A tribal people in an industrial setting', *Journal of American folklore* 71(281), July-Sept. 1958, p. 422-445. [Santal, India.]

PAUVERT, J.-C. 'Note sur quelques aspects du "développement communautaire"' in: CONSEIL INTERNATIONAL DES SCIENCES SOCIALES. *Les implications sociales du développement économique*, p. 143-152. Paris, Presses universitaires de France, 1962, p. 143-152.

PIATIER, A. *Équilibre entre développement économique et développement social*. Paris, Éditions Génin (for the Conseil international des sciences sociales), 1962, 181 p. [Bibliography p. 105-181.]

PIEGEAY, C. 'Industrialisation en habitat', *Encyclopédie mensuelle d'outre-mer* 5(59), July 1955, p. 325-329. [Antilles.]

POZAS, R. 'Los cambios sociales y la industrialización (Social change and industrialization), in: *Actas del XXXIII Congreso internacional de los americanistas*, vol. I, p. 373-379. San José, 1959. [Mexico.]

RAMA, C. M. 'Aspectos sociales de la industrialización en el Uruguay' (Social aspects of industrialization in Uruguay), *Sociología (São Paulo)* 21(4), Oct. 1959, p. 418-433.

RIBADEAU-DUMAS, J. 'Industrialisation outre-mer et problèmes humains', *Association de cadres dirigeants de l'industrie pour le progrès social et économique. Bulletin.* 120, Jan. 1958, p. 19-26.

RICHARDSON, S. A. 'Technological change: some effects on three Canadian fishing villages', *Human organization* 11(3), Aut. 1952, p. 17-27.

RONDOT, P. 'Les musulmans devant la technique', *Cahiers de l'ISÉA* 106, série V, no. 2, Oct. 1960, p. 37-63.

——. 'Les musulmans et l'Islam devant la technique', *Revue de la défense nationale* 16, June 1960, p. 1011-1027.

SALGADO, P. 'Australia: progreso material y problemas de población' (Australia: progress and population questions), *Boletín trimestral de informacion economica (Quito)*, Jan.-Mar. 1954, p. 109-136.

SALZ, B. R. *The human element in industrialization; a hypothetical case study of Ecuadorean Indians*. Menasha, Wis., American Anthropological Association, 1955. IX + 256 p.

SETON, F. 'Industrialization in overpopulated areas, a geometric interpretation of certain aspects', *Oxford economic papers* 12(2), June 1960, p. 202-214.

SHANNON, L. W. 'Social factors in economic growth. A trend report and bibliography / Les facteurs sociaux du développement économique. Tendances de la recherche et bibliographie', *Current sociology / Sociologie contemporaine* 6(3), 1957, p. 171-238. [See chapter XI, 'Social effects of economic development'.]

SHIRI KANWAR SAIN. 'Social repercussions of hydraulic projects in India', *Civilisations* 5(2), 1955, p. 183-191.

SIMAO, A. 'Industrialisation et syndicalisme au Brésil', *Sociologie du travail* 3(4), 1961, p. 66-76.

SIMKIN, D. B. 'Industrialization. A challenging problem for cultural anthropology', *Southwestern journal of anthropology* 8, 1952, p. 84-91.

SMITH, R. J. 'Comparative studies in anthropology of the interrelations between social and technical change', *Human organization* 16 (1), Spr. 1957, p. 30-36.

SOARES BARATA, O. 'As implicações sociais dos grandes projectos na Africa ao sul do Sara' (Social implication of important projects in Africa South of the Sahara), *Estudos ultramarinos* 2, 1960, p. 119-139.

SPITAELS, G. 'Considérations sur le chômage à Léopoldville', *Revue de l'Institut de sociologie* (1), 1960, p. 55-72.

STRAUS, M. A. 'Family role differentiation and technological change in farming', *Rural Sociology* 25(2), June 1960, p. 219-228.

TEICHERT, P. C. M. *Economic policy revolution and industrialization in Latin America*.Mississipi, University of Mississipi, Bureau of Business Research, 1954, 282 p.

TEXTOR, R. B., et al. *The social implications of industrialization and urbanization. Five studies of urban population of recent rural origin in cities of Southern Asia*. Calcutta, Unesco Research Centre on the Social Implications of Industrialization in Southern Asia, 1956. XIV + 268 p.

THORSRUD, E. 'The social consequences of technical change from the psychological standpoint', International social science bulletin 4(2), Summer 1952, p. 300-309.

TOURAINE, A. 'Industrialisation et conscience ouvrière à São Paulo', *Sociologie du travail* 3(4), 1961, p. 77-95.

ULKEN, H. Z. 'La répercussion sociale de l'agriculture mécanisée en Turquie', *Transactions of the 3rd World Congress of Sociology*, vol. 2, p. 319-325. London, International Sociological Association, 1956.

URBAIN, Y. 'L'incidence sociale des facteurs économiques', *Revue nouvelle* 7(12), 15 Dec. 1951, p. 532-542.

VAKIL, C. N. 'Social implications of technological change at the level of the community', in: CONSEIL INTERNATIONAL DES SCIENCES SOCIALES. *Les implications sociales du développement économique*, p. 167-178. Paris, Presses universitaires de France, 1962.

VANDERLINDEN, R. 'Industrialisation et évolution sociale', *Belgique d'outre-mer* 12(269), July 1957, p. 665-667.

VERSLUYS, J. D. W. 'Social implications of industrialisation in South Asia', *Industrial relations* 9(5), Sept.-Oct. 1957, p. 181-183.

VITO, F. 'Quelques problèmes au sujet de la transformation économique, sociale et culturelle des nouveaux États africains', *Justice dans le monde* 2(2), Dec. 1960, p. 147-161.

WERTHEIM, W. F. *Indonesian society in transition, a study of social change*. The Hague, W. van Hoeve, 1956. XIV + 360 p.

WILKINSON, T. O. 'Urban structure and industrialization', *American sociological review* 25(3), June 1960, p. 356-363. [The case of Japan.]

WRIGHT, R. 'Tradition et industrialisation', *Présence africaine* 8-10, June-Nov. 1956, p. 347-360. [Africa.]